Oregon, This Storied Land

OREGON

THIS STORIED LAND

William G. Robbins

OREGON HISTORICAL SOCIETY PRESS
PORTLAND

Visit our website at www.ohs.org.

Printed in the United States of America

Distributed by the University of Washington Press

COVER DESIGN: Jennifer Viviano
PRINTER: Thomson-Shore, Inc.

COVER ART: Charles E. Heaney, *Road to Shaniko*, 1977, oil on panel, 6 1/2 x 40", collection of Marge Riley. Used with permission. Aaron Johanson, photographer, through the courtesy of the Hallie Ford Museum of Art, Willamette University, Salem, Oregon. TITLE PAGE PHOTOS: Women and Children at Farm Labor Camp (OHS neg., OrHi 97809), Klamath Families (OHS neg., OrHi 35789), Kaiser Shipyard Workers (OHS neg., OrHi 24146). CHAPTER TITLE PAGE PHOTOS: Port Orford Cedar near Wooden Rock Creek, 1922 (OHS neg., CN 004724), xiii; Cascade Rapids (OHS neg., OrHi 105344), 1; Ft. Vancouver, detail, Gustavus Sohon, artist (OHS neg., CN 008519), 19; Residents of Agness (OHS neg., CN 021026), 39; Construction of Cascade Canal and Locks (OHS neg., OrHi 351-A), 65; William U'Ren defending Labor Communist Party members (OHS neg., CN 009663), 87; CCC Camp (OHS neg., OrHi 59523), 111; Logs on Rail Car (OHS neg., OrHi 96577), 135; Portland Symphony Orchestra (OHS neg., OrHi 48710), 157; Downtown Beaverton (OHS neg., OrHi 66941), 179; Klamath Falls, John Bauguess, photographer (OHS neg., OrHi 105221), 201.

∞ The paper in this publication meets the minimum requirements of the American National Standard for Information Sciences—Permanence of Paper for Printed Library Materials, ANSI Z39.48-192.

Library of Congress Cataloging-in-Publication Data

Robbins, William G., 1935-
Oregon : this storied land / William G. Robbins. p. cm.
Includes bibliographical references and index.
ISBN 0-87595-286-0 (pbk. : alk. paper)
1. Oregon--History. 2. Oregon--Social conditions. 3. Oregon--Historiography. I. Title.
F876.R63 2005
979.5--dc22   2005016294

*To my trail-running friends
and their love of the western outback*

Bob Andersen, Chris Andersen, Meghan Arbogast, Brian Arbogast, Jim Archer, Marilyn Bailey, Anna Bandick, Dana Bandy, John Bandur, Mary Barron, David Bateham, Rod Beckner, Karen Bennett, Melissa Berman, Jon Boyd, Mike Burke, Ellen Burnes, Phil Brownell, Cathy Cafazzo, Dian Cummings, Andy Dale, Joe Dana, Devon Dobek, Kelly Donegan, Rich Duncombe, Nancy Dunton, Eb Englemann, Lee Fields, Jan Finley, Susan Fox, Joe Fulton, John Gillis, Cambria Martin Gilsdorf, Rick Hafer, Larry Halford, John Hart, Irv Horowitz, Peter Idema, Vicky Idema, Ruth Johns, Chris Johnson, Melanie Johnson, Boone Kauffman, Erin Knutson, Ricky Knutson, Scott Kruis, Amy LaCava, Clem LaCava, Jan LaCava, Scott Leonard, Ross Leonard, John Liebeskind, Els Lofgren, Jim Lofgren, Steve Loitz, Bob Lynes, Nate McDowell, Sean Meissner, Kathy Morelock, John Morelock, Clint Morrison, Bruce Moser, Josh Munk, Andy Nelson, Sander Nelson, Ken Osher, Pam Otley, Steve Payne, Tim Peterson, Jim Pittman, Karon Pittman, Jim Ridlington, Barbara Ringstad, Kurt Ringstad, my children (Aubrey Jody, Kelly, and Larry), Gabriela Rosales, Jim Roy, Mary Jo Rutten, Linda Samet, Theresa Schut, Reenie Schwallie, Mike Shaughnessy, John Simon, Jeremy Smith, Amy Smoker, Justin Soares, Mark Spence, Bruce Stevens, Mary Stevens, Phil Vaughn, Marc Vomocil, Ken Ward, and Greg Wheeler

Contents

Illustrations

Acknowledgments

This book had its beginnings in the summer of 2001 with the Oregon Historical Society's (OHS) outreach efforts to promote a better understanding of the state's history, especially in the public schools. The Society's former executive director, Norma Paulus, led a successful fund-raising effort to support what became known as the Oregon History Project. The Society's education director, Marianne Keddington-Lang, guided the early development of the project as it expanded and advanced along several fronts.

Beginning in the fall of 2001 and continuing through the next year, I drafted a multiple-chapter outline of Oregon history and then turned the seven-chapter outline into a short narrative. Paralleling this effort, OHS staff constructed an Oregon History Project Web site that featured the historical narrative and links to appropriate documents, photographs, and maps. As part of this collaborative effort, historian Bill Lang and I presented a few history workshops for public schoolteachers at various sites around the state.

With 144 pages of print manuscript already in the bank—and with the enthusiastic support of Marianne Keddington-Lang—I decided to purge more than 30 years of files and extend the Web narrative into a book-length history of Oregon. Karen Hoppes and Eckard Toy provided valuable input in framing the original outline. Eckard and Katrine Barber offered helpful and perceptive critiques of the full manuscript. My greatest debt is to Katrine for her constructive suggestions and probing review of the manuscript. Her advice is reflected especially in the more careful consideration of social issues. As usual, this book owes much to Bill Lang and our ongoing discussions about how to properly frame a compelling history of Oregon. And finally, my gratitude to my wife, Karla, for tolerating my enthusiasm for doing history.

INTRODUCTION

Of Forests, Water, and Sky

Oregon's spectacular Silver Creek Falls State Park was born of receding oceans, colossal volcanic lava flows, and pathways cut by water flowing through the numerous streams in Silver Creek Canyon. Kalapuya Indians frequented the steep canyon hillsides as a fruitful hunting and gathering grounds, a place to collect berries, camas bulbs, cedar roots and bark, and, perhaps, a place to seek spirit quests. To the practiced eye and with the help of old boundary surveys, Indian trails are still recognizable in the park. Evidence of early logging activity is visible in springboard scars, notches cut in the sides of slowly decomposing stumps, from a time when loggers stood on the strong boards to pull long crosscut saws through huge Douglas fir, cedar, and hemlock. Today's park reflects cataclysmic natural and human events and actions, including state and federal conservation initiatives during the Great Depression and the boom in recreation following the Second World War. Only 15 miles east of Salem, Silver Creek Canyon had long been a recreational sanctuary for Marion County residents, but increased automobile travel, a booming economy after 1945, and the expansion of the park brought a dramatic increase in the number of visitors.

The story of Silver Creek Falls State Park provides a window to Oregon history during the 20th century. The pictorial artistry of Silverton's June Drake, whose photographs document Silver Creek Canyon, was of major importance in bringing the park to the public's attention. The work of Drake's contemporary, Samuel H. Boardman, Oregon Parks superintendent from 1929 to 1950, was even more significant. The charismatic Boardman, dubbed the "father of the Oregon state parks," negotiated the state's first piecemeal purchases of Silver Creek Falls in 1931, the nucleus of the nearly 9,000 acres in today's park.

No single event shaped Silver Falls' recreational splendor more than the crisis of the Great Depression. In an effort to put unemployed people to constructive work, President Franklin D. Roosevelt's New Deal administration established the Civilian Conservation Corps (CCC) in 1933, camps of young men who labored in wide-ranging conservation activities, especially federal and state outdoor rehabilitation projects. The first CCC contingent at Silver Creek Falls State Park began work in March 1935, and over the next several years "CCC boys" built roads and trails, rock walls, bridges, fences, picnic shelters, water and sewer systems, and the magnificent Silver Falls Lodge. With materials from nearby timber stands and rock quarries, workers created two impressive fireplaces for the lodge and crafted myrtlewood tables, chairs, and benches designed by Margery Hoffman Smith of the Oregon Arts Project, an affiliate of the Works Projects Administration (Smith also directed the interior decorations for another federal project, Timberline Lodge on Mount Hood). The federal government vastly expanded the park's boundaries when the National Park Service deeded 6,000 acres—designated as a Recreational Demonstration Area—to the state in the late 1940s. Silver Falls Lodge, at the center of the South Falls day-use area, was restored in 1978 and now serves as the park's visitors' center.

With its rustic lodge and outbuildings, its magnificent waterfalls, and its wondrous rock formations, Silver Creek Falls State Park is a magnificent public space. To visit the park today is to see a vibrant cross-section of Oregon's diverse social and cultural worlds—minority ethnic groups, colorful dress and music, and friendly people enjoying a beautiful setting. Those who visit the park include people from all walks of life, from affluent suburbanites to working-class Hispanics to Russian Old Believer families from the mid-Willamette Valley. To a historian's critical eye, however, Silver Creek Falls State Park is much more. It is a living monument to the farsighted civic-mindedness of generations of people who believed in creating beautiful public places for everyone.

With its vast distances and magnificent vistas, southeastern Oregon's Steens Mountain is a strikingly different place. Set in classic basin-and-range topography, Steens Mountain slopes gently upward from the Malheur National Wildlife Refuge to its eastern rim, which drops precipitously more than one vertical mile to the Alvord Desert below. Unlike Silver Creek Canyon, where volcanic action and vast lava flows shaped the landscape, geological uplifting between 16 and 23 million years ago gave birth to the Steens. For thousands of years, the ancestors of today's northern Paiute bands walked the western slopes of the Steens, digging bulbs, gathering berries, and hunting for game. In the late 1860s and early 1870s, the Paiutes' world was dramatically changed when cattle drovers from California, Nevada, and northeastern Oregon began moving their herds to the virgin grasslands in the deep valleys.

The activities of the cattle drovers and the successive waves of immigrant farmers reduced the Paiutes to a desperate resistance. The U.S. Army captured the small bands and forced them onto already established reservations. The head foremen and their great herds then engaged in a Darwinian competitive struggle with small farmers to control water rights and access to grazing land. By the 1880s, nomadic sheepherders compounded the problem of overgrazing, driving their herds to less accessible recesses of Steens Mountain in search of browse. At the beginning of the 20th century, federal surveyors reported too many cattle, too many sheep, denuded grasses, and eroded streams on the Steens. Although the cattle barons, including Peter French's famous "P" Ranch, staked out several large holdings, the federal government through the General Land Office controlled much of the Steens area. With modest grazing restrictions introduced under the federal Taylor Grazing Act of 1934, authorities were able to reduce the size of the herds that once grazed in the bottoms of the mountain canyons. During the Great Depression, there were also sporadic discussions about designating the area as a national park.

Since the Second World War, ranchers have continued to graze cattle on the more than 230,000 acres of privately owned land and on federal lease-holdings managed by the Bureau of Land Management. But Steens Mountain has always been more than a cattlemen's feed lot. With improved roads and automobiles, especially after 1945, an increasing number of visitors began making the long drive to the remote mountain to take in its scenic wonders, to fish the Donner und

Blitzen River and other streams, and to hunt the mule deer that frequented the high, isolated canyons. With the emergence of the environmental movement in the 1970s and the formal organization of the
Oregon Natural Desert Association in 1989, some groups urged federal
protective status for the Steens. In June 2000, with his second term in
office nearing its end, President Bill Clinton signed into law a complex
and multifaceted piece of legislation establishing the Steens Mountain
Cooperative Management Protection Area, which embraced 425,550
acres of federal land. The Cooperative Management Area, a mediated
compromise negotiated by Interior Secretary Bruce Babbitt, includes
the 97,071-acre Steens Mountain Wilderness Area, federal land that is
off-limits to cattle grazing. The Management Act also includes provisions for land exchanges between private owners and the federal government to protect the ecologically diverse habitat on the Steens.

Although the number of visitors to Steens Mountain pale beside
those who travel to Silver Falls State Park, this magnificent natural
treasure in Oregon's high desert country has become part of our common heritage. Crater Lake in the southern Cascades, Multnomah Falls
in the scenic Columbia River Gorge, wild rivers such as the Umpqua
and Rogue, the Wallowa Mountains in the northeast, and special
places along the Oregon Coast testify to inspirational public places
that provide citizens with the opportunity to enjoy a wonderful in-
heritance. Oregon's story has always been more than the logging de-
tritus that once littered Silver Creek Canyon or the ravaged slopes of
Steens Mountain. In Oregon—as the history of Steens Mountain and
Silver Creek Canyon illustrates—citizens have the capacity to restore
desecrated landscapes and to refashion special environments into aes-
thetic and healthy places.

After he left the governor's office in 1975, Tom McCall continued to
speak of the "Oregon mystique," the state's capacity for pioneering
imaginative ideas and the notion that livability and a healthy economy
were one and the same. Governor John Kitzhaber made similar statements. There is "an Oregon identity—and ethic," he said, that gives
the state a character that makes it different from other places. Among
those qualities are "a strong identity with the land," a belief in clear air
and water, and a commitment to healthy natural systems. McCall and
Kitzhaber were echoing testimonials about Oregon and the Northwest that date from the early 19th century, when the region seemed
to promise the good life to all comers. Obviously, not all of Oregon's

public places share in the kind of restorative attractiveness of Silver Creek Canyon and Steens Mountain. Portland's polluted Columbia Slough, for example, has been a dumping ground for industrial and human waste for more than a century. Such degraded places span the state in varying degrees of disturbance—from the Willamette River's Superfund site in Portland Harbor, to the severely eroded Sumpter Valley hillsides that suffer from 19th-century hydraulic mining, to the nerve gas stored on the bleak landscape of the Umatilla Army Depot near Boardman.

Scratch the surface, and you will find evidence of historical events and circumstances scripted across Oregon's more than 61 million acres. The stories of Silver Creek Canyon and Steens Mountain represent only a small part of the changes brought about by humans in the Columbia River corridor, in the extensive western valleys, on the coast, and across the high desert and mountainous interior. Archaeological evidence, cultural artifacts, documented materials, federal and state statistical compilations, and oral histories help us tease out the details of the past. The qualitative human side of this equation is revealed through anecdotal and journal reports; the federal census and tax lists; records of births, deaths, and marriages; and miscellaneous data collected by local, county, state, and federal governments. Making sense of those details is the discrete, selective, and highly personal work of historians.

*O*regon, This Storied Land is a select and interpretive exploration of Oregon's past. It represents a rummaging through of more than 30 years of collecting, cutting, and filing away sometimes obscure, yet fascinating details and observations about Oregon and Pacific Northwest history. Even though I have developed a deep affection for the state since emigrating here from the East in 1963, this book attempts to remain true to a historian's commitment to critical inquiry, to interrogate the past with a critical lens, to raise uncomfortable questions, to approach Oregon's history with an open-mindedness and a healthy dose of skepticism about the claims of its boosters. At its very best, history seeks neither to condemn nor to celebrate but to critically analyze. Historians, I have always told my students, are often contrarians, playing devil's advocate by continually raising new questions. When the American Historical Association attempted to draft national history standards for public schools in the mid-1990s, for example, some politicians loudly denounced the effort for devoting too much time to minorities and for presenting what they considered a "depressing" story. In the aftermath of the controversy, a *Newsweek* reporter asked acclaimed historian Eric Foner: "When did historians stop relating facts and start all this revising of reinterpretation of the past?" Foner responded: "Around the time of Thucydides."

This book will examine and question conventional notions about "discovery," "exploration," and "progress." There is no understanding the place that became Oregon, I believe, without knowing something about the first people to inhabit the land. Because Native peoples have persisted as active players through more than two centuries of incredible population losses, forced removal from their homelands, and continued repression, *Oregon, This Storied Land* tries to tell that story over time.

While the state's success stories should be remembered, it is also important to examine the darker side of Oregon history: early statutes, especially the racial exclusion clause written into the state constitution, the Democratic Party's equivocation over the ratification of the 14th Amendment, the state's culpability in the violent removal of Chinese during the 1880s, and the Japanese question during the first half of the 20th century. Similar hostility has been directed toward Hispanics, Southeast Asians, Middle Easterners, and others who immigrated to Oregon. In a sense, this book is an effort to follow a precept of the great British historian Eric Hobsbawm, who said that historians are the "professional remembrancers of what their fellow citizens wish to forget."

But *Oregon, This Storied Land* is more than what Oregonians wish to forget. It is a narrative of innovative political and cultural initiatives, courageous public decision-making, and people working hard to make a better world for themselves and future generations. It is also a story of false starts, dead-end policies, flawed personalities, narrow-minded social agendas, economies of greed, and civic principles gone astray. History, William Appleman Williams wrote, "is a way of learning." We should not study the past, he cautioned, "in search of reassurance and security." To do so would be misleading and dangerous, especially if it was an effort to use the past to justify present or future decisions. Rather, history is an enterprise whose great tradition "is to help us understand ourselves"—both our successes and our failures —so that we can make reasoned decisions about the future. It is my hope that this book will provide some understanding of who we are as Oregonians.

Oregon, This Storied Land

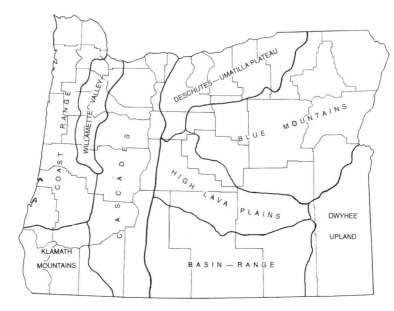

Reprinted from Samuel N. Dicken and Emily F. Dicken, *The Making of Oregon* (Portland: Oregon Historical Society, 1979)

The landform regions of Oregon

CHAPTER ONE

Beginnings and Native Cultures

The places and stories that became Oregon evolved slowly through geological and historical time, beginning millions of years ago amid cataclysmic volcanic eruptions, huge basalt flows, and the folding and faulting of tectonic plates. When the earth's surface cooled about one million years ago, a continental ice sheet formed over North America, spreading southward until it embraced the upper Columbia River drainage. One lobe of the glacial sheet pushed down the Okanagan Valley, while another farther to the east created an ice dam across Idaho's panhandle country. In the mountainous region east of the Cascade Range, cooling conditions created large alpine glaciers that remained in place until the great ice mass began to retreat and the climate began to warm around 18,000 years ago. The retreating ice sheets and glaciers released huge volumes of water that blasted into eastern Washington with a flood tide 1,000 feet high. As the waters followed the Columbia's westward course, they pushed through the Columbia Gorge at more than 800 feet deep. The Missoula Floods were catastrophic in nature, reoccurring in cyclical flooding events for more than 3,000 years. The Missoula ice dams burst more than 100 times between 18,000 and 14,000 years ago, creating the largest flows of water ever recorded on earth.

The powerful Late Pleistocene floods shaped and reshaped the great Columbia River landscape, sweeping down the river in great deluges that moved literally everything in its wake. The floods scoured what are known today as the channeled scablands of eastern Washington, including the Grand Coulee, which today holds waters that irrigate the interior Columbia Basin. The great walls of water rushed through the Columbia Gorge, and then, slowed by the ocean tides and the precipitous banks on the lower river, the glacial wash backed into the Willamette River system, giving shape to the valley's landscape. When the floods were at their peak, the Willamette lowland was turned into a great inland sea. As the waters retreated, settling ice masses left in their wake giant granite boulders on the valley floor. The pooling waters also created the Portland Basin, a 50-by-15-mile marshy lowland extending along both sides of the Columbia River between the Columbia River Gorge and the Coast Range.

Pollen samples from the immediate post-glacial period indicate that spruce, fir, and other conifers emerged at higher elevations in the interior Northwest as the glaciers retreated and inland lakes slowly drained. As the climate warmed, Pleistocene lakes in the northern basin-and-range country disappeared, leaving behind remnants such as Summer Lake, Lake Abert, Malheur Lake, and the Warner Valley's marshy lake terrain. With the rapidly warming conditions of the early Holocene, interior forest ecosystems and plant life advanced northward (and correspondingly became more conspicuous in the archaeological record). Across Oregon's high desert country, grassland and sagebrush began to replace alpine plant communities between 7,000 and 4,000 years ago. With the exception of Mount Mazama's violent eruption about 6,000 years ago, the post-glacial climate regime in the Pacific Northwest has remained relatively stable for roughly 10,000 years.

Because there is no scientific evidence that *Homo sapiens* evolved in the Western Hemisphere, scholars have long debated the origins and timing of New World humans. The most reliable explanations are based on the ebb and flow of glaciers and the existence of a land bridge linking Asia with North America. As the global climate cooled and water amassed in Northern Hemisphere glaciers, the scientific evidence suggests that the ocean level lowered to the point that an extensive land bridge was exposed between Asia and western Alaska. Over thousands of years, first vegetation, then large mammals, and finally human hunters and gatherers moved onto and eventually across the land bridge. People who were already adapted to arctic environments slowly migrated southward, following a route along the eastern slope of the Rocky Mountains and perhaps along the coast (although there is no archaeological confirmation for this).

The scientific argument is only one explanation for the peopling of the Americas. Native American peoples have traditions that differ sharply from the archaeological and scientific explanations. Creation stories provide metaphorical and supernatural accounts about human origins and migrations that carry powerful meaning. Although tribal origin stories vary across North America according to place and environmental circumstances, they often have common themes centered in catastrophic events such as volcanic eruptions, earthquakes, and floods. Indian creation stories in the Pacific Northwest usually involve supernatural forces or creatures who bring humans into being.

The Columbia River Chinook, for example, tell several stories about the origins of their people, with each account fixed to a specific geography. The magnificent 19th-century storyteller James Swan recorded several stories told to him by Chinooks on the lower river. One involves an old man who was a giant and an old woman who was an ogress. When the old man catches a fish and attempts to cut it sideways, the woman cries out that he must cut the fish down the back. The man ignores her pleas and proceeds to cut the fish crossways. Immediately the fish changes into a giant bird that flies away toward Saddle Mountain on the northern Oregon Coast, and the man and woman go in search of the bird. One day while picking berries, the woman discovers a thunderbird's nest full of eggs. When she begins to break the eggs, humans appear out of the broken shells. Such stories, which have been told in Native communities for hundreds of years, personalize the origins of specific tribal groups.

There is considerable evidence that humans lived in the Pacific Northwest at least 15,000 years ago. The archaeological record conclusively places people on the landscape that would become Oregon sometime toward the close of the Pleistocene, a period when the great ice-age glaciers were retreating from the mountainous interior. Archaeological evidence in the Fort Rock area, The Dalles, and on the Oregon Coast indicates that people were beginning to occupy several locations in the region during the early Holocene epoch, from 10,000 to 5,000 years ago. Evidence from Malheur Lake indicates human occupation at least 10,000 years ago. The 75 sage-bark sandals that University of Oregon archaeologist Luther Cressman found at Fort Rock Cave in 1938 provide evidence of human habitation as early as 13,200 years ago, a time when several species of giant megafauna, such as mastodons and mammoths, were disappearing from the landscape. Scientists continue to debate the factors contributing to the extinction of the large herbivores and carnivores, with some positing that humans were killing off the megafauna. Other scientists find the "overkill" hypothesis outrageous, arguing instead that changing climate conditions better explain the extinctions.

Archaeological finds in Oregon's western valleys are less conclusive, suggesting that humans were present from 6,000 to 10,000 years ago. Clovis spear points recovered from the upper Willamette Valley date to at least 10,000 years ago. Several other Willamette Valley archaeological sites dating to nearly 8,000 years ago reveal that people were subsisting on camas bulbs, a food source that is still important to indigenous peoples. The post-glacial environments in the western valleys—the Willamette, Umpqua, and Rogue, for example—were conducive to human occupation because of the great variety of plant foods, including camas, acorns, hazel nuts, tarweed and sunflower seeds, cattail rhizomes, and several varieties of berries. The western valleys also supported diverse insect and animal populations and a wealth of aquatic resources.

Oregon's western valleys were also slowly evolving into the ecosystems that were described in the earliest historical accounts: the Douglas fir, grand fir, ponderosa pine, lodgepole pine, and western hemlock on the slopes of the Cascades and the Coast Range, with some coniferous species extending to lower elevations. With some variation, the Rogue, Umpqua, and Willamette valleys also took on ecological assemblages—oak savannas and grasslands—as reported by early United States reconnaissance expeditions. It is also strikingly obvious that the Oregon environments described in the early historical literature were humanized landscapes, physical settings shaped through human and natural fire regimes. The archaeological record reveals that Pleistocene hunters burned their surroundings thousands of years in the past, and there is clear evidence that Native peoples both east and west of the Cascade Mountains used fire to enhance their gathering and subsistence needs. In the western valleys, several millennia of purposeful, strategic burning sustained vast open prairies interspersed with occasional open stands of fire-resistant white oak. George Emmons, a surveyor with the U.S. Exploring Expedition in 1841, provides a wonderful eyewitness account of the Indian-fashioned Willamette Valley landscape from the vantage of the Eola Hills northwest of Salem:

From the top of these at an alt. of about 1000 feet—had a panoramic view . . . prairie to the south as far as the view extends—the streams being easily traced by a border of trees that grew up on either bank . . . white oak scattered about in all directions.

According to most scientists, people have lived in Oregon's diverse landscapes for at least 15,000 years. By the 16th century, dozens of Indian bands were scattered across the future state, with concentrated populations living along the lower Columbia River, in the western valleys, and around coastal estuaries and inlets. In about 1800, before the ravages of Old World diseases dramatically reduced their numbers, the Native population of the Pacific Northwest was about 300,000 people. Even this educated guess fails to consider how many people may have lived in the region before the first smallpox epidemics struck in the mid-1770s. The disease was brought to the Pacific Northwest by Spanish ships voyaging along the North Pacific Coast. There is also a likelihood that carriers of such diseases traveled through the interior of the continent to the Northwest.

These widely differing Native peoples spoke a multitude of languages, with the greatest diversity along the rugged Pacific Coast. Coastal archaeological sites also indicate that people relied on the marine environment for subsistence from a very early period. In Oregon's interior valleys, and especially east of the Cascade Range, common language patterns covered much broader geographies, with each cluster of people practicing its own cultural traditions and skillfully adapting to available resources. Political autonomy across the Pacific Northwest, however, was limited only to the local village or band, the unit that served as the basis for social and political reckoning. Despite those circumscribed political boundaries, coastal people carried on extensive trade and social and cultural interactions with other villages.

Native cultures were dynamic, periodically making cultural adaptations when new material items were introduced through trade and exchange networks. There is also evidence of population movement, with groups such as the interior Numic speakers, the Northern Paiute, and the Shoshone replacing a people who once inhabited Oregon's high desert country. Linguists have also determined that the Athabascan-speaking people who inhabited the southwestern Oregon Coast were relative newcomers to the area, arriving perhaps sometime between 2,000 and 1,000 years ago. Such population dynamics parallel similar movements elsewhere in North America, where groups such as the Apache and Navajo did not arrive in the Southwest until sometime after Christopher Columbus reached the New World.

Following the work of James Mooney in the early 20th century, anthropologists began dividing North America's indigenous populations into culture areas representing large expanses of the continent where people supposedly shared common cultural and subsistence traits. For the Pacific Northwest, scholars have identified three major culture areas—the Northwest Coast, the Plateau, and the Great Basin—biogeographical landscapes that share common features. Such classifications have always been arbitrary, reductive, and controversial, with people frequently sharing cultural traits with adjacent groups. There are special problems in understanding the cultural world of Native peoples in the Willamette, Umpqua, and Rogue river valleys, because they occupied transitional zones and shared cultural traits with both coastal and Plateau groups. Moreover, like Native American groups across the continent, the valley people developed special ways of adapting to their own biotic settings. With these caveats in mind, it is useful to inquire into the cultural and material worlds of the people who inhabited Oregon in about 1800.

Because of their proximity to abundant food sources, coastal Oregon people tended to live in fixed villages around estuaries or in riverine tidal zones. During the summer season, there was considerable movement to upstream places to gather berries, camas, and other edible plants that were pounded, dried, and stored for winter consumption. The work of both men and women was critical to village survival, with men being responsible for hunting and women gathering plants and preparing food. Coastal people lived in modified semi-subterranean, cedar-plank houses—with some structural variation from south to north—that might provide shelter for several families. Chinook houses on the lower Columbia could be more than 120 feet in length and 25 to 50 feet wide. A central ridgepole, 20 feet above ground level, was used to support the largest of those spacious dwellings. Archaeologist Kenneth Ames has excavated one Chinook house at Cathlapotle Village near Ridgefield, Washington, that was occupied continuously for 400 years. Because the site was used for such a lengthy period, timbers and cedar planks were cared for and replaced at regular intervals. For the Chinook occupants of the house, those were clearly labor-intensive activities.

Coastal households were the basic social and economic points of reckoning for villagers, providing a place where children were con-

OHS neg., OrHi 446a

Interior of a large Chinookan winter lodge, 1841, sketch by Alfred T. Agate

ceived and raised and where traditions were passed on from one generation to the next. The cedar dwellings also furnished space for food processing, manufacturing clothing and tools, spiritual rituals, winter storytelling, and shelter for domestic dogs. Racks or frames suspended above the hearths preserved salmon and other foods in the smoke rising from the fires. Households also existed in relation to other village households and to more distant spheres of trade and commerce, marriage ties, and ceremonial observances.

These complex coastal villages enjoyed relatively mild winters and a wealth of easily obtainable fish and shellfish from nearby streams and estuaries. At low tide, the rich intertidal zones offered up a variety of shellfish (cockles, snails, mussels, and clams), while salmon-bearing streams provided an essential seasonal staple and an important source of protein. Using an assortment of digging sticks, women and children foraged for shell foods, while men fished for salmon using various techniques, including dip nets, weirs, and traps. Although salmon usually appeared in predictable places at predictable times, the runs were vulnerable to changing environmental conditions, especially on smaller streams. Men and boys used deadfalls and pits to capture the occasional deer or elk. Women and girls picked salmonberries, huckleberries, and blueberries, which they dried, pounded into cakes with animal fats, and preserved for later use. While coastal people occasionally experienced periods of hunger, the region's lush marine surroundings precluded long periods of suffering.

Northwest Coast Indians, from Alaska's Prince William Sound to California's Klamath River country, were a true wood-culture people who used wood for housing, transportation, utensils, vessels for preparing food, weaponry, a variety of art forms, and clothing. Although coastal people north of the Columbia River created the more elaborate artistic items out of wood—including totems, masks, and canoe carvings—tribal groups along the Oregon Coast were also remarkably skilled in working with wood. Men constructed cedar canoes and used a combination of fire and wedging to split cedar logs into long planks for housing. Women were highly skilled weavers, who shredded cedar bark into strands that they wove into clothing. They also used tules, grasses, and reeds to create matting material and spruce roots and cedar strips to weave baskets.

Social inequality was a long-standing and universal characteristic of Northwest coastal life. Villagers lived in highly stratified social worlds in which there were essentially two classes of people—free and slave—and little room for social mobility. Free villagers also recognized a ranking system that further governed social distinctions. Although slavery was not widespread and had no economic rationale, people who had been captured in warfare or kidnaped from distant places lived in many villages. Without rights and at the bottom of the social order, slaves eked out a miserable existence subject to the arbitrary power of village headmen. The highest ranking free persons in the village were the chiefs who possessed special knowledge, accumulations of wealth, and inherited privileges. These were the people who directed village affairs. Next in rank were individuals related to the chief who possessed some wealth. Finally, there was a large group of "commoners" who were free but possessed no privileges. Although chiefs were usually male, high-ranking women occasionally held such positions and exercised considerable authority. Older women sometimes joined the deliberations of village elders in advising on important matters.

Along the lower Columbia River, high-ranking individuals practiced head-flattening as a symbol of status. A baby was placed in a cradleboard with a piece of cedar bark pressed against his or her head to force a straight line from the slant of the nose to the top of the head.

Although the practice apparently did no harm to the brain, it could damage the auditory canal. This method of identifying nobility was most important to lower Columbia River people.

The western interior valleys marked a cultural transition zone where people gathered seasonally available roots, nuts, seeds, and berries from the prairies, oak savannas, and foothills. They also hunted deer, elk, and waterfowl and fished local streams for salmon and freshwater fish. The most numerous of those groups was the Kalapuya, who occupied the broad expanses of the Willamette Valley, with some of the bands living in the upper Umpqua basin. The Kalapuyas lived in permanent villages during the rainy winter season and moved about to temporary camps in the valley and foothills during the summer. During their seasonal rounds, people in the Willamette, Umpqua, and Rogue valleys and the Klamaths and Modocs in the upper Klamath Basin harvested camas, acorns, wapato, hazelnuts, arrowroot, tule, cattails, and great varieties of berries. Camas, the most widespread and important of the root bulbs, was collected in great quantities in June, roasted in underground rock ovens, and then dried and pounded into cakes and preserved for winter use. Large and small game, waterfowl, and fish—depending on location—were also important components of the interior valley diet.

Indians in the western valleys also lived in fire-nurtured landscapes, strategically set annual burns that enhanced the growth and production of certain plants and animals. The Kalapuyas burned some areas season after season to improve their food-gathering prospects. Burning nurtured camas fields, increased the quantity of other edible plants, made seed harvesting such as tarweed more efficient, and controlled underbrush. When the rains returned in the fall, the valleys sprouted fresh grass, providing tender greenery for migrating waterfowl. Both scientific and eyewitness accounts indicate that Native peoples in the interior valleys manipulated the landscape on a grand scale to advance their chances for survival. Tree-ring studies in Oregon State University's McDonald Forest show that regular burning began in about 1647 and ended in the late 1840s, when the ravages of introduced disease attacked the Kalapuyas and large numbers of Euroamericans arrived in the Willamette Valley.

Until they acquired a few horses sometime after 1800, the Kalapuyas followed trails that linked the Willamette Valley with the coast and the western Cascades to exchange trade goods with neighboring groups. Cedar dugout canoes, modest by comparison with those on the northern coast, provided water transportation on the major rivers, and Kalapuya bands traveled down tributary streams and followed the Willamette River to the falls, where they exchanged camas for smoke-dried meat, huckleberries, eels, and pounded and dried salmon. Occasionally, goods from far beyond the valley—such as highly valued dentalia (slender mollusk shells that were found off Vancouver Island), bone and shell beads, and animal hides—were exchanged at the falls. Individuals who possessed many dentalia were usually wealthy or village chiefs. Although social distinctions among people in the western valleys were less obvious than those on the coast, material wealth usually symbolized band leadership.

In the interior Plateau region, Native people moved opportunistically through a variety of habitats and ecological zones—from the Columbia River to high mountain meadows—gathering plant foods as they matured. Inhabiting the vast interior area east of the Cascades, from central Oregon to southern British Columbia, Plateau peoples such as the Yakama, Umatilla, Walla Walla, Cayuse, and Nez Perce lived in permanent winter villages in low-lying, protected areas. Their seasonal rounds took them through complex habitats in the spring to gather bitterroot and other starchy foods and then to important fishing places such as Celilo Falls and the Long Narrows when the Chinook salmon were running in the Columbia River. During the hot summer months, families traveled to mountain-meadow huckleberry grounds that were kept productive through regular burning. While women gathered and dried berries for winter use, men hunted for game animals in the high country. Plateau Indians had to preserve and dry substantial food surpluses for winter use, employing a variety of subsistence strategies that varied with habitat across the Plateau region. Although fish provided an important source of protein for all Columbia River peoples, the Sahaptin speakers who lived east of The Dalles, including the Cayuse and the Nez Perce, placed much greater emphasis on hunting deer and elk than the Chinookan people who lived along the lower river.

Although diets varied with location, estimates suggest that salmon provided from one-third to one-half of the protein consumed by Plateau people. Beginning in the early spring and continuing until fall, mid-Columbia Indians had access to predictable and prodigious runs of a variety of species of salmon. Because the salmon harvest was

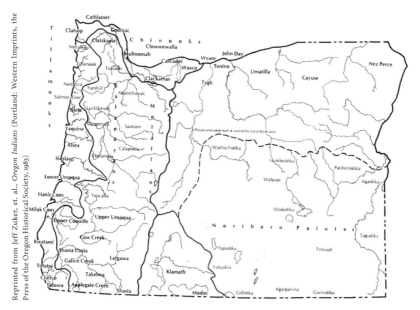

Reprinted from Jeff Zuker, et. al., *Oregon Indians* (Portland: Western Imprints, the Press of the Oregon Historical Society, 1983)

Native territories in Oregon

abundant and seasonal, the annual runs attracted people from distant places on the Plateau to the vicinity of Celilo Falls. People came to exchange goods and socialize at the Long Narrows, a section of the river that fur-trader Alexander Ross called "the great emporium or mart of the Columbia." Lewis and Clark in 1805-1806 and Alexander Ross in 1811 reported great quantities of salmon drying on racks near The Dalles. When the captains passed Celilo Falls on October 22, 1805, William Clark noticed large quantities of pounded fish wrapped in blankets lined with dried salmon skin:

> those 12 baskets of from 90 to 100 w. each (basket) for a Stack. thus pre-
> served those fish may be kept Sound and Sweet Several years, as those
> people inform me, Great quantities as they inform us are Sold to the
> whites peoples who visit the mouth of this river as well as the nativs
> below.

When Alexander Ross passed upriver through the Long Narrows in August 1811, he estimated that more than 3,000 people came to the mid-Columbia during the peak of the salmon runs. According to Ross, only about 100 persons—the Wyams—were permanent residents; the others were "foreigners" from different parts of the country. Visi-

tors from the coast and the interior came to the great falls to gamble
and trade for such goods as bison hides from the Great Plains, camas
loaves from the interior valleys, and marine shells from the Pacific
Coast. Upper Klamath Basin Indians came to The Dalles with wocas
lily seeds, beads, and freshwater shells to exchange for hides from the
Plains and marine items from the coast. Although the acquisition of
horses sometime in the mid-1700s revolutionized life for Plateau peoples, archaeological evidence indicates that the mid-Columbia summer trading rendezvous was a long-standing one, perhaps predating
the arrival of the horse culture by several generations. As the Lewis
and Clark journals make clear, the Indians the captains met during
their autumn passage through the mid-Columbia region in 1805 were
sophisticated and experienced traders. On the lower river, Lewis referred to the Clatsops in January 1806 as "great higlers in trade and
if they conceive you anxious to purchase [they] will be a whole day
bargaining for a handful of roots."

The Indian bands that lived across Oregon's basin and range country moved seasonally to favored fishing, hunting, and gathering
places. More than any other human groups, however, their rugged
basin and high-desert homelands forced them to travel considerable
distances to hunting and gathering sites, and they had to extend those
distances when climatic conditions were especially severe. Inhabiting an area from the southern fringes of the Blue Mountains south
into Nevada and beyond, Great Basin Indians lived in an arid and demanding environment with extreme diurnal and seasonal tempera-
ture fluctuations. Although the Great Basin was a demanding and
difficult place to live, archaeologist C. Melvin Aikens contends that
the environment was also rich in material resources for a people well-
adapted to the region.

Indians in the northern Great Basin wintered in sheltered camps
near such places as Malheur Lake, where they subsisted on preserved
foods and occasional game animals. Sometime during April, the
Northern Paiute bands would begin their seasonal round, setting out
for the high country and circling the northeastern rim of the Great
Basin in search of roots and bulbs. While root digging was still in full
swing in late May and early June, men headed for the Malheur River,
where chum salmon were making their seasonal upstream journey to
spawning grounds. At the same time, women shifted their attention
to the purple-blue camas fields between Malheur Lake and the sur-

rounding mountains. July was cricket month, the time to collect, dry, pound, and store the protein-rich insects. During August and September, people hunted for game, gathered ripening berries, and began collecting the seeds of the wada plant, a low-growing shrub that grew in abundance around the shores of Malheur Lake. By October and November, Paiute families were back in their winter camps, and the men continued to hunt for game animals. Elevation, the availability of water, and a keen sensitivity to the seasons dictated the movements of the Northern Paiute. Knowing precisely when to collect bitterroot, chokecherries, Indian ricegrass, camas, cattail, and wada seeds was critical to survival.

When he died during a malaria epidemic in 1830, the powerful Chinook chief Comcomly was 66 years old. When Lewis and Clark arrived on the lower Columbia 25 years earlier, in November 1805, Comcomly lived in Qwatsa'mts, a plankhouse settlement along Bakers Bay on the north side of the river. The captains counted 28 houses in the Chinook village and estimated the population to be 400 people. Before the Corps of Discovery left for the southern shore of the Columbia estuary to establish their winter encampment in a sheltered inlet along what is now the Lewis and Clark River, Meriwether Lewis presented Comcomly with a medal and perhaps an American flag. Lewis and Clark were not the first outsiders to traffic in commerce with the Chinooks, however. Long before American Robert Gray arrived on the lower Columbia in May 1792, the Chinooks and their Clatsop neighbors on the south side of the river had participated in an extensive trading network that extended north to Nootka Sound, south along the coast to the present California-Oregon state line, and upriver to the great falls of the Columbia. Still, it is fair to say that Robert Gray's entry into the Columbia estuary initiated regular trade between the Chinooks and Clatsops and the British and Americans. When the British sloop *Ruby* anchored in Bakers Bay in May 1795, the Qwatsa'mts Chinooks bargained for three days with the ship's officers before the two parties struck a deal, with the Indians trading 100 sea-otter pelts for valued metal and cloth items.

Although Comcomly never visited Fort Clatsop during the winter of 1805-1806, the Chinook chief eventually emerged as the most influential Indian leader on the lower Columbia, forming strategic alliances with other groups, carrying on regular diplomacy with fur traders at Fort Astoria and Fort Vancouver, and marrying the daughters in his extended family to trading company officials such as Duncan McDougall. David Thompson, the inveterate North West Company partner and explorer who journeyed down the Columbia River in 1811, described Comcomly as strong, muscular, with dark brown hair, and "naked except a short kelt around his waist to the middle of the thigh." Thompson also met one of Comcomly's wives, who was "well dressed with ornaments of beads and shells, [and] had a fine appearance." The 40-year-old Chinook chief and his wife, Thompson reported, "were in the prime of life." Even at that early point in his contacts with the land-based fur traders, Comcomly had already forged strategic marriage alliances with several other coastal villages.

Comcomly's Clatsop neighbor, Coboway, exercised a similar influence at Point Adams on the opposite shore. Coboway was a principal chief in a smaller Clatsop community of eight cedar plankhouses, where about 100 people lived. When Isaac Stevens surveyed the mouth of the Columbia River for the United States government in 1854, he referred to the area as "a perfect Indian paradise in its adaptation to canoe travel, and the abundance of sea and shell fish." Across the mist, rain, fog, and great cultural divide of that winter with Lewis and Clark, Coboway was a regular visitor at Fort Clatsop, gaining the respect of the captains, who referred to the village headman as "the most friendly and decent savage that we have met with in this neighborhood." Coboway continued social and trading exchanges with the Corps of Discovery and allowed village women to interact with the Corps until the group departed upriver in late March 1806. With at least two decades of expanding exchanges with British and American ships that trafficked in the sea-otter trade, coastal villagers were far from novices in their negotiations with outsiders. When Coboway made his way by canoe from Point Adams to the Corps' crude fort on the Netul (Lewis and Clark) River in early December 1805, it was clear that he came to trade.

The trade goods Coboway was seeking, according to historian James Ronda—goods such as ironware, pots, fishhooks, metal tools, and western clothing—were familiar items to the Clatsop people through the maritime trade. In exchange for the limited stocks that Lewis and Clark had to offer, the Clatsops offered wapato roots, berries, salmon, and elk. A late 19th-century Clatsop informant told anthropologist Franz Boas that the village had become wealthy by trading salvaged material from a shipwreck with people who lived upriver. While Lewis and Clark's trade goods paled against the wealth offered up by a shipwreck, the presence of the Corps on the lower river that winter provided the Clatsops with a potential ally against attack. What Lewis and Clark failed to grasp, according to Ronda, were "the rituals of exchange," the ceremony, the "dance of offer and counter-offer" that was integral to the coastal trading world. For the Indians, the exchange experience was as important as any goods that might be acquired.

William Clark thought the Clatsops were "close deelers" who refused to come to a trade agreement "except [when] they think they have the advantage." While the Clatsops negotiated in Chinook jargon with the merchant ship captains who stopped along the coast, the overland captains and their party were unfamiliar with the recently cultivated but limited trade language. The Fort Clatsop commanders further restricted exchanges and socializing with the Clatsops when they established guards and sentries and required all the Indians to leave the fort before nightfall.

The November 1805 arrival of Lewis and Clark represented the opening salvo in a contest for control, the assertion of power and influence over the world of the lower Columbia. The captains offered up new meanings about places in the heart of Clatsop country, especially when they declared the encampment off-limits to Coboway and his people. As the Corps' supply of trade goods dwindled, Lewis and Clark faced increasing difficulties of another kind—acquiring the goods they needed for their return trip upriver. Because they lacked enough canoes, the captains set out to purchase some from the Clatsops, an effort they were unable to accomplish because they lacked goods that the Indians valued. To solve their transportation problem, Lewis and Clark dispatched a small contingent of men to Point Adams, where they stole a canoe and then returned clandestinely to the fort. Four days later, as the party was ready to embark on the upriver journey, Lewis presented Coboway with a certificate of good conduct, a list of the expedition members, and possession of Fort Clatsop. In his journal on March 19, 1806, Lewis commended Coboway for "his good conduct and the friendly intercourse which he has maintained with us during our residence at this place."

Lewis and Clark's escape upriver with the pilfered canoe left the Clatsops with impressions of another kind about the newcomers who had wintered with them. Coboway's name disappears from the written record shortly after John Jacob Astor's Pacific Fur Company built the rough-hewn Fort Astoria in the late spring of 1811. His name resurfaces in December 1813 after Fort Astoria was renamed Fort George and transferred to the British-based North West Fur Company during the War of 1812. A company trader reported that the Clatsop chief regularly visited the post to sell salmon and elk. Sometime later, when a friendly Coboway showed the list that Lewis had given him to North West Company personnel, a clerk threw the paper into a fire and presented the Clatsop chief with a new document representing the power of the North West Company. In a later assertion of British sovereignty—one that Coboway most likely did not witness—the Hudson's Bay Company's chief factor at Fort Vancouver, John McLoughlin, ordered the recovery of shipwrecked goods at Point Adams in 1829 when the Hudson's Bay Company frigate, *William and Ann,* ran aground and split open on Clatsop Spit. In confusing circumstances, a small flotilla and 60 men from Fort Vancouver killed several Clatsops, including village leaders, and pillaged and burned all the houses.

The persistent Point Adams villagers rebuilt their dwellings following the Bay Company assault and lived on in the area into the early 1850s. During his reconnaissance of the West Coast in 1841 for the United States government, Lt. Charles Wilkes reported the existence of several plankhouses with smoked salmon and venison hanging in the interior. Wilkes also observed that a heavy wooden palisade surrounded the houses, the Clatsops' response to the Bay Company attack of 1829. Oregon's Methodist missionaries arrived on the lower Columbia in 1840 when Rev. John Frost established a post near Point Adams. Frost, who counted 160 Clatsops living in the vicinity, failed in his mission effort and left in frustration and failure three years later. Following the influx of immigrants on the Oregon Trail in the 1840s and 1850s, however, the steady flow of white settlers to the Clatsop Plains proved to be a much more numerous and formidable force.

The establishment of farming operations, federally legal land claims, and logging and sawmilling further circumscribed the traditional lifeways of the Clatsop people. In 1852, an executive order set aside Point Adams as a strategic military reserve to protect the mouth of the Columbia River. The U.S. Army began building Fort Stevens during the Civil War. As for the surviving Clatsops, a few intermarried with whites, others went to the newly formed coastal reservations, and some remained near Point Adams and adjusted to the new political and cultural realities by becoming wage laborers.

The arrival of John Jacob Astor's Pacific Fur Company in the spring of 1811 marked the beginning of a permanent Euroamerican presence in the Columbia River country. Comcomly and the Qwatsa'mts villagers had extensive contacts with the Astor party and later with the North West Company. Comcomly's people also rescued Duncan McDougall and six Astorians in April 1811 when their small boat capsized inside Bakers Bay. When the Astor crew set about the demanding task of clearing a site for buildings on the south side of the river, company personnel were suspicious of both the Clatsops and the Chinooks. Company clerk Alexander Ross reported that every member of the crew "was armed with an axe in one hand and a gun in the other," the one for chopping away at the huge trees and the other to ease their apprehensions about the local Indians. Despite the Astorians' uneasiness, Comcomly's name appears regularly in Astorian and later North West Company records as a powerful middleman in the fur trade, controlling transactions north and south along the coast and the delivery of furs to the post on the south shore of the Columbia.

Comcomly and the lower Columbia River Chinook were effective middlemen who exercised their long-time practice of controlling access to trade on the lower Columbia and along the coast. The Chinook headman shrewdly negotiated his way to a dominant role in the delivery of furs to Astoria. For their part, Pacific Fur Company clerks were instructed to establish good relations with local Indians to enhance the firm's trading prospects. While the company was attempting to treat the Chinooks, Clatsops, and other tribes equitably, however, the officials in charge of Astoria were turning the fort into an armed garrison, much to Comcomly's alarm. Through all the cultural misunderstandings and intrigues, the Chinooks continued their lucrative trade with the Astorians. Under the short-lived Astor venture, company clerk Duncan McDougall observed that relations between company employees and the Chinooks and other Indians had been remarkably friendly.

The new flag flying from the fort and the transfer of the Astor company's holdings to the North West Company in December 1813 did little to disrupt daily routine at Fort George. Relations with Comcomly and the Chinooks went on much as before, and Fort George in 1814 was much like Astoria had been in 1811. Comcomly's daughter had married Duncan McDougall, further advancing ties of culture and commerce between the Chinook chief and the newcomers. The bride-price included 15 guns, 15 blankets, and other property. The chief subsequently married three other daughters to fur-trade personnel. When Fort George employees plied Comcomly's son with rum, the headman angrily demanded that no more alcohol be distributed to the Chinooks. Comcomly lived on for more than a decade, making a strategic decision to move 90 miles upriver to live near Fort Vancouver when the Hudson's Bay Company began erecting buildings there in 1825. When the first in a series of seasonal malaria outbreaks took place near the fort in August 1830, the disease proved lethal to Comcomly and virtually all of the other Indians living near the HBC post.

Comcomly's death did not end the Euroamerican fascination with the Chinook chief. Five years after Comcomly died, Meredith Gairdner, a physician at Fort Vancouver, sneaked into an Indian burial ground under cover of darkness, decapitated Comcomly's corpse, and took ship for Hawaii, where he sent the boxed skull to a friend in England for scientific study. His daring act of thievery was linked to an intense 19th-century interest in craniometry, a belief that measuring heads would explain racial and class differences. Comcomly's head was housed in the Royal Naval Hospital Museum in England for 117 years until, at the request of the Clatsop County Historical Society, the skull was returned to Astoria in 1952. It was loaned to the Smithsonian in 1956. When Comcomly's descendants requested his remains in 1972, the head was returned and buried near the chief's village site at Ilwaco, Washington.

Beginning with Lewis and Clark and then with the establishment of Fort Astoria in 1811, power relations on the lower Columbia River were rapidly beginning to shift to other locales. Although the Clatsops and Chinooks were likely aware of the coastal trading ships well before Robert Gray crossed into the Columbia River in 1792, with the exception of the introduction of smallpox in the 1770s their villages remained autonomous political entities, untouched by Euroamerican traders. Dispossession and disaster loomed ahead, however, with an increasing numbers of immigrants coming by sea and by land.

CHAPTER TWO

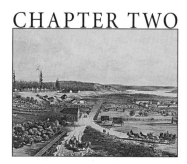

The Coming of Other People

As the 18th century drew to a close, Indian groups along the Oregon Coast were living in well-known and familiar surroundings, trading with people who lived in nearby villages and occasionally with voyagers in seagoing canoes from the north. For centuries they had traveled well-worn trails to upriver fishing places and to berrying grounds in the nearby mountains. The Tillamooks on the northern Oregon Coast knew the terrain and the paths that traversed the headlands and the villagers who lived to the north and the south. They knew intimately the plants and animals that provided sustenance for their survival and the special places for spirit quests, and they understood the proper behavior necessary to appease spiritual guardians. Some coastal groups were also aware, perhaps as early as the 1640s, of the European sailing ships that occasionally touched landfall along the coast. By the last quarter of the 18th century, Europe's interests in the North Pacific quickened as Spanish, British, French, and eventually American vessels came into increasing contact with people who lived in coastal estuaries.

Representing an expanding imperial geography of Old World and New World powers in search of national aggrandizement, mineral riches, and profits, the ships encountered places of long-standing trade and commerce. Described as "discovery" in the historical literature of the Western world, those voyages were in the process of making known to Europeans and Americans a distant corner of the world. But discovery rests in the eye of the beholder. To Native people, European discovery and exploration had few immediate consequences beyond expanded trading opportunities to acquire metal goods and other valued items. While that distant imperial contact with the Northwest Coast ultimately introduced devastating diseases to Native people, its immediate effect merely augmented existing trading prospects for local villages. Slowly and incrementally, the expanding trading networks also brought indigenous peoples within the embrace of global market exchanges.

The Europeans' suspicion and anxiety about the ambitions of their imperial rivals quickened their interest in the Northwest Coast. The earliest pretenders to empire in western North America were Spain and Russia. Spain, with colonial enclaves in Mexico, was in the beginning stages of establishing missions along the southern California Coast, while the Russians were operating a few trading posts along the Alaskan littoral. Worried that Russian advances southward from Alaska threatened its colonial aspirations in California, Spain ordered Capt. Juan Perez to sail to 60 degrees north latitude. Although scurvy aboard his ship forced Perez to retreat, in 1774 he and his crew made landfall in Nootka Sound, where they exchanged trade items with villagers.

One year later, Juan Francisco de Bodega y Quadra and Bruno de Hezeta voyaged northward, only to have both their ships turned back, again by the dreaded scurvy. The Quadra and Hezeta ventures were not without incident. When the two ships made landfall off the Quinault River, local Indians attacked a small landing party. The Spanish ships retaliated by firing on an Indian canoe, initiating the first known instance of blood revenge between Europeans and Native people along the Northwest Coast. Although Hezeta observed a powerful current in the vicinity of the Columbia River, he decided against entering what he called the Rio de San Roque because of his crew's weakened condition. While the Spanish faltered in their secret strategies to counter the southward advancing Russians, their longtime imperial rival, England, presented the more immediate and significant challenge.

British voyages to North Pacific waters in the late 18th century marked the onset of the imperial claiming and bounding of geopolitical space in the Northwest. There were significant differences, however, between early European scientific explorations in the region and the flood of trading ships that followed. The voyages and cartographic contributions of British naval captains James Cook and George Vancouver and American ship captain Robert Gray offer up important contrasts. Cook's third and last official passage through Pacific waters, from 1776 to 1780, has been heralded as one of the most significant events of the Enlightenment, gaining the British captain a revered place as a humanitarian and a prominent place in the annals of maritime history. Although his ships touched several places along the Northwest Coast and wintered in Nootka Sound on the west coast of Vancouver Island, Cook's geographic reconnaissance failed to locate the entry into the Columbia River or to recognize that Nootka Sound was located on the outer coast of a large island and not on the North American mainland. Cook's greatest failure, however, and the central objective of his mission, was his inability to locate the Northwest Passage, the mythical water route across North America.

Cook's voyage into North Pacific waters represented much more than disinterested Enlightenment probing of the far corners of the Earth. Cook was in the employ of the Royal Navy and an ambitious British government eager to challenge Spain for supremacy in the Pacific. During his winter season at Nootka, he was intruding into Native space, triangulating and drafting charts for imperial-minded visionaries in the British Admiralty. While Cook represented wealth and opportunity to the empire-brokers in London, he represented something quite different to the people who lived on Nootka Sound. Even with the vantage of more than two centuries of time, however, many historians still treat Cook's stay at Nootka as one of the principal building blocks for Pacific Northwest history, granting too much attention to Cook and ignoring the people who occupied and were in possession of those places. Such histories condition readers to privilege the heroic stories of the Europeans.

George Vancouver, who had served with Cook on his second and third voyages, sailed into the North Pacific in 1792 on an official cartographic surveying mission for the British government. The Admiralty had instructed him to carefully chart Pacific Northwest waters and to provide detailed descriptions of "every principal object whose position is either wholly or even thro' Accident only partially and incompletely determined." Vancouver was charged with producing an authoritative and accurate geography, with special attention to the elusive Northwest Passage. Leaving England in 1791 and arriving in Pacific waters the following year, the domineering and controversial captain carefully mapped the Pacific Coast from Cape Mendocino to Vancouver Island, including an exacting survey of Puget Sound.

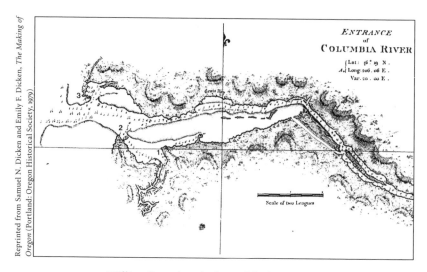

William Broughton's chart of the lower Columbia

Vancouver's crew carried out their work with clinical, scientific precision and in the end concluded that the Northwest Passage was indeed a myth. It is worth mentioning that Vancouver's survey acknowledged only a few of the place-names bestowed by earlier Spanish mapping efforts and made only passing mention of a few Native villages. In keeping faith with the British Admiralty's instructions, he gave "significant and Characteristic Names" to major Northwest landmarks, including Bellingham Bay, Whidbey and Vashon islands, and Mt. Hood and Mt. Rainier, volcanos named after Admiralty friends who would never see the Pacific Northwest. He bestowed on the big island his own name, emphasizing, as geographer Daniel Clayton tells us, "his—and Britain's—presence" on North America's Pacific Coast. Despite the obvious scientific precision of Vancouver's enterprise, his cartographic accomplishments for the British Admiralty illustrate the close ties between exploration and empire.

The coming of American sea captain Robert Gray to Northwest waters is a very different story. Gray's place in the region's history is complex and falls far short of the heroic achievements that some writers have attributed to him. A privateer captain during the American Revolution, Gray was without a ship and looking for work in the mid-1780s when word arrived in Boston of the discovery by James Cook's crew that sea-otter pelts from the Northwest Coast could be sold for great profits in China. With the support of New England maritime investors, in 1787 Gray and Capt. John Kendrick set sail in the *Lady Washington* and *Columbia Rediviva* for Northwest waters, where they spent the winter trading for sea-otter pelts. Because Kendrick proved inept when the two ships sailed for Macao on China's southern coast, Gray assumed command of the *Columbia,* the larger of the two ships. In Macao, Gray sold his furs and returned to Boston in 1790. Within a month and freshly outfitted with Indian trade goods, Gray was once again bound for the Northwest Coast, where he would make every effort to gain maximum returns for his investors as well as himself.

After wintering at Adventure Cove in Clayoquot Sound, Gray headed out in search of sea otters, eventually sailing south along the Washington Coast. The *Columbia Rediviva* cleared the entrance to present-day Gray's Harbor on the evening of May 10, 1792, and continued south toward a bay where the captain had noted a strong outflow several weeks earlier. On the morning of May 11, the ship crossed the bar into the great waterway that Captain Gray named Columbia's River in honor of his ship. Contrary to scholars who have argued otherwise, Gray made no claims of possession but proceeded to carry on a brisk trade with local Natives who canoed out to meet the ship. The *Columbia Rediviva* departed on May 20 with 300 beaver and 150 sea-otter pelts.

In truth, Robert Gray was little interested in exploration and geography, other than the prospect that such knowledge might enhance his profits. He was first and foremost a trader, and nothing in the historical record indicates that he was aware of the estuary's significance. Historian Dorothy Johansen characterized Gray as "a hard man, strictly attentive to the 'two-penny objects' of his business—to get sea otter skins and invest them in China goods." The captain's dealings with Native peoples, especially during his second voyage, were contentious, and on several occasions—with only the slightest provocation—he ordered his crew to destroy villages and blow Indian canoes out of the water. Before leaving his winter quarters in Clayoquot Sound in March 1792, Gray directed his crew to demolish a village with some 200 dwellings. John Boit, a mate aboard the ship, confided to his journal: "am grieved to think Captain Gray should let his passions go so far." Three days before the *Columbia* made its historic crossing of the Columbia bar, his ship directed musket and canon fire on several canoes, sinking one large craft and killing all its occupants. This action was repeated again in May near Clayoquot when Gray's ship destroyed

Trading Vessels in the Northwest		
	England	*United States*
1785-1794	25	15
1795-1804	9	50
1805-1814	3	40

another canoe, killing everyone aboard. Although his "discovery" of the Columbia River would eventually be treated as one of the founding events of the region's history, there is ample reason to question his role as an explorer-hero.

By the close of the 18th century, the Northwest Coast had become a distant corner of an expanding world economy. Yet, the coastal areas of Oregon, Washington, and British Columbia were also places where Native and non-Native people interacted, sought power and influence, and carried on complex exchanges of goods and services. For a considerable period of time, the coastal fur trade involved negotiations among equals, with each party contesting for advantage in the exchange relationship. For Native people, there were also fundamental differences between the maritime and land-based fur traders and the settlers who followed. The traders needed the Indians to provide them with furs and local knowledge, to serve as a labor force in transporting furs, and to act as guides through unfamiliar country. In very distant places, however, imperial nations were beginning to joust for advantage and influence in the Northwest, taking initiatives that eventually would bring great changes to what would become the Oregon country.

The maritime fur trade, which lasted from 1785 to 1815, centered primarily on sea-otter trafficking and brought coastal Indian groups into market-exchange networks. When Capt. James Cook's crew discovered the high prices that sea-otter pelts brought in Chinese markets, the hunt was on. James Hanna, the first British trader to touch landfall along the Northwest Coast in 1785, exchanged metal trade goods in Nootka Sound for furs and then reaped huge profits when he sold the pelts in Canton. By the time Hanna returned to Nootka, other ships had already traded for all the available furs from people who lived in the extensive harbor area. With British and an increasing number of American ships participating in the coastal exchanges, the sea-otter business continued to increase until 1805, when a drop in market demand and diminishing numbers of sea otters contributed to a decline in the trade. During the winter of 1801-1802, 15 vessels along the Northwest Coast took approximately 15,000 furs. Between 1785 and the close of the trade in about 1812, ship captains took an average of 12,000 furs per season, or a total of 200,000 pelts. Hampered by the restrictive monopoly of the British East India Company, British traders eventually lost out to the "Bostons" who dominated the trade.

Transactions between British and American ship captains and Native people did not represent classic market intercourse, because Indian groups took part in the exchanges for their own purposes. Village headmen proved to be shrewd bargainers, demanding more in the way of trade items—especially highly valued metal goods—when furs became scarce. The onset of the fur trade also underscored the extractive nature of the region's fledgling market economy, one that slowly expanded during the first half of the 19th century. Although Indians provided the primary labor force and in many respects controlled the terms of the trade, trouble lay ahead. When the fur-bearing animals became scarce, those who had come to rely on the trade for their livelihoods were left with few alternatives. And then there was the disease factor. As ships from Europe and the United States came into increasing contact with people on the Northwest Coast, they left in their wake Old World contagions that were disastrous for Native people. The maritime and then the interior fur trade regularly placed an unprotected people in direct contact with carriers of global disease pools.

At some point during the 1770s and 1780s, the European voyagers to the North Pacific Coast introduced viruses and bacteria to people who had no immunological defenses against them. The consequences were catastrophic. Demographers argue that there was a hemisphere-wide population decline of at least 90 percent in the centuries following the Columbian voyage of 1492. Smallpox and other Old World diseases probably arrived relatively late on the Northwest Coast because the region was generally distant and beyond the major routes of European travel. The evidence suggests that, beginning in the mid-1770s, mariners from Spanish ships landing along the Oregon, Washington, and British Columbia coasts spread smallpox among the people they encountered.

Based on painstaking research, geographer Cole Harris contends that a devastating smallpox outbreak reached the Strait of Georgia in 1782, leaving in its wake a fearful loss of life. Harris traces the epidemic northward from the lower Columbia River to Puget Sound and then

into the Strait of Georgia in 1782-1783. Anthropologist Robert Boyd
cites the spread of smallpox in the 1780s from the Tillamooks on the
Oregon Coast to the Tlingits in the north. The social and cultural
upheavals were profound, and Boyd estimates a mortality in excess of
30 percent from the initial outbreaks. Although there were no eyewit-
nesses to record in writing the effects of the disease, when Lewis and
Clark wintered on the lower Columbia River in 1805-1806 they found
that smallpox had already greatly reduced the population of local
Clatsop villages.

The coastal and interior fur trade also provided the beginnings for
capital accumulation in distant places, especially in London, Montreal, Boston, and New York. There is considerable evidence that the
sea-otter trade—eventually dominated by ships sailing out of Boston—launched several family fortunes, surplus capital that may have
been invested in New England's early textile industry. The trade also
resulted in shifting imperial claims to the region, with Spain controlling only remnants of its empire south of the 42nd parallel. Russian activity was increasingly confined to Alaska, and American and
British interests emerged dominant across much of the Columbia
Basin and beyond. Between 1800 and the settlement of the Oregon
boundary dispute in 1846, however, those distant claims were largely
empty boasts on paper. Indian peoples from coastal villages to the
interior Plateau were still autonomous groups, enjoying freedom of
movement and association, with many of them only peripherally involved in the developing market economy. With Thomas Jefferson's
election as president of the United States in 1800, however, forces were
set in motion that would initiate a great immigrant movement to the
Northwest that eventually would marginalize Native people in their
own homelands.

No two explorers are more firmly imprinted in the American con-
sciousness than Meriwether Lewis and William Clark. There are
campgrounds, rivers, towns, highway markers, monuments, two institutions of higher education, books, and even a formal association—
the Lewis and Clark Trail Association—named after them. Lewis and
Clark are part of the organic narrative of the American West, one of
the nation's great founding stories. Their expedition is also central
to understanding Oregon and United States history and to explain-
ing the links between exploration and an expanding American empire. The captains were advance agents of an imperial-minded United

States, emissaries for a government headed by political figures who looked on the American West as an area to enter and occupy. To historian Richard White, they were "first white men," akin to Columbus, Daniel Boone, Davy Crocket, and John C. Frémont.

No American political figure is more central to that story of westward expansion than Thomas Jefferson, the third president of the United States. Jefferson is generally associated with the Declaration of Independence, the establishment of a republican government, and the development of democratic institutions. But historian Richard Dillon argues that "if George Washington is the father of our country, then surely Jefferson is the father of our American West." The Virginia founding father was the architect of American democracy, a linguist, a natural scientist, the designer of the University of Virginia, a philosopher-statesman, an inventor, "and [a] vicarious explorer." He was first interested in the West immediately beyond the Appalachian Mountains; but by the time he was elected president, his vision and ambitions had stretched across the continent. One of Jefferson's grand designs was to locate a land-based Northwest Passage, a land and water route that would link the Mississippi Valley to the Pacific. Soon after he became president, Jefferson invited his neighbor, the young military officer Meriwether Lewis, to join his staff as personal secretary. The president had written Lewis' commanding officer that he wanted a secretary who understood both the army and the "Western Country."

From the moment Lewis arrived in Washington, D.C., Jefferson put him to work learning about western North America—its people, topography, river systems, flora and fauna, climates, and the like. Jefferson, who was widely conversant with existing knowledge about the West, was already familiar with Alexander Mackenzie's 1793 trek across present-day Canada. Historian Stephen Ambrose tells us that Jefferson was especially concerned with Mackenzie's recommendation that British fur-trading companies move quickly and decisively to gain control of the Indian trade in the Columbia River country. Jefferson, who had been interested in promoting exploration as early as the 1790s, moved to action in the fall of 1802, informing Lewis that the captain would lead an exploring journey to the Pacific. Shortly thereafter, the president requested a secret congressional appropriation to fund the expedition. Because the Louisiana Territory was still part of the French empire, the president found it necessary to conceal his objectives. Respected journalist-historian Bernard DeVoto concludes that sending the Lewis and Clark expedition was "an act of imperial policy." Ambrose paints Jefferson in even larger terms: "In an age of imperialism, he was the greatest empire builder of all. His mind encompassed the continent." As for the residents of the West, Ambrose claims that Jefferson was ruthless: "Join us or get out of the way." "Hypocrisy," Ambrose concluded, "ran through [Jefferson's] Indian policy."

Jefferson's motivations and ambitions explain part of the background to the authorization and objectives of the mission. President Jefferson made his initial—and secret—request for funding for the expedition in February 1803, a few months before the United States purchased Louisiana from France. Lewis had asked William Clark to join the expedition, and while he was waiting for his decision, Jefferson sent Lewis his instructions about the purposes of the undertaking:

> The object of your mission is to explore the Missouri River, & such principal stream of it as, by its course and communication with the waters of the Pacific Ocean, whether the Columbia, Oregon, Colorado or any other river, may offer the most direct and practicable water communication across this Continent for the purposes of commerce.

Jefferson's orders make it clear that expansion, trade, and future settlement were the mission's principal objectives.

Lewis and Clark's epic journey up the Missouri River, through the rugged Bitterroot Mountains, and down the Columbia River has become the stuff of folklore, legend, and television documentary. Master storyteller Ken Burns' widely viewed film, *Lewis and Clark: The Journey of the Corps of Discovery*, calls the trek one of the greatest exploring adventures of all time. While historians might quarrel with the film's morality tale of heroic achievement and fulfillment of national purpose, it is fair to say that the Corps of Discovery was immensely successful in carrying out Jefferson's instructions. The geographic and natural science findings, the ethnographic information, and the journals themselves—first published in 1814—have served as primary sources for a corpus of writing for more than 150 years. It is also significant, as historian James Ronda reminds us, that Lewis and Clark were among Indians throughout their journey to and from the Pacific. With great skill, the Corps successfully navigated through several Indian nations and a rugged, uncharted geography with the loss of only one expedition member's life.

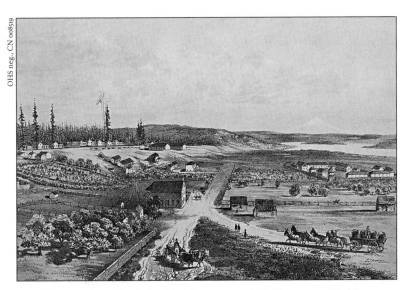

OHS neg., CN 008559

Fort Vancouver on the Columbia River, near today's Vancouver, Washington,
1854 lithograph by Gustavus Sohon

In spite of this success, there is little in the Lewis and Clark journals
to suggest that the captains were any different from their countrymen
in the way they stereotyped Indians. Both were military men with extensive experience in Indian country (and Clark was a slaveholder).
The Lewis and Clark journals, therefore, present a largely negative
commentary on Native people, racial and cultural assessments that
were familiar to their contemporaries in the United States. Their accounts of thieving and treacherous Indians on the mid- and lower Columbia are prime examples. Because of their considerable influence
in shaping perceptions about Indians, Lewis and Clark contributed
to fixing in our historical literature fundamental notions of superior-
ity and dominance over Native Americans. The leaders of the Corps
of Discovery were infinitely more positive in seeing bright prospects
along their route of travel: the promise of the Indian trade, the multitude of fur-bearing animals, the agricultural prospects of some areas,
and the potential for transportation on the Columbia River.

Lewis and Clark were much more than disinterested scientist-geog-
raphers in their reporting about the Columbia River country. Like the
earlier voyages of British sea captains James Cook and George Van-

couver, the American officers provided the young United States with
strategic information about the western reaches of the continent. In
his recommendations to President Jefferson, Lewis urged the United
States to establish fur-trading posts on the Columbia River to counter the designs of the "British N. West Company of Canada." Taking such action would counter Mackenzie, Lewis predicted, and give
the Americans an advantage in controlling trade on the Missouri and
Columbia rivers. He further warned that the ambitions of the North
West Company in expanding the Indian trade "must be vigelently
watched." But the expedition's immediate influence focused on the
region's rich natural resources. In a news article on the Corps of Discovery's return to St. Louis, the *National Intelligencer* reported that
Lewis "speaks of the whole country furnishing valuable furs" and that
the Columbia River system abounded in salmon. In the end, Lewis'
advice to Jefferson was prophetic. According to geographer John Allen, the "American response led to the Astorians, the Rocky Mountain
fur trade, and ultimate American victory in the imperial conflict over
the Oregon country."

Those who followed Lewis and Clark to the Columbia River built
on the captains' narrative descriptions to fix in the public imagination
what would become familiar images of the far-western landscape and
Native people. The increasing activities of land-based fur traders in
the opening decade of the 19th century marked the onset of accelerating change in the Pacific Northwest. Several of these operatives—the
clerks, factors, and traders—left journal accounts and narrative descriptions that shaped what would soon become standard representations of the Oregon country. In an effort to take advantage of the
rich fur resource hinted at in Lewis' report to the president, New York
entrepreneur John Jacob Astor sent two groups of clerks—one by sea
and the other by land—to the Columbia River. Arriving at the mouth
of the river in 1811, fur-trader Ross Cox saw the magnificent "productions of the country, amongst the most wonderful of which are the
fur [*sic*] trees." Eventually traveling upriver and into the Willamette
Valley, he confided to his journal that the land possessed "a rich and
luxuriant soil, which yields an abundance of fruits and roots."

Fellow Astorian Alexander Ross thought the Willamette Valley held
excellent potential for agriculture, with an ideal climate that would
"ripen every kind of grain in a short time." The Willamette, he reported, "fertilizes one of the finest valleys west of the Rocky Mountains" and predicted that with its "salubrious and dry" climate it

would prove to be "the garden of the Columbia." Despite the valley's rich soils, however, Ross feared that "the remote distance and savage aspect of the boundless wilderness along the Pacific" would deter colonization until some future generation. As the Astor party entered the Columbia Gorge, Ross reported that the river narrowed, the current became turbulent, and the clerks struggled to make slow headway upstream. "A dense, gloomy forest" cloaked both sides of the river and left little room for agricultural enterprise.

After portaging around the Cascades, the countryside soon opened up as Ross and the Astorians moved toward The Dalles. At this point in their upriver trek, Ross reported the great runs of salmon in the Columbia River, a potential bonanza "were a foreign market to present itself." He also recorded that while more than 3,000 people gathered along this section of the river "during the salmon season," the permanent inhabitants numbered no more than 100. As the Astorians moved upriver past the Long Narrows and Celilo Falls, Ross saw the great fishery where people came from great distances to "trade and traffic" in horses, buffalo robes, and beads and items from the coast. He called it "the great emporium or mart of the Columbia."

The Americans were not alone in attempting to secure a foothold in the Columbia River country. The North West Company, based in Montreal, was the first business organization to profit from the interior fur trade. Company personnel such as Alexander Mackenzie, Simon Fraser, and David Thompson traversed and mapped much of the interior Columbia Basin and described for the outside world the region's major mountain ranges and river valleys. They also established several fur-trading outposts at strategic interior travel corridors, such as Fort Colville. When the North West Company received word about Astor's ambitions, it dispatched David Thompson to give the Nor'westers a presence on the lower river. In a remarkably rapid descent, Thompson canoed down the Columbia with seven men "to explore this river in order to open out a passage for the interior trade with the Pacific Ocean." By right of "discovery," Thompson claimed for Great Britain the country north of the confluence with the Snake River and announced the intentions of "the N W Company of Merchants from Canada" to establish a trading post to carry on commerce. When Thompson paddled into the lower Columbia estuary, Astor company clerks—who were equally ambitious to move into the interior in search of furs—had further cause for worry. With the outbreak of the War of 1812 and the expected arrival of a British sloop of war, Astor officials agreed to sell the fort to the North West Company, which renamed the post Fort George.

Although the North West Company now dominated the Columbia River fur trade, it too fell victim to outside pressure in 1821, when the British government ordered the firm to merge with the company's larger and more powerful competitor, the Hudson's Bay Company (HBC). The HBC (which still operates department stores across Canada as "The Bay") immediately set about reorganizing its continent-wide fur-trading activities under the ruthless but efficient administration of George Simpson, the new governor for the Northern Department. After an amazingly speedy tour of inspection from the Canadian interior to the lower Columbia River in 1824, Simpson ordered HBC employees to build a major regional trading center on the north shore of the Columbia at the river's confluence with the Willamette. Situated 100 miles upriver from Fort George, Fort Vancouver became a focal point for trade and commerce, a place where local Indians came to trade and negotiate agreements, residence to a remarkably multicultural cast of people, and ultimately a setting that served as a place for transmitting exogenous diseases.

Under Simpson, HBC pursued a geopolitical strategy of trapping out areas south and east of the Columbia, including the great Snake River drainage, to slow the advance of Americans into the region. The result was the creation of an uninviting "fur desert" designed to keep the ambitious Americans east of the Continental Divide. The company's directive of 1824 recognized the realities of maintaining the Columbia River as a southern boundary in any potential agreement with the United States. The calculating Simpson directed that "it will be very desirable that the hunters should get as much out of the Snake Country as possible for the next few years." Settling the boundary along the Columbia River would retain Puget Sound for the British and provide free access to the Columbia for transportation. The success of the HBC brigades in carrying out the fur-desert policy between 1823 and 1841 denuded the Snake River Basin of beaver, increased friction between trappers and Natives, and contributed to lasting changes to stream ecology in the region. As historian Jennifer Ott points out, "to read the journals from the Snake country expeditions is to read a story of creating scarcity."

More than most entrepreneurs of his time Simpson was alive to the potential profits to be made in the northwestern fur trade. He took note of the Columbia River's abundant salmon runs, the fertile soil and "salubrious" climate on the lower river, and Fort Vancouver's strategic location. Simpson was optimistic that Indians living along the river could "be civilized and instructed in morality and Religion at . . . a moderate expence," an achievement that would make them eligible as "runners Boatsmen &c and their services in other respects turned to profitable account." Religion, to Simpson's thinking, had the potential to serve the larger interests of the Hudson's Bay Company, integrating Native people—and especially their labor—into the firm's expanding market networks. Although his expanded responsibilities increasingly kept him in Montreal, Simpson continued to direct the company's policies in the region well past 1846, when the Oregon Boundary Treaty set the American border at the 49th parallel.

With the tall, rawboned John McLoughlin serving as chief factor, Fort Vancouver (1825-1846) became one of imperial England's most distant outposts. Born in Quebec, McLoughlin was 39 years old when Simpson appointed him to head the Columbia Department. Cruel and ruthless on occasion, the calculating McLoughlin shrewdly guided the HBC's Columbia District activities to keep Native people within the embrace of the firm's trading network. He ordered the construction of a small water-powered sawmill upstream from Fort Vancouver, followed Simpson's orders to make the Columbia District self-sufficient in producing its own foodstuffs, encouraged the company to "salt" salmon for external markets, and worried that the Americans "will attempt something in this way." In addition to seeking new markets for the company's productions, McLoughlin carried on business with Russian posts along the Alaskan coast and with the Spanish/Mexican missions in California. The chief factor turned Fort Vancouver into a welcoming international port of call for visitors, who included natural scientists, missionaries, and an occasional American empire-builder.

Under McLoughlin, the Hudson's Bay Company used arbitrary, even severe methods to force recalcitrant employees to carry out their work. The isolated nature of the trading posts meant lengthy and tedious assignments, so fur traders, according to McLoughlin, had "no alternative but to make them do their duty." The favored punishment for slackers was flogging, a widely practiced form of discipline among both the British and the Americans. McLoughlin and the HBC also followed even more forceful procedures, seeking wholesale retaliation when individuals and tribes in the region were deemed particularly obstreperous. McLoughlin and his fur-brigade leaders retaliated for killings with quick dispatch, for example, punishing the perpetra-

tors in a kind of blood-feud reciprocity. When the Clallam along the
south shore of the Strait of Juan de Fuca killed a small company party,
McLoughlin dispatched a force of 60 men and a ship to the area. After the company vessel, *Cadboro,* cannonaded the Clallam village into
oblivion, HBC personnel destroyed 30 Native canoes and burned the
village. McLoughlin reported to company officials that the Indians of
the Northwest Coast "can only be restrained from Committing acts of
atrocity and violence by the dread of retaliation." His larger strategic
objective, however, was to limit violence in the interests of trade.

For the new economy settling on the Oregon country, Fort Vancouver became the central clearinghouse for business activities that
treated animals and other natural resources as extractive commodities, items of exchange that could be traded for profit. As an expression of Great Britain's expanding commercial and imperial power, the
post served as a middle ground between Indian and western worlds,
a place where the terms and volume of trade could be mediated. Until
the 1840s, when American immigrants trekking west on the Oregon
Trail began to overrun the lower Columbia and Willamette valleys,
Fort Vancouver was a colonial outpost among still-dominant Indian
communities. The post had a full complement of skilled craftspeople
who fashioned metal goods, built containers for shipping furs, and
constructed vessels for trading along the coasts. It also was the command center and headquarters for the Columbia Department's relations with outlying posts in the interior—Fort Colville, Fort Nez
Perces, and Fort Umpqua.

Fort Vancouver represented dramatic change for the region—
steamboats, fields and pastures, and the chief factor's handsome white
house (with two cannons mounted in front), where meals were served
on elegant blue china. John McLoughlin lived in the house with his
common-law wife, a half-Ojibwa woman, and their four children. Beyond the stockade in the extensive forest clearing along the Columbia River, an always transient group of French Canadian *voyageurs,*
Iroquois trappers, Hawaiians, and Indians were part of a community
of some 700 people. The fur brigades were a polyglot of British and
Scottish nationals, French Canadians, and their Indian and métis
wives. Marriages between Indian women and white fur traders created economic and functional social alliances. Although the brigade
leaders' journals only hint at the makeup of trapping parties, there is

Klamath Indian families in dugout canoes

considerable evidence that women contributed to the success of the seasonal ventures.

While wives regularly accompanied the engagés and freemen who made up the annual trapping parties, brigade leader John Work's métis wife, Josette Legace, and their children also occasionally traveled with her husband's fur-gathering expeditions. Women performed critical labor, making moccasins and snowshoes, picking berries and pounding them with dried meat to produce pemmican, and carrying supplies and beaver pelts. Trapper journals also report that brigade women were responsible for skinning beaver and dressing pelts, drying salmon, and gathering root bulbs. In brief, women were indispensable to the efficient management of the expeditions and enabled parties to cover vast distances during the trapping season.

John McLoughlin and George Simpson differed in their assessment of the severity of the threat that Americans posed to the Bay Company's hegemony in the Northwest. Simpson, who was prepared to accept a boundary settlement along the Columbia River, worried that American missionaries were making more progress in extending and improving their farms "than in the ostensible objects of their residence in this country." Although he directed the bulk of the Americans to settle south of the Columbia, McLoughlin believed that it was good business to provide the increasing number of newcomers with seeds, supplies, and other necessities. The chief factor—who had converted to Catholicism as a youth—also encouraged Roman Catholic missionaries to establish posts in the Willamette Valley to "prevent the American Missionaries acquiring influence over the Canadians." In the end, however, McLoughlin was a realist, and he staked out a sizable claim of his own at Willamette Falls well in advance of the boundary settlement.

Because Fort Vancouver served as an imperial outpost with an extended overland and seagoing trading network, the constant goings and comings of people left McLoughlin with a delicate balancing act—pacifying the imperious George Simpson and the company's board of governors on the one hand and dealing with the arrival of increasing numbers of Americans on the other. While he was generous in selling and loaning seeds and supplies to the incoming Americans, McLoughlin was careful to point the newcomers south into the Willamette Valley at the end of their journey to protect the company's strategic interests north of the Columbia River. Directives from HBC officials who worried that missionaries were more interested in forming a U.S. colony on the lower Columbia than they were in converting Indians to Christianity further complicated McLoughlin's task.

More than any other factor, disease contributed to reversing the demographic balance between Indian and Euroamerican populations in the Pacific Northwest. Because of Fort Vancouver's strategic location astride the region's major trading corridors—the Columbia and Willamette rivers—the post provided ideal conditions for transmitting lethal pathogens to Native people. This underscores the signal feature of the fur trade—its role as prelude to white settlement. Until the close of the 18th century, the Columbia River country existed in relative isolation from the exogenous disease pools—smallpox, measles, whooping cough, typhoid, malaria, and cholera—that had proved so deadly to people lacking immunities to Old World contagions. While the Rocky Mountains and ocean barriers limited travel and access to the region for centuries, that isolation began to erode when Russian, Spanish, British, and American ships increasingly touched base along the Northwest Coast. Brought to the Pacific Northwest by coastal fur traders, first smallpox and then a succession of Old World (including African) biological disease pools struck down

Native villagers in large numbers. Geographer Cole Harris argues that the disease factor "turns the story of the contact process away from the rhetoric of progress and salvation and towards the numbing recognition of catastrophe." A disease-induced depopulation brings into question the widespread Euroamerican belief that the introduction of western cultural values and religious principles brought enlightened civilization to Native people. It is clear that the immigrants traveling the trails to the Northwest represented agents of destruction as well as the genesis of a new society.

The best documented of the major epidemics—and a major cause of Native depopulation—was a series of seasonally recurring malaria outbreaks on the broad wetlands of the lower Columbia River and in the Willamette Valley between 1830 and 1833. Coming first from West Africa to Central America, the initial outbreak in the Oregon country took place around Fort Vancouver in August 1830. Fever and ague first appeared at Fort Vancouver in July 1830, coincident with the departure of the *Owyhee*, an American trading ship. Spread by an insect vector—in this case mosquitoes—the "fever and ague" returned annually to ravage Indian and white populations alike. But the malarial infections affected the two peoples in dramatically different ways. While whites usually developed fevers and sickness and survived, malaria was lethal to the Chinookan and Kalapuyan people. Anthropologist Robert Boyd suggests that for the humid sections of the Oregon country the seasonal epidemics were the most significant epidemiological happening during the early contact period.

The malaria epidemics were devastating to Indians. In a letter to Hudson's Bay Company officials in September 1830, Chief Factor John McLoughlin expressed alarm at the toll of the disease: "The Intermittent Fever is making a dreadful havoc among the natives & at this place half our people are laid up with it." McLoughlin estimated the Native death toll at 75 percent in the vicinity of Fort Vancouver. Company trader Peter Skene Ogden reported the devastating toll at Native villages on Sauvie Island across from the fort: "Silence reigned where erst the din of population resounded loud and lively. . . . The fever ghoul has wreaked his most dire vengeance; to the utter destruction of every human inhabitant." Visiting botanist David Douglas left a similar description in the fall of 1830: "A dreadfully fatal intermittent fever broke out in the lower parts of this river about eleven weeks ago, which has depopulated the country." Boyd estimates an Indian mortality on the lower Columbia River and in the Willamette Valley of 90 percent out of a pre-epidemic population of 14,000 people by the time the epidemic had run its course. When Lt. Charles Wilkes of the U.S. Exploring Expedition visited the region in 1841, he counted 575 Chinook survivors on the Columbia and 600 Kalapuyans in the Willamette Valley.

The well-documented malaria epidemic was only one among several exogenous diseases that struck down Native people. The ever-increasing traffic on the Oregon Trail after 1844 brought new diseases, especially those associated with childhood, such as chicken pox, measles, and whooping cough. These later pathogens struck disproportionately against Indian children, skewing the average age of the Indian population. Anthropologist Eugene Hunn points out that Indian-white relations in the Pacific Northwest "has been first and foremost a history of the ravages of disease which drastically reduced native populations." By the close of the American Civil War, disease had reduced the Native population in the region by about 80 percent, a catastrophic decrease that parallels similar declines elsewhere in the Americas. The pathogens unquestionably weakened the ability of Indian groups to resist the increasing numbers of Euroamericans who were entering the lower Columbia and Willamette valleys in the 1830s and 1840s. By mid-century, Oregon stood on the threshold of immense demographic, cultural, economic, and ecological change.

CHAPTER THREE

Creating an Immigrant Society

The 1830s and 1840s marked a critical turning point in the place that would become Oregon. Sometime during the mid-1830s, the Willamette Valley passed through a demographic, cultural, and economic divide of sorts. When the inquisitive John McLoughlin visited the valley in 1832, he judged that it deserved "all the praises Bestowed on it as it is the finest country I have ever seen." To the south along the meandering Willamette River, former employees of Astor's company, the North West Company, and HBC trappers were establishing rudimentary farmsteads and raising a few livestock. People were also coming to Oregon for other reasons. In a lengthy and fascinating letter to Hudson's Bay Company officials in November 1834, McLoughlin reported the arrival at Fort Vancouver of Boston merchant Nathaniel Wyeth, Methodist missionaries Jason and Daniel Lee, and naturalists John Kirk Townsend and Thomas Nuttall.

These newcomers to Oregon's big western valley were beginning the slow and difficult work of imposing a new order on the valley landscape, initiating a transformation that differed in kind and quality from Native practices. The 1830s and 1840s marked the onset of resettlement in the Oregon country, the beginnings of establishing a largely immigrant society with new social, cultural, and geopolitical reckonings. For the most part, those French Canadian, British, and American settlers were oblivious that they were displacing and marginalizing another people. The immigrants also brought with them familiar animals and plants, cattle, pigs, sheep, wheat, fruits—species that adapted especially well to the valley's humid climate. The growing number of American citizens on their way to the Oregon country during the 1830s were the vanguard of what would become a floodtide of overland immigrants entering the Willamette Valley in the 1840s and the Umpqua and Rogue valleys during the next two decades. The non-Indian population in the valley numbered about 150 in 1840 and burgeoned to about 6,000 by 1846. This process of resettling and displacing the Native population took place first in Oregon's western valleys and then, after 1860, advanced eastward into the interior. During those decades, Indian survivors were increasingly pushed to the margins through local pressures and arbitrarily dictated federal treaties that established land reserves in areas less desirable for agriculture.

Why did they come, these Americans? What prompted them to pull up stakes in such great numbers and travel nearly 2,000 miles on a difficult journey to seek out new homes? What motivated them to leave their home places for another, very different land? These were people, especially the men, who gladly accepted the prospect of extreme displacement, who severed themselves from their former homes to relocate to a distant corner of the continent. The background to the increasing interest in the Oregon country was vested in events and circumstances that gathered momentum in the aftermath of the Lewis and Clark expedition. Using the Corps of Discovery for both commercial and geopolitical purposes, expansion-minded American politicians and publicists began to actively promote the occupation and settlement of the Oregon country. The growing American interest in the region prompted Secretary of State John Quincy Adams to negotiate a treaty with Great Britain in 1818, an agreement that extended the Anglo-American boundary along the 49th parallel to the Rocky Mountains and granted joint occupancy to both nations for ten years. The Adams-Onis Treaty with Spain established the Oregon country's southern boundary at 42 degrees in 1819. In essence, that treaty symbolized the contest between an ambitious and expanding American empire and a diminishing Spanish presence in North America.

The American nation-state was becoming more aggressive in its ambitions. A committee in the U.S. House of Representatives issued a flattering and greatly exaggerated report in 1820 characterizing the Columbia region from "a commercial point of view . . . of the utmost importance." The committee singled out for special praise the area's proximity to China, its lucrative fur trade, agricultural potential, and excellent fisheries. As editor of the *St. Louis Enquirer* and later as U.S. senator, Missouri's Thomas Hart Benton urged the occupation and settlement of the Oregon country. Writing for his newspaper, Benton called for enterprising Americans to lead the way: "The children of Adam . . . should march to the Pacific." With the publication of the House report, he declared, "the first blow was struck . . . in the public mind which promised eventual favorable consideration." Benton was one of the earliest to call for a railroad to the West, an accomplishment that would bring into existence a "long line of farms and houses, of towns and villages, of orchards, fields, and gardens." For nearly two decades, Benton and his fellow Missouri colleague, Lewis F. Linn, described the Northwest as an earthly paradise, a place where prudent and ambitious American citizens could turn their dreams to reality.

There were still others, visionaries and mythmakers with even greater imaginations, who were even less hinged to reality. The most single-minded and obsessive American promoting Columbia River settlement was Harvard-educated Hall Jackson Kelley. After reading the Lewis and Clark journals in 1817, he reported, "the word came expressly to me to go and labor in the field of philanthropic enterprise and promote the propagation of Christianity in the dark and cruel places about the shores of the Pacific." The imaginative Kelley promoted the Oregon country as a "New Eden," a land with "sublime and conspicuous" mountains, a "salubrious" climate, a place "well watered, nourished by a rich soil, and warmed by a congenial heat." Kelley publicized Oregon in letters to major eastern newspapers; and in *A Geographical Sketch of that Part of North America Called Oregon* (1830), he published a wildly imaginative pamphlet plagiarized from earlier journals. He also put his promotional talents to work in Boston when he established a society to encourage the establishment of Christian settlements on the Columbia River. While historians have ridiculed him as eccentric and out of touch with reality, it should be noted that Boston entrepreneur Nathaniel Wyeth, who made two abortive efforts to establish business enterprises on the Columbia, and Presbyterian missionary Henry Harmon Spalding, who built a mission house and school at Lapwai among the Nez Perce, were both members of Kelley's society.

Taking their cue from the perceptive John McLoughlin, historians have long been aware that missionaries greatly aided in disseminating information about the Pacific Northwest, especially their favorable descriptions about the agricultural potential of places such as the

Willamette Valley. Published in Protestant religious journals, their glowing stories described the bright prospects of a promised land and offered up visions of a limitless future. Marcus Whitman, who represented the ecumenical American Board of Commissioners for Foreign Missions outpost at Waiilatpu in the Walla Walla Valley, praised the region's fertile soil, its "mild equable climate," and its superior "advantages for Manufactories and Commerce." Although mission organizations directed the Whitmans, the Spaldings, and Jason and Daniel Lee to convert Indians to Christianity, in virtually every instance their greatest efforts were directed toward urging the white settlement of the region. The aging McLoughlin was prophetic when he wrote in 1847 about why the Americans came: "It always seemed that the great influx of American missionaries and the statements of the Country these missionaries sent to their friends circulated through the United States in the public papers were the remote cause."

Missionaries did far more than serve as publicists for the Oregon country. Protestant missionaries in particular ridiculed and undermined the authority of Indian spiritual leaders and insisted that implementing an agricultural economy was the proper route to salvation and Christianity. Narcissa Whitman was one of those who became disillusioned in her efforts to save "the heathen" and by the 1840s turned her energies toward promoting white immigration. Missionaries served immigrants in other ways: guiding wagon parties, providing advice to Oregon-bound travelers, and carrying on experimental agricultural enterprises. Faced with abysmal failures in their efforts to convert Indians, the Whitmans, Spaldings, Lees, and others looked to white settlement as the great hope for their newly adopted homelands. The new immigrants firmly believed that they represented forward advance in the noble effort to extend the boundaries of civilized space. Because Indians failed to obey "the command to multiply and replenish the earth, . . . they cannot stand in the way of others," Marcus Whitman wrote to his parents in 1844.

People have always made decisions about migrating to new lands— if they have the option—based on certain assumptions and values. A review of most population movements in 19th-century America indicates that they followed in the wake of shifting social and economic conditions. "Motive," geographer William Bowen argues, "is fundamental to migration," and motivation becomes increasingly important the more distant and difficult the move. Until the 1840s, there were only a few isolated Euroamerican settlements in the Columbia River country—Fort Vancouver and its scattered outposts, a few former trappers in the French Prairie area, and the mission establishments in the Willamette Valley and the interior. A series of events and circumstances during the 1830s and 1840s, however, irrevocably changed the demographic profile of the Oregon country. First there were the glowing descriptions of the region's agricultural potential, Edenic stories that had special appeal to midwestern farmers who were suffering through a floundering agricultural economy and a prolonged period of depressed prices in the wake of the Panic of 1837. But there was more to the emigrant movement to the Northwest than the simple Eden-like descriptions of the region.

For some time scholars have deliberated about the factors contributing to the "Oregon fever" of the 1840s, the real reasons that prompted families to head west on the Oregon Trail. William Bowen discounts Fourth of July oratorical themes of patriotic idealism and the immigrants' "inspired nationalism" to win Oregon away from the British. He lists instead the lingering effects of the Panic of 1837; several years of flooding in Missouri, Iowa, and Illinois; the lure of free land; the promise of economic betterment; the quest for adventure and excitement; and, finally, physical health, which is repeatedly referred to in overland journals and reminiscences. Chronic sickness and disease in the Mississippi Valley, he concludes, rank ahead of economic considerations and all other factors as motives for immigrating to Oregon.

Historian Carlos Schwantes sees different motivations, arguing that hard-pressed midwestern farmers found the promise of abundant and fertile land in the Willamette Valley a sufficient attraction to undertake the arduous 2,000-mile journey. Still others ventured to the Oregon country to distance themselves from failed personal or business enterprises. The Jacksonian period in American history also featured riots over religion and slavery, the dislocations associated with early industrialization, and a floodtide of Irish and German immigrants who were reshaping eastern cities. In the South, real and potential slave rebellions and the westward press of slaveholding states and territories created additional uncertainties.

The immigrants came with a rush. During his reconnaissance of the Oregon country in 1841, Lt. Charles Wilkes estimated a population of between 700 and 800 people of "whites, Canadians, and half breeds" in the western valleys. Of that number, about 150 were Americans, most of them associated with the mission settlements at Willamette Falls and farther up the valley. By the early 1840s, Hudson's Bay Company

OHS neg., OrHi 2591, Carleton Eugene Watkins, photographer

Oregon City and Willamette Falls in 1867,
shortly after the first portage railroad was built there

personnel who had lived in the region for nearly two decades were expressing amazement at the number of overlanders suddenly in their midst. A company trader at Fort Nez Perces on the Walla Walla River reported that the Americans were getting "as thick as Mosquitoes in this part of the world." When the large immigrant group of about 800 people—known as the "Great Migration"—arrived in the Willamette Valley in 1843, McLoughlin himself expressed alarm that the country was "settling fast."

The growth of Oregon City is indicative of the transformation that was taking place in the valley. McLoughlin established a land claim at Willamette Falls in 1829, and two years later the HBC opened a saw-mill at the site. After the Methodists established a mission at the falls, the small settlement grew from a single building in 1840 to several more early in 1843. The newly named Oregon City had 75 structures by the close of that year. In an article published in the New York *Weekly Herald* in 1844, Peter Burnett reported that the new settlement had four stores, two sawmills, one gristmill, and another under construc-tion. "There is quite a little village here," he wrote. When Joel Palmer arrived in 1845, Oregon City had taken on the appearance of a village of about 100 houses, "most of them not only commodious, but neat." The town now had about 300 residents, two conspicuous public buildings, a Methodist church and a Catholic chapel, and the usual array of services.

With only a remnant of the Kalapuya people scattered across the valley, the intruding whites experienced little resistance in staking out generous land claims for themselves. And people kept coming. In 1843, 1,500 Euroamericans lived in the valley. By 1845, the number had increased to 6,000 and then climbed to 9,083 in 1849 and 13,294 in 1850. By 1860, 52,000 non-Natives called the Willamette Valley home.

It is nearly impossible to estimate Oregon's Native American population based on the first territorial census in 1850. The Indian population was in sharp decline, and the Bureau of the Census issued confusing instructions about counting them. In the Willamette Valley, where most white settlers were concentrated, there were an estimated 500 Kalapuyas, according to William Bowen. Until the settlement of the boundary issue, the shrewd McLoughlin had directed most of that early stream of Americans south into the Willamette Valley, with only a few pushing north into the Cowlitz Valley and to the southern tip of Puget Sound where the Bay Company had established agricultural enterprises. With the increasing number of United States citizens in their midst, HBC officials initiated moves to attract Canadians to settle the disputed area north of the Columbia River. When the company invited Roman Catholic missionaries to come to the Columbia River country in 1838 to counter the influence of Protestant missions, the American mission settlements deemed the move subversive. After the Cayuse attack on the Whitman Mission in 1847, Presbyterian missionary Henry Harmon Spalding, in a fit of religious bigotry, blamed Roman Catholics and the Hudson's Bay Company for the assault.

Coming to terms with the new immigrant society in the Oregon country is to understand something about the restless nature of sizable segments of the American population. The Americans trekking westward on the Oregon Trail were representatives of a young but rapidly growing nation-state who carried with them the core values and conflicts associated with a modernizing, capitalist world. They were largely landseekers, looking to establish community structures that would provide security for their landed property and a degree of economic opportunity for later arrivals. Those first comers in the resettlement process were less interested in striking out in bold new directions—creating new social institutions—than they were in affirming long-held values and legal precedents in a fresh setting. Although the immigrant society emerging in the Pacific Northwest developed a few unique traits, the host of traditions and ideas the migrants carried with them on the western trails proved remarkably adaptable to the Pacific Slope. As Cole Harris has written about British Columbia's resettlement, those who came west brought with them "everyday ideas about social organization, work, and the details of daily life." Even the long overland journey could not erase those deeply conditioned ideals.

With the sudden inrush of United States citizens in the early 1840s, the immigrant population quickly established a new legal landscape, imposed first in the Willamette Valley and then in outlying areas as the number of migrants swelled in the next decade. The earlier Euroamerican settlers in the valley—French Canadians, retired HBC personnel, and Methodist Mission personnel—held land through simple preemption and occupation and by forcibly removing the Kalapuyas who had survived the malaria epidemic. But the increasing number of immigrants arriving in the valley threatened existing land claims and prompted a search for legal mechanisms to protect them. With advance notice that a large group of immigrants were expected in the Willamette Valley in the fall of 1843, Euroamerican residents gathered together in a series of celebrated meetings in the spring and early summer and fashioned what became known as the Provisional Government. The neophyte organization's legal enactments highlight how new property relations were imposed in lieu of the simple preemptive practices of the previous decade. Article 3 of the Provisional Government's Organic Code established the basis for land ownership:

> No individual shall be allowed to hold a claim of more than one square mile, of 640 acres in a square or oblong farm, according to the natural situation of the premises; nor shall any individual be allowed to hold more than one claim at the same time.

The code granted citizenship to "every free male descendant of a white man who has resided in the territory for 6 months," wording that enfranchised the sons of white males and their half-blood offspring. The newly adopted Provisional Government's legal principles—which existed independently of both the United States and Great Britain—also prohibited slavery, a provision driven by the desire to avoid conflicts over the slavery issue rather than any idealistic or humanitarian principle. Still left unresolved, however, was imperial resolution of the boundary question.

After much bluster, breast-beating, and threats of war, the United States and Great Britain signed a treaty in 1846 establishing a natural boundary along the 49th parallel, exclusive of the southern tip of Vancouver Island. Despite the Democratic Party's 1844 campaign slogan, "Fifty-four-forty or fight," the United States did not press its claim to present-day British Columbia. Already at war with Mexico in the spring of 1846, American negotiators limited their ambitions to the area south of the 49th parallel. With beaver largely trapped out south of the Columbia River, the influential Hudson's Bay Company did not pressure the British government to strike a more favorable agreement. Moreover, the company had already moved its Columbia Department headquarters from Fort Vancouver to Fort Victoria on Vancouver Island. The British were also moved to compromise because of persisting troubles in its far-flung empire, especially the potato famine in Ireland and problems on the Indian subcontinent.

Settlement of the boundary issue, however, still left law and governance to the Provisional Government, which had no legal constitutional relation to the United States government. The boundary treaty with Great Britain also guaranteed Indian rights to property and specified that immigrants were prohibited from settling on Indian land "so long as such rights shall remain unextinguished by treaty." The issue of territorial status for the American Northwest continued to remain in limbo, with the slavery issue delaying congressional action to create a new territory. Congress finally took action following the Cayuse attack on the Whitman mission in November 1847, passing the Oregon Territorial Act the following year to provide civil institutions to protect citizens. The measure implicitly prohibited slavery by acknowledging an anti-slavery section of the Ordinance of 1787 and put off to a future date the resolution to the Provisional Government's generous land-law arrangements. The territorial act also guaranteed Native rights to landed property unless those rights were "extinguished" by formal treaties with tribes.

By the autumn of 1847, Oregon's immigrant population had soared to 9,000 people, with most of them settling in the lower Willamette Valley. That fall, a group of Cayuses and Walla Wallas returned from the Sacramento Valley infected with measles, an exotic pestilence to Native people that quickly spread through the interior Columbia Basin and beyond. According to estimates by Fort Vancouver officials, by the time the disease had run its course the epidemic had killed nearly one-tenth of the Indian population between Fort Hall and

Puget Sound. When more than 200 Cayuses died in the vicinity of the Whitman Mission at Waiilatpu, the Cayuses became suspicious that Marcus Whitman, trained as a physician, was the cause of the alarming mortality. Believing that Whitman had loosed poisons upon their people, the Cayuse struck against the mission on November 29, 1847, killing both Whitmans and 11 other whites. What became known as the Whitman Massacre, anthropologist Robert Boyd argues, was directly related to the introduction of a devastating disease and its calamitous consequences for the Cayuse. The Whitman killings also marked the onset of more than 30 years of intermittent conflict between Native peoples and the region's newly dominant immigrant population.

Slavery and questions of race were more than academic issues to Oregon's white citizenry. While many who took the western trails were from slaveholding or border states, the great majority of them were neither slave holders nor of the slave-holding class. That said, whether they were from the North or South, most of them carried cultural baggage that included deeply seated prejudices against Indians and African Americans, and a small number even traveled to Oregon with their human chattel. Although those mostly white, property-owning immigrants wanted to avoid competition with slave labor, they also sought independence and the opportunity to reestablish themselves as landowners. Historian Robert Bunting argues that white settlers confronted the contradiction "between freedom and slavery with legal statutes of exclusion and racist appeals to biological imprinting." Oregon's white immigrant population, historian David Johnson concludes, feared losing its cultural and racial homogeneity.

Despite its distance from the slave-owning states, the slavery issue was embroiled in politics in the Pacific Northwest. Balloting on Oregon's proposed state constitution in 1857 reveals the deeply ingrained cultural values of the largely border-state immigrant population. It also provides a fair reflection of the territory's attitudes toward the slavery/race question. The constitutional delegates drafted three questions for the ballot: "Do you vote for the constitution?" Approved 7,195 to 3,195. "Do you vote for slavery in Oregon?" Defeated 7,727 to 2,645. "Do you vote for free Negroes in Oregon?" Defeated 8,640 to 1,081. Enforcement aside and despite amendments to the U.S. Constitution, Oregon did not rescind the prohibition against "free Negroes" until 1926. The race/ethnicity issue would prove to be an acrimonious and persistent legacy that Oregonians would grapple with into the 21st century.

Reprinted from Samuel N. Dicken and Emily F. Dicken, *The Making of Oregon* (Portland: Oregon Historical Society, 1979)

Section of J.J. Abert's territorial map, 1838

The race question was also linked to the most important piece of land legislation to leave a permanent imprint on the Oregon landscape. Because the territorial act of 1848 said nothing about the existing land situation, Willamette Valley settlers commissioned Oregon's territorial delegate, Samuel Thurston, to secure the passage of a federal law that would legitimate the existing land claims, most of them in the western valleys. The problem for Congress, which historically limited claims to 160-acre grants, was the enormous size of the 640-acre claims allowed under the Provisional Government. But the persistent Thurston achieved remarkable success when Congress passed the Oregon Donation Land Law in September 1850, a near replica of the bill that Thurston carried with him to Washington, D.C. With some modifications, the act legitimized the Provisional Government's land claims of 640 acres. For settlers in Oregon by 1850, white male citizens were eligible for 320 acres. If the man was married, his wife could also claim 320 acres in her own right. For citizens arriving after 1850, the acreage limitation was halved for a husband-wife total of 320 acres. To gain title to the land, a person was required to live and make improvements on the claim for four years. Section 4 of the law established the question of eligibility:

> ... granted to every white settler or occupant of the public lands, American half-breed Indians included, above the age of 18 years, being a citizen of the United States, or having made a declaration according to law, of his intention to become a citizen.

The Oregon Donation Land Law benefitted incoming whites and dispossessed Indians. In his lobbying efforts in Washington, D.C., Thurston informed Congress that the "first prerequisite step" to settling the land issue involved the removal of Indians. To meet constitutional requirements, he argued, it was necessary to extinguish Indian title to land before it could become part of the public domain. Because the Oregon Territorial Act of 1848 guaranteed Indian rights to their homelands "so long as such rights shall remain unextinguished by treaty," Congress passed legislation authorizing the appointment of commissioners to negotiate treaties with Oregon tribes "for the Extinguishment of their claims to lands lying west of the Cascade Mountains." The commissioners were empowered to negotiate treaties, "and if they find it practicable, they shall remove all these small tribes and leave the whole of the most desirable portion open to white settlers."

Those federal initiatives set in motion strategies that forced treaties on Indian tribes throughout the Northwest. The treaty-making spree that took place in the region during the 1850s was part of a broader, more ambitious effort being pursued to gain access to Indian lands across the American West. Treaty-making of this kind did not represent a diplomatic give-and-take between equals but an aggressive nation-state dictating terms to a subject people. Everywhere across the continent, treaties meant a progressive erosion of the Indian land base and a diminution of Native sovereignty. In the Pacific Northwest, the removal policies that followed enjoyed the wholehearted support of the region's immigrant settler population, who wanted security in their claims to property and new lands opened to settlement.

By expropriating Indian land through the treaty process, much of Oregon was made part of the Public Domain and became available to United States citizens under federal land laws. The Donation Land Law validated white settler claims in the Willamette Valley and brought a rush of people spilling over into the Umpqua and Rogue valleys. It stimulated an even greater settler movement to Oregon, with the number of immigrants peaking in 1852. Before the donation law lapsed in 1855, some 25,000 to 30,000 people entered the territory, a population increase close to 300 percent, with approximately 7,000 individuals making claims to 2.5 million acres. Until the onset of the railroad era in the 1870s, the Donation Land Law had a greater influence in shaping the course of Oregon history than any other event or legislative enactment.

By attracting large numbers of settlers to the Umpqua and Rogue valleys, the Oregon Donation Land Law helped trigger something akin to a race war, especially in Oregon's southernmost valley. For more than a decade Euroamerican fur-trading encounters with Indians in the Rogue Valley involved trade, sexual liaisons, and negotiations that established what historian Nathan Douthit calls a "limited accommodation and adaptation" between the two cultures. This "middle ground" cultural relationship involved unions between Hudson's Bay Company personnel and Native women and the mixed-blood progeny of those partnerships. That small mixed-blood group served a limited role as cultural intermediaries until their world was irrevocably changed in a crescendo of racial violence in the mid-1850s. A white volunteer militia, comprised of prospecting miners who worked the tributaries of the Rogue River and white settler-farmers, embarked on a war of extermination in 1852 and 1853 to drive Rogue bands from their hunting and gathering grounds. After a series of bloody search-and-destroy forays, the volunteer forces and regular U.S. Army troops succeeded in removing most of the Rogue Indians from the valley.

For western Oregon Indian tribes, the 1850s were tragic, involving the relocation of most Native people to the newly established Siletz and Grand Ronde reservations. Because these were executive-order reservations and not subject to treaty stipulations, it took only a presidential decree to open Native lands to white settlement. The architect of the coastal reservations, Oregon Superintendent of Indian Affairs Joel Palmer, justified the reserves, arguing that they were isolated and away from the Willamette Valley, inaccessible by sea, and lacked agricultural potential. The establishment of the reservations marginalized Native peoples and severely limited their hunting and gathering and communitarian mode of existence. The removal policy also opened millions of acres of land—under federal land laws—to market forces, large sections that were transferred eventually to private, non-Indian ownership.

Confined to reservations and suffering the persisting ravages of disease, Indian numbers continued to spiral downward. Native people from the interior Rogue and Umpqua valleys found the coastal reservation wet and cold and lacking in traditional food sources. Because the Bureau of Indian Affairs failed to provide adequate food and shelter, the coast reservation became home to suffering, starvation, and disease. Moreover, the Indian Bureau's effort to promote agriculture proved futile, because it was impossible to grow conventional crops such as wheat, corn, and potatoes in the peat-bog soils of the coastal estuaries. Farther inland at the Grand Ronde agency, Douglas fir flourished on the red clay-like soils, but the infertile lands produced anemic agricultural crops. With soil science still in its infancy, the Bureau pursued a questionable policy of promoting crop production in areas ill-suited to agricultural enterprise.

Population losses offer striking testimony to the inhumanity of reservation policy. The records for the Siletz and Grand Ronde agencies indicate that annual deaths exceeded births rates until the early 20th century. The number of enrollees on the Siletz reservation dropped from 2,026 in 1856 to 438 in 1900; at Grand Ronde, the population declined from 1,826 in 1857 to 298 in 1902. These numbers do not account for people who left the reservation to pursue wage-labor jobs, some to the Willamette, Umpqua, and Rogue valleys, others to Portland's small service-sector industry. As early as the 1860s, enrollees began taking seasonal leaves from the reservation as a kind of migratory work force, a practice, according to historian E.A. Schwartz, that had some parallels to their traditional seasonal travels to sources of food. "Instead of gathering the products of nature," he argues, "people now ensured their survival by collecting wages from farmers involved in the market economy."

In the midst of such hardships and Indian Bureau dictates, however, Native people on and off the reservation were working through their own informal adaptations to the future. In other cases, interracial unions produced a generation of mixed-bloods who lived uneasily between Indian and white worlds. As the federal government progressively opened sections of the extensive coastal reservation to white settlement, Indians began returning to their old homelands in southwestern Oregon. Some families moved to remote areas in the Siuslaw watershed, while others returned to the Umpqua estuary and the lower Smith River. As the decades passed, men continued to seek seasonal employment working in coastal mills and other small enterprises as Native peoples made cultural adjustments to survive in a new and difficult world.

OHS neg., CN 021026

Residents of Agness in the Rogue River Valley in front of the post office

The decades of the 1850s and 1860s were tumultuous ones for Oregon's new immigrant society. Faced with a contentious politics, much of it centered on issues such as slavery, rival newspapers indulged in unrestrained attacks on political opponents and their journalistic competitors. The most notorious practitioners of "Oregon style" journalism were the Salem *Statesman*'s Asahel Bush, the Portland *Oregonian*'s Thomas Jefferson Dryer, and the Oregon City *Oregon Argus*'s William Lysander Adams. Bush, the "Ass of Hell" to his enemies, served the interests of the Democratic Party; Dryer spoke for the Whig/Republican Party; and Adams for the fading Whigs. With their incessant and noisome editorial invectives, the three newspapers contested with the major issues of the day: the location of the territorial/state capitol, political appointments, statehood, and slavery. When language failed to evoke the most venomous epithet, the three editors created new vocabulary to skewer their opponents. In an age without libel laws and few restraints on journalist haranguing, Oregon newspapers indulged in a series of "take no prisoners" colloquies, with Bush indicting the *Oregonian*'s Dryer on one occasion for engaging in "the grossest personal abuse, the most foul mouthed slander, grovelling, scurrility, falsehood and ribald blackguardism." Such vitriolic exchanges began to moderate in the 1870s when the state legislature adopted a libel law and newspaper publishers formed a state press association and established a professional ethics code.

Oregon voters defeated statehood initiatives three times before approving a measure in June 1857 that called for a constitutional convention. The constitution-makers who descended on Salem that summer represented a familiar cast of characters. Orchestrated primarily by the Democratic Party, the convention elected Territorial Supreme Court Justice Matthew P. Deady (who ran on a pro-slavery platform) as president. Historian David Johnson, who refers to Deady as "a cerebral and enigmatic figure," contends that the Douglas County jurist was committed to 18th-century notions of statesmanship and public service. After his arrival in Oregon in late 1849, he became the territory's most prominent defender of the South and a proponent of slave society. In a letter to a colleague just before the convention opened, Deady argued that slaves owned as property were "just as much property as horses, cattle or land." In the same letter, he urged his friends to support "the white race, the Constitution, and the institutions of [the] country."

The Democratic and anti-Democratic factions in the convention debated the addition of a bill of rights to the constitution, the nature of the judiciary, suffrage limitations, and the regulation of corporations. The majority Democrats also closed ranks in their determination to avoid the slavery issue, preferring instead to offer voters a variety of options. Democrats representing the counties upriver from Oregon City wanted references to religion left out of the constitution, while anti-Democrats, representing downriver counties (including populous Multnomah County) favored the Indiana charter, which included references to Godly ordination and Christian fidelity. In this and in debates over placing additional citizenship restrictions on suffrage, the majority Democrats prevailed. But on the issue of race, Johnson argues, the opposing factions were of one mind—suffrage should not be extended to nonwhites: "Oregonians treated race lightly because they could not conceive of nonwhite suffrage ever coming to pass." No one in the convention raised the question of women's suffrage.

Reflecting the principles of Illinois Senator Stephen A. Douglas' ideas about "popular sovereignty," the statehood initiative touched deeper themes related to race and slavery: as a state Oregon would be free of both slavery and free blacks. President James Buchanan signed the congressional Enabling Act admitting Oregon as the 33rd state in early 1859. Although several states had similar statutes, Oregon was the first to include a provision excluding free blacks in its constitution.

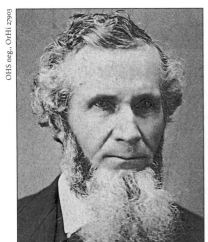

Joel Palmer, Superintendent of Indian
Affairs for Oregon Territory

Asahel Bush, editor of the *Oregon
Statesman*

There was nothing particularly innovative in the state's founding body
of law—most of its legal principles were modeled after the constitutions of Indiana, Iowa, and Michigan—but the precepts adopted in
1857 (with congressional approval in 1859) proved to have exceptional
staying power. Given the frequency with which Oregon citizens have
acted to amend the constitution in the last few decades, it is ironic that
the document approved in 1857 went without amendment until the
Progressive Era in the early 20th century.

Events in California have always loomed large in Oregon. The celebrated California Gold Rush was the great catalyst for agricultural growth in Oregon and for all kinds of commercial development.
The hundreds of thousands of people who flocked to the goldfields in
1849 and the early 1850s created an instant market for timber, wheat,
and other goods. To add to the frenzy, miners working through the
northern Sierra Mountains spilled over into the Rogue and Illinois
valleys, making new gold discoveries and expanding markets for
food and other supplies. Scottsburg, at the head of tidewater on the
Umpqua River, enjoyed a brief period as a jumping-off place for the
southern Oregon mining country. Oregon City and Portland on the
lower Willamette River developed an instant lumber and flour trade,
with the number of ships entering tidewater multiplying severalfold

in a brief period of time. Where only two ships crossed the Columbia River bar in 1847, 50 ships entered into the Columbia in 1849 to load high-priced wheat.

Portland's emergence as a leading trade center was directly tied to the booming California trade. The self-styled "stump town" enjoyed strategic advantages because of its location at the confluence of the Columbia and Willamette rivers, water routes that extended east and south into the interior and west to the Pacific's ocean highways. Incorporated in 1851, the city's deep-water port and favorable location below Willamette Falls enabled its merchants to dominate the emerging trading networks between Willamette Valley farms and San Francisco, the redistribution center to California's goldfields. With a population of 800 people in 1850, Portland expanded from five commercial buildings in 1850 to more than 40 business establishments by 1853, including four steam-powered sawmills and several small manufacturers. Oregon's leading city on the lower Willamette continued to add wharves and steamboats with the discovery of additional gold deposits in the upper Columbia River Basin during the 1860s.

To satisfy San Francisco's insatiable demand for goods and building materials, capitalists ventured north to the maze of sloughs and tidewater streams around Coos Bay estuary and its wealth of Douglas fir, Sitka spruce, and white cedar timber. With the construction of mostly California-owned mills during the 1850s, the Coos Bay region began a century-long link with the growing cities and towns around San Francisco Bay, providing lumber, coal, and other resources. Already sharply reduced in numbers from Old World diseases, the Coos Indians witnessed their homeland being made over into a resource-extractive economy to serve San Francisco interests. Although immigrants established a scattering of small farms in low-lying areas around the Coos estuary, timber harvesting became the region's bread-and-butter industry. In the next several decades, Coos Bay's extensive waterways were turned into industrial transportation arterials to float log rafts to the big mills. It can also be argued that the Coos Bay communities became the most timber-dependent area in Oregon, operating in an economic environment that fluctuated dramatically with the rise and fall of lumber prices.

Far removed from Oregon's coastal region, mineral discoveries in the interior districts in the early 1860s and an inrush of miners to the Snake River/Clearwater country enhanced Portland's position as a major transportation hub. The increase in Columbia River traffic

OHS neg. OrHi 946

Corner of Front and Stark streets, Portland, 1852

boosted The Dalles, already a vital military and trading location, and led to the establishment of several small interior towns adjacent to the mines, including Lewiston, Baker City, and John Day. One of the more fascinating of these short-lived enterprises was the discovery of gold less than ten miles southwest of Baker City in October 1861. By the following summer, the newly minted town of Auburn was the center of frenetic mining and building activity as more than 5,000 miners swarmed through the hills in the vicinity of Blue Canyon Creek and Freezeout Gulch.

As stores and buildings quickly went up, Auburn became the center of several different mining districts that embraced nearly 100 square miles. As the first sizable Euroamerican settlement in eastern Oregon, Auburn became the official seat for Baker County. Cynthia Stafford, who arrived with her husband in the fall of 1862, described a rough-hewn town where "the main object is making money." As the future would show, neither Stafford nor the town survived for long. She died in March 1863 after a brief illness, and Auburn dwindled to about 100 people in 1864. Today, only a stone foundation and a few remnant fireplace rocks hint at the bustle of activity that took place there in the summer and fall of 1862.

This great spurt of human activity in eastern Oregon served as the opening wedge for systemic environmental change, especially to min-

eral-bearing streams where entire hillsides were sluiced away, riparian habitat degraded, and salmon-breeding grounds silted over. When
gold was discovered on Canyon Creek, a tributary of the John Day
River, more than 300 miners rushed to the area in the summer of 1862
to work the placer deposits along the lower sections of the stream.
Miners sluiced away the riverbank searching for gold, destroying
most of the streamside vegetation. As mining developed into a true
industrial activity, especially with the construction of underground
tunnels, loggers began the first large-scale cutting of inland forests to
satisfy the demand for timber trusses and lumber for mining ditches.
To capitalize on the sudden increase in traffic on the Columbia River,
a group of Portland entrepreneurs formed the Oregon Steam Navigation Company (OSN) in 1860. The enterprise soon gained a monopoly on river transportation, moving miners and supplies upriver
and mineral wealth on return trips and reaping handsome profits for
investors. OSN dividends also provided start-up capital for Portland
bankers such as John C. Ainsworth, the president of OSN. During the
peak of prospecting in the mid-1860s, as many as 75,000 miners may
have been working interior streams.

Except for those who lived in Portland, Salem, and Eugene, the
immigrants to Oregon following the Civil War were scattered in
clusters of small communities and outlying farming districts in the
Willamette, Umpqua, and Rogue valleys and in isolated communities
such as Tillamook and Hood River. Farmsteads began as subsistence
operations, where production and consumption were joint family un-
dertakings; but they slowly shifted into the commercial arena, where
production and consumption became separate enterprises mediated
by exchanges in money. Kin relationships and groups of people who
emigrated from common geographic areas in the Midwest and upper
South defined Oregon's rural settlements from the 1840s through the
1860s. The names of some Willamette Valley counties also reflect those
immigrant populations and bear the names of famous individuals
from the border states (Washington, Polk, Benton, Linn, and Lane).
Still other counties carry Indian names (Multnomah, Clackamas, and
Yamhill). Portland and other larger towns were given New England
or New York names and had a different demographic profile, a larger
percentage of single males and a greater percentage of the foreign born
and people from the Northeast.

Despite the continued infusion of new migrants, Oregon's development through the 1860s was remarkably homogenous, mirroring

mostly midwestern political, social, and cultural values. Many scholars have emphasized the conservative nature of 19th-century Oregon, a people more interested in building stable and secure communities than in pursuing the main chance. Yet, a careful reading of local newspapers reveals some interesting alternatives to this view. Safe and secure settlements, editors agreed, would lend constancy to local life and attract capital and new residents. The *Weekly Times*, one of Portland's earliest newspapers, insisted that a central requirement for attracting more immigrants was "always [to] give the world to understand that Oregon is a land of law and order." Mercantile and professional classes from Portland south to Roseburg, who represented the ambitions and class interests of community boosters, enthusiastically promoted orderly development and growth.

With a mild and humid environment ideally suited to the cultivation of wheat, a variety of other grains, and fruit orchards, the Willamette Valley became a major producer of foodstuffs marketed outside the region. With the end of the annual Indian fires, the valley landscape began to take on a different appearance. Fenced fields, cropland, and farmsteads occupied areas that were less prone to seasonal flooding. Beyond those cultivated tracts, brush and small trees slowly colonized the valley's lower hills, dramatically altering the open, savannah-like appearance of the early 19th century. Farmers were also making slow headway in clearing the dense floodplain forests for row-crop production.

To meet the increasing demand for foodstuffs and to speed production, farmers purchased mowing machines, threshers, plows, and seed drills. The acreage planted to wheat along the Willamette River grew, marking the final push toward commercial agriculture. Valley producers formed agricultural societies, supported a weekly newspaper, the *Willamette Farmer*, and took advantage of the most progressive advice in farming techniques. To speed the transport of goods to Portland warehouses, especially wheat, farmers pooled their resources to remove snags and to deepen some of the more troublesome bars in the Willamette River. But those alterations were only the initial efforts to reshape the waterway into a channelized commercial corridor. The completion of the Oregon and California Railroad through the valley in the early 1870s provided a fast and efficient means of transportation, but steamboats continued to ply the Willamette River and the waterway served as an important traffic way well into the 20th century.

The federal population census for Oregon reflects the significance of wheat production to the Willamette Valley economy. The state's population increased from 52,465 in 1860 to 90,923 in 1870. The Oregon and California Railroad brought new ethnic groups to the state, especially Chinese laborers, who provided most of the construction force that laid the tracks and blasted the tunnels. Hiring what were deemed "cheap" workers suggests the way particular occupational categories were racialized. Western Oregon's demographic profile also was most heavily weighted toward those Willamette Valley counties with the greatest agricultural output. Lane and Linn counties, listed as two of the more heavily populated counties in the 1870 census, ranked first and second in "improved land," with Linn County ranking first in wheat production. The importance of wheat to the burgeoning valley economy was apparent to everyone and a cause for concern to some. Valley farmers produced 200,000 bushels in 1850 and 660,081 bushels in 1860. Then, in 1870, output swelled to more than 2 million bushels. As construction workers were laying the first rails south of Portland in the autumn of 1869, the *Oregonian* cautioned farmers against overreliance on wheat and urged them to seek alternative crops. The state's most widely circulated newspaper advised business investors to diversify the state's economy so it could produce more "of the other necessities of life."

Well before railroad connections linked the western valleys with Portland, Oregon's expanding commercial enterprises were tied to distant markets, places far removed from the Columbia country. Following the fur-trade era, the California market, which centered on San Francisco Bay, shaped and directed Oregon's emerging resource-based economy. Newspapers constantly reminded farmers that they must produce goods that would find convenient and paying markets. With the hint that Pacific coastal wheat markets were becoming saturated in the late 1860s, Portland shippers arranged to send a cargo of wheat directly to Liverpool, England. The *Oregonian* called the effort important to the state's "agricultural and commercial progress," an attempt to "secure constant and remunerative markets for our products." Portland merchants had already sent consignments of flour to New York City in yet another undertaking to establish new outlets for valley wheat farmers. The move to secure overseas markets indicates the increasing interdependence of the Oregon economy.

Once the federal government had resolved the western Oregon Indian question to its satisfaction, officials turned their attention to the vast areas of central and eastern Oregon. Repeating the practices

OHS neg., OrHi 96629

Unidentified women from the Warm Springs Reservation, around 1880

carried out in Oregon's western valleys, federal officials again moved to forcibly relocate Indian groups to reservations far removed from main routes of travel. The objective of Indian Bureau policymakers (and Oregon politicians) was to open eastern Oregon and Washington rangelands to white settlement. The process involved forced treaties with several tribes and establishing two major reservations: the

Reprinted from Jeff Zuker, et. al., *Oregon Indians* (Portland: Western Imprints, the Press of the Oregon Historical Society, 1983)

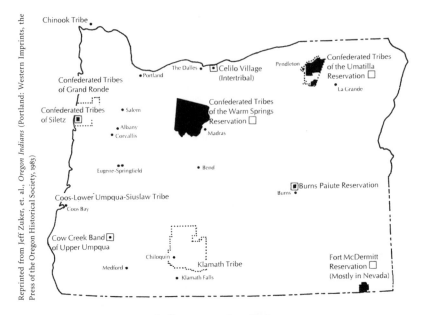

Indian reservations in Oregon

Confederated Tribes of the Umatilla Reservation (Cayuse, Umatilla, and Walla Walla) and the Confederated Tribes of the Warm Springs Reservation (Wasco, Warm Springs, and Paiute).

The Umatilla Reservation, established as part of the 1855 Walla Walla Treaty Council, was arbitrated by Washington Territorial Governor Isaac Stevens and Oregon Superintendent of Indian Affairs Joel Palmer. The treaty ceded huge areas to the federal government and reserved to the three tribes specified areas in southeastern Washington and northeastern Oregon. The tribes also reserved the right to hunt and fish "in their usual and accustomed places." Palmer pursued a similar strategy on the mid-Columbia River, negotiating a treaty that established the Warm Springs Reservation. In return for the reserved lands and the right to fish and hunt "in their usual and accustomed places," the tribes were forced to relinquish approximately 10 million acres to the federal government.

During the 1860s and 1870s, white immigrants began establishing a few small settlements across the vast stretches of central and eastern Oregon. The gold-seekers were first, setting up camps in narrow canyons throughout the greater Blue Mountain region. Because of the increasing demand for meat products, stock farmers in the western valleys began moving their cattle and sheep herds east of the Cascades to graze on the semi-arid sage grasslands in the Deschutes, John Day, and Umatilla valleys. Cattle and sheep grazed everywhere across the region by the 1870s, with the largest and most spectacular herds in Oregon's southeastern quadrant. For the upland areas south and east of the Columbia River—along the Deschutes-Umatilla Plateau—the era of the range-cattle industry was relatively brief. With the completion of the Northern Pacific Railroad along the Columbia River in 1883 and the Oregon Short Line across northeastern Oregon the next year, the rolling hills of Sherman and Umatilla counties were turned to wheat production. With sufficient seasonal precipitation during most years, the district's loess soils were ideally suited to growing winter wheat. Within two decades, Sherman County farmers had increased the area planted to wheat by nearly 400 percent, establishing the single cash crop that continues to dominate the area's economy.

As farmers in the northern districts turned sage country to the plow, grazers increasingly concentrated their herds in more marginal areas, especially in the southeastern part of the state—the Harney Basin and the Malheur and lower Owyhee river valleys. The coming of the range cattle industry to southeastern Oregon was tied to events in California, where the state legislature enacted a series of herd and fence laws in the 1860s that sharply restricted access to the open range. Two immigrant groups moved into the Harney Basin in the late 1860s—a few subsistence farmers from the Willamette Valley and California and cattle herders in search of good watering places and virgin grasslands. Representing large corporate interests, foremen staked out claims along streams that drained the northern and southern slopes of Steens Mountain. Through those methods, cattle barons such as Peter French and his California backer, Hugh Glenn, developed largely self-sufficient empires centered on controlling the few streams that emptied into the Harney Basin.

The rapidly growing livestock herds, including thousands of sheep driven into southeastern Oregon in the 1880s, brought systemic ecological change to the region. When the Oregon Short Line was extended along the Snake River in 1884, cattle interests shifted some of their sales to Huntington and Ontario and, ultimately, Chicago rather than Winnemucca, Nevada, and the regional market in San Francisco. With the new rail line in place, the livestock barons greatly increased the size of their southeastern Oregon herds. These were speculative enterprises, designed to maximize profits with the least expense. A listing of the preeminent corporate groups and the number of cattle grazed across the region suggests the environmental impact of the huge herds:

Todhunter and Devine	40,000
French-Glenn	30,000
Thomas Overfelt	30,000
Riley and Hardin	25,000

According to the federal census for agriculture in 1880, southeastern Oregon's major problem was the cattle barons' monopoly on water supplies. By the turn of the 20th century, a series of United States Geological Survey (USGS) scientific reports clearly indicated that the grazing practices of the large cattle interests were unsustainable. Environmental writer Nancy Langston points out, however, that USGS surveys documenting overgrazing had little effect. The absence of regulations and conflicts over access to unfenced rangelands meant that the stresses on grazing land would continue.

With the forces of the Industrial Revolution firmly established in the state and the resettlement of its vast landscape proceeding apace, Oregon began to take on the trappings of a flawed but modernizing American state. With a few murmurings of dissent, Oregon's dominant white population continued to discriminate against Indians, the newly arrived Chinese, and the small number of African Americans and other minority groups in the state. The majority of women toiled in the home and contributed mightily to the agricultural and service economy, but they were still mostly removed from active participation in politics. At the onset of the railroad age, Oregon's bedrock extractive industries—agriculture, mining, and lumbering—emphasized the state's natural resource dependence and its relationship to distant markets. Those circumstances would bedevil the state for more than a century.

CHAPTER FOUR

Emerging Social, Economic, and Political Relations

She was born in a log cabin in Tazewell County, Illinois, when Andrew Jackson was president and died in Portland, Oregon, during Woodrow Wilson's first term in office. From the 1870s until 1915, Abigail Scott Duniway was the public face of the women's rights movement in Oregon and the Pacific Northwest. Publisher and editor of the pragmatic weekly suffrage newspaper *New Northwest* from 1871 to 1886, Duniway was a schoolteacher and millinery shopkeeper before she became known as the region's leading suffragette. She was a skilled business-woman who became her family's principal breadwinner after her husband was permanently disabled by an accident in 1862. She gave birth to the last of her six children in 1869 at the age of 35. Despite her outspoken positions on suffrage and other women's issues, Duniway was at one with conventional Oregon boosterism in the last 30 years of the 19th century, defending property rights and promoting a variety of economic development activities.

Abigail Scott Duniway is an appropriate representative for the emergence of modern Oregon. She lived through a dizzying period of change in American society, one that included the emergence of the United States as the world's leading industrial power as well as profound changes in the women's movement. In addition to her tireless efforts to gain voting rights for women, Duniway was also a no-

table literary figure—publisher and editor of widely read newspapers
and author of fictional works. She was a regular contributor to reform
newspapers such as the *Oregon City Argus* and occasionally wrote for
the weekly *Oregon Farmer*, a progressive agricultural publication. Her
adult life spanned Oregon's great age of railroad development, and she
delighted in promoting rail lines into the interior districts and supporting the establishment of new businesses and settlements in the
outback. Because Duniway's background was steeped in Jeffersonian
agrarianism, historian Ruth Barnes Moynihan contends, she was a
believer in entrepreneurial pragmatism, values consistent with small-
scale capital and cooperative enterprises. Duniway was also at one
with Portland's leading (Republican) business and political figures,
who actively promoted regional economic development.

Beginning with the portage lines that bypassed the rapids and falls
on the mid-Columbia River in the 1860s, railroad construction
over the next half century vastly extended the region's economic geography. In the several decades following the Civil War, Oregonians
viewed railroads as indispensable symbols of civilization and progress,
the mark of a truly advanced people. The rapidly expanding networks
of railroads—from Portland to the California state line, eastward
along the Columbia River corridor, and across the Blue Mountains
and along the Snake River into Idaho were "engines of empire," in
Carlos Schwantes' words. Reflecting the world of industrial capital-
ism, railroads required the pooling of enormous financial resources,
some originating in international banking centers in New York, London, Paris, and Berlin. When officials drove the famous Golden Spike
joining the Central Pacific and Union Pacific lines in Utah's Great Basin in the spring of 1869, the *Oregonian* boasted that "time and space
have been actually annihilated by the industry of man."

The completion of the nation's first continental railroad preceded
construction of the Oregon and California Railroad (O&C) by only
a year. The O&C line, the work of transportation tycoon Benjamin
Holladay, involved corruption, bullying, and extravagant entertainment and was rooted in a politics that included the purchase of votes
to ensure that the Oregon legislature would award the company the
large land grant that Congress had bestowed on Oregon to subsidize
rail construction. Holladay's O&C—originally called the Oregon
Central—reached Salem and Eugene in 1871. Holladay extended his
rail line south to Roseburg, and then the national economic crash of

the mid-1870s halted construction and forced him into bankruptcy. As the southernmost terminus for the railroad, Roseburg's economy boomed, its new warehouses bulging with grain products and a sizable wool clip.

Joseph Gaston, a competitor in the contest to build the north-south line (and the author of *The Centennial History of Oregon, 1811-1912*), castigated Holladay for his unethical behavior: "He was energetic, untiring, unconscionable, unscrupulous, and wholly destitute of fixed principles of honesty, morality or common decency." Because the O&C was built on unfulfilled expectations—that the company could parcel off its huge land grant to settlers and that agricultural goods would sustain the line—Holladay eventually fell victim to his own risk-taking and daring. Much of the land grant was heavily forested, agricultural production was inadequate, and southern Oregon's mines were in sharp decline. Because he had vastly overextended his financial reach, Holladay lost control of the O&C to Henry Villard, the Northwest's first significant railroad magnate, who represented German bondholders.

Although the O&C line was not completed through to Sacramento until 1887, it was an enormous success in expediting the shipment of people, agricultural commodities, and incoming manufactured goods and supplies. The railroad was especially effective in speeding the movement of farm products to Portland's big waterfront warehouses. The new line also attracted a rush of immigrants to the Willamette, Umpqua, and Rogue valleys, boosted agricultural production, and enhanced Portland's commercial importance. The O&C ushered in what some have referred to as the golden age of Willamette Valley agriculture. The valley's population grew by 62 percent during the first railroad decade, and wheat production more than doubled. In the midst of the euphoria over the O&C's benefits to the state and its economy, the *Willamette Farmer* bragged that railroads were true measures of progress, symbols of advancement and improvement. To Frances Fuller Victor, Oregon's preeminent historian of the late 19th century, railroads were "the dream of [Thomas] Jefferson and [Thomas Hart] Benton realized."

The transforming magic of new steel rails resonated across Oregon's landscape after 1870. The railroads were powerful centralizing and dispersing forces, contributing to the concentration of populations in urban areas and, at the same moment, scattering people and small communities across Oregon's extensive outback. Railroads also rep-

resented outside capital, such as Villard and his German bondholders, with distant investors buying up mineral rights, timberland, and
town lots and investing in the construction of new rail lines. Even
when railroads did not bring direct economic benefits to communities, the mere idea of its potential spurred business activity and ex-
cited the imaginations of developers, dreamers, and town promoters.
In both a physical and psychological sense, railroads helped break
down regional isolation, freeing passengers and freight from difficult
geography and closing both time and space with distant places such
as California and the Midwest. Tunneling through mountain barriers
and building bridges and trestles across deep ravines were great technical feats; but better than anything else, railroads made raw materials more accessible to investment capitalists. Those new human reckonings created the physical infrastructure to develop resources over a
vast and rugged geography.

Railroads set off a demographic explosion in the Pacific Northwest.
Portland was the region's undisputed metropolitan center in 1880,
with a population of 17,500, while Seattle was a mere stump town of
3,500. Although Portland was still a modest and somewhat parochial
city in the 1870s, the community was also exhibiting the trappings of
financial fortunes and affluence; an establishment that valued wealth
accumulation, business and family ties, and an upper class of "first
families" who believed they were the proper repositories of political
authority. Led by white males with wealth and social standing, Portland's power elite defined themselves "largely in terms of money," in
historian E. Kimbark MacColl's words. Those merchants-turned-en-
trepreneurs founded what would become the Arlington Club in December 1867, a restricted-member organization that emphasized the
power and riches of the privileged few. That exclusively male group
represented the wealthiest people in the community, including power-
brokers Simeon Reed, John C. Ainsworth, Robert R. Thompson, William S. Ladd, and Henry W. Corbett.

During Portland's first decade as a rail center, its greater urban population increased from 8,000 to nearly 21,000 people. One indication of
the city's growing prosperity was the increasing number of expensive,
highly ornate, and pretentious commercial buildings. The overblown
architecture drew disparaging comments from visitors such as Lon-
doner Wallis Nash who was in Portland in 1877: "To one who has seen
real cities, . . . [Portland] is but a little place; but some of its 21,000 or

22,000 inhabitants raise claims to greatness and even supremacy that make it difficult to suppress a smile." Portland's business community behaved like "toll gate" functionaries, Nash judged, exacting tribute from all goods and people passing through the city. Nash also pointed out that local capitalists—including the Oregon Steam Navigation Company, the region's largest firm—held monopoly control over waterfront property and blocked public access to the river.

The OSN was an appropriate fit for Nash's description of a "toll gate" enterprise. The company prospered and vastly extended its water-borne transportation dominion during the interior gold rushes of the 1860s. During the next decade, the OSN added new ships to its fleet, until it was operating 26 powerful and stylish sternwheelers on the Columbia River and its tributaries. By building 6-and-14-mile-long rail portages at the Cascades and The Dalles along the Washington shore, the company was able to monopolize transportation by coordinating the arrivals and departures of steamers, stagecoaches, pack trains, and smaller boats reaching into the vast interior of the Columbia River country. The OSN's sole owners by 1870—Simeon Reed, John Ainsworth, and Robert Thompson—made Portland the centerpiece of its transportation empire. The company's cash machine brought rich dividends to the principal stockholders and boomed activity on Portland's waterfront.

Charging all that the market would bear caused outrage in the agricultural sectors east of the Cascade Range. The Baker City *Bedrock Democrat* referred to Reed, Ainsworth, Thompson, and new partner William S. Ladd as "codfish aristocrats." The OSN leadership was filled with avarice and greed, the newspaper charged, accusations that had little effect on Simeon Reed, the company's front man. Because the OSN diverted traffic and immigrants to Portland, western Washington politicians and business interests accused the company of impeding the territory's development. When Washington's territorial legislature chartered its own company and attempted to exercise the power of eminent domain to condemn OSN's portage railroad, Reed persuaded Congress to rescind the legislature's act. He boasted that in the future the Washington legislature "will be reminded that there is a 'power above them.'"

The OSN partners were involved in several interrelated business ventures in Portland and beyond. Robert Thompson, who moved to Portland from The Dalles, accumulated savings in the hardware business before joining with other investors in founding OSN. John

Ainsworth held investments in banking enterprises and several construction companies that contracted to build the British Columbia
section of the Canadian Pacific Railroad and the branch line linking
the Northern Pacific between Portland and Tacoma. Simeon Reed and
William Ladd each operated Portland mercantile houses before ven-
turing beyond the city as transportation magnates and bankers. They
also partnered in several Willamette Valley agricultural operations,
including the 7,000-acre Broadmead experimental farm in Yamhill
County. While there were other Portland entrepreneurs of equal or
greater wealth, Reed, Thompson, Ainsworth, and Ladd were among
the more notable in the variety and reach of their investments.

The transcontinental railroads that linked the Northwest with the
rest of the nation during the 1880s began to change the region's urban dynamics. Although Portland's population more than doubled to
46,385 by 1890, Seattle burgeoned to 42,837 during the same period. By
1900, Portland had 90,426 residents to Seattle's 80,871. Despite Seattle's
tremendous growth spurt, Portland remained the leading metropolis
of the Northwest, a preeminence that continued at least through the
First World War. Ray Stannard Baker, the Progressive journalist who
visited Portland in 1903, liked what he saw:

> . . . not a crude western town; Portland really is a fine old city, a bit, as
> it might be, of central New York a square with a post office in the cen-
> ter, tree-shaded streets, comfortable homes and plenty of churches and
> clubs, the signs of conservatism and respectability.

Portland remained a major power broker in Oregon politics, and the
city's business community continued to command a banking influence
that extended into the Columbia Basin and beyond the Willamette
Valley to the south.

The Pacific Northwest's railroad ties to a broader geography brought
new people, new ideas, and new ethnic groups to the Northwest.
Even before the completion of the Northern Pacific, the O&C im-
ported large numbers of Chinese laborers to build its line from Portland to Roseburg in the early 1870s. Originally contracted to work on
the Central Pacific Railroad, many of the Chinese moved north after
1869 to take construction jobs on the O&C line. The virulent anti-Chinese sentiment that developed in Oregon and the Northwest emerged
early on, especially during economic downturns such as the Panic of
1873 and the short-lived depression of the mid-1880s. When the Or-

egon legislature passed a bill to tax and restrict Chinese workers from public employment in 1868, Governor George Woods vetoed the measure. With the end to construction on the O&C railroad, Chinese immigrants settling in Portland surpassed Germans as the city's largest foreign-born group. And Chinese women, working as prostitutes in River City bawdy houses, experienced arrest rates much greater than their Caucasian sisters, a less-than-subtle suggestion of discriminatory action by local police.

The anti-Chinese phobia involved sometimes violent antagonisms of one segment of the working class against another. In the midst of rising unemployment, white workers feared that the continued importation of cheap labor threatened their livelihoods; and for a people intolerant of racial and cultural differences, the Chinese provided convenient scapegoats. At the same time, many in the business community hired Chinese workers as domestic help or common laborers. Although the most violent of the "Chinese Must Go" activity took place on Puget Sound, similar threats occurred in every Oregon town along the O&C line from Portland to Roseburg. When the Northern Pacific Railroad was completed in 1883, many of the out-of-work Chinese moved to Portland and lesser Oregon cities in search of employment. Within a few months, Portland had more than 4,000 Chinese residents, flooding an already glutted labor market. Irish immigrant workers, eager to give voice to their patriotism, opposed Chinese employment in the city, along with a Harvard-educated labor advocate with political ambitions, Democrat Sylvester Pennoyer.

Portland's anti-Chinese fervor followed even more violent incidents in Seattle and Tacoma, where white workers made several attempts to drive Chinese laborers from their communities. Tacoma labor unionists and leading citizens combined forces in November 1885 to expel some 700 Chinese people from the community. Similar violence in Seattle led to street clashes, the declaration of martial law, one death, and several injuries. The "Chinese Must Go" mania reached fever pitch in Portland during the early months of 1886 when Knights of Labor union organizer Daniel Cronin arrived in town to urge the business and labor community to rid Portland of the Chinese. Speaking to a packed hall in the New Market Theater on January 27, Cronin promised that within a few months there would "not be a working Chinaman in Portland." Following three months of protests, street marches, violence against the Chinese, and finally a few arrests, the turbulence gradually spent itself as some Chinese left for San Francisco's large

OHS neg. OrHi 856

Portland's Chintown, around 1890

Chinatown. There are few heroes to this story. Even Portland's most prominent leaders, such as *Oregonian* editor Harvey Scott, served as deputy sheriffs to enforce the rule of law. But whether workers were white or Chinese, as Abigail Scott Duniway pointed out, the local establishment was primarily interested in cheap labor. Chinese and white female workers, she reported, received less than half the wages paid to white males in Oregon's woolen mills.

Because of the ethnic violence and hatred directed toward the Chinese in far western states, Congress—with the support of organized labor—passed the Chinese Exclusion Act in 1882. The measure reflected the nation's racial prejudice, the realities of economic hard times, and the labor-related agitation in California, Oregon, and Washington. The anti-Chinese prejudice also reflected the influence of powerful business establishments that benefitted from a plentiful and inexpensive supply of labor. The exclusion measure declared the Chinese ineligible for citizenship and banned them from industries such as mining. As Oregon's Chinese population decreased, Japanese immigrants began to replace them in labor-intensive industries. And as they grew in numbers, they, too, would be subject to similar kinds of discrimination.

Although the 1880 census lists only 148 Japanese in the United States, that number would swell during the next three decades, with most of the immigrants coming as migratory workers to the Pacific states. Many of the earliest Japanese emigrated first to Hawaii, where they worked as contract laborers on sugar plantations before making the move to the mainland. The federal census for Oregon lists 2 Japanese in 1880, 25 in 1890, and 2,501 in 1900. Oregon's Japanese immigrants worked as contract laborers on railroads, in the fishing and logging industry, and as agricultural fieldworkers, jobs formerly held by the Chinese. Many of those mostly male immigrants returned to Japan and then made second and third trips to the United States.

By the early 20th century, a few Japanese began to pool their resources and started small family-operated truck farms on the fringes of major cities, supplying fresh fruits and vegetables to residents of Portland, Tacoma, and Seattle. Several eventually managed hotels and related enterprises in Portland. "Birds of Passage," as Yamato Ichihashi called them, these early Japanese immigrants saw themselves as temporary sojourners in the United States, with a vision that through hard work and diligence they would be able to return to Japan with a respectable savings. Between 1900 and 1910, Issei (first-generation Japanese) began settling in green, mist-shrouded Hood River Valley, where they sought work in the lumber industry and as orchardists and field hands. Issei families settled in the upper reaches of the valley in Odell, Pine Grove, and Oak Grove outside Hood River proper. The valley's Japanese numbered 468 in 1910, or 6 percent of the population, the largest settlement of Japanese outside Portland. A few of them, such as Masuo Yasui and his two brothers, became business owners and large landholders in Hood River County.

International geopolitics singled out Japanese immigrants for special attention when Japan emerged as a major world power after defeating Russia's far-eastern forces in 1905. Jingoistic West Coast newspapers played up the Japanese threat and pointed to the immigrant Japanese as a potential menace to American security and welfare. Large corporations competing with Japan for Pacific markets helped fan those anti-Japanese fears. While California and Washington's Japanese population dwarfed the number in Oregon, the concentration of Japanese in Multnomah and Hood River counties subjected them to the same abuses, injustices, and denial of civil rights that had been visited on the Chinese 25 years earlier. The successes of Japanese farmers and the fact that, after 1910, the mostly male immigrants were increasingly joined by women through "picture-bride" arrangements further fanned racial hostilities. Writer Lauren Kessler estimates that 45,000 Japanese women immigrated to the United States through such agreements.

European immigrants to the Pacific Northwest tell similar stories, but absent the racial acrimony and rancor directed against the Japanese. Many of those who rode the rail cars to Portland during the 1880s came from the Midwest, some of them only recent arrivals to states such as Minnesota. Immigrants from Scandinavia (especially Sweden and Norway), Great Britain, and Germany dominated Oregon's foreign-born at the turn of the 20th century. They made up 16 percent of the state's population in 1900, placing Oregon slightly above the national average of 14 percent. The new immigrants gravitated in large numbers to specific occupations: Germans, British, and Jewish newcomers to urban jobs such as artisans and store clerks; Scandinavians to logging and mill work in places such as Coos Bay; Scandinavians and Finns to Astoria and the booming fishing industry; and Danes to towns such as Junction City, where they raised grain crops or operated dairies. A significant group of Finnish orchardists settled in Hood River County, where they still proudly sponsor an off-beat celebration to counter St. Patrick's Day.

Scandinavians and Finnish workers dominated the lower Columbia River fishing industry by the 1880s. Settling sometimes temporarily in Astoria, Ilwaco, Cathlamet, and Deep River, they labored as fishermen and cannery workers during the peak of the salmon runs, from April through the early fall and sought work in lumber camps during the off-season. Finns who immigrated to the United States did so to escape poverty, crop failures, famine, and later conscription into the Russian army. During the early years, they were an especially transient population, fishing the seasonal runs and then returning to their winter base in Berkeley, California. Although the first Finnish immigrants gradually migrated westward from the eastern seaboard, by the 1890s a new generation of emigrés, attracted by the stories of those who had ventured to North America before them, began making the trek directly to towns on the lower Columbia River. One turn-of-the-century promotional pamphlet aimed at immigrants featured photos of teeming salmon runs, pleasant homes, and illustrations of the prosperous Finnish communities in Astoria and Deep River.

Between 1880 and 1910, the Northwest underwent remarkable urbanization. Propelled by the new steel rails that penetrated its hin-

OHS neg., OrHi 48921

Japanese at a work camp near Hood River, around 1920

terland, the region was alive with venture capitalists and free-booters of all kinds, investors seeking to take advantage of the region's natural bounty. The most striking urban growth took place in the state of Washington, with Oregon's population following a similar if less spectacular tendency. Until 1950, when the Census Bureau changed its calculations to people per square mile, the agency's definition of "urban" included cities and towns with 2,500 or more residents. Based on that formula, Oregon was 14.8 percent urban in 1880, 26.8 percent in 1890, 32.2 percent in 1910, and 45.5 percent in 1910. Washington provides an interesting contrast. With only 10 percent of its population living in urban areas in 1880, 53 percent of the state's residents lived in cities and towns by 1910.

The federal census also indicates that between 1880 and 1910 many Oregon newcomers settled in Multnomah and Marion counties, the state's two most urban political jurisdictions. While Portland experienced a remarkable growth spurt between 1900 and 1910, other towns underwent even more dramatic increases, with Salem's population increasing by more than 300 percent and Eugene by nearly the same amount. When the Southern Pacific Railroad was completed from the Rogue Valley to California, Ashland's population increased by nearly 200 percent; and nearby Medford, a mere post office stop in 1880, grew

by almost 500 percent between 1900 and 1910. The development of re-
frigerated rail cars accelerated those developments, contributing to a
fruit-growing boom in the greater Medford area and in the Hood River
Valley. The emergence of foreign markets proved a great boon to Hood
River orchardists whose most important crops were Yellow Newtown
Pippins, Spitzenberg, Ben Davis, and Baldwin apples. While British
buyers preferred Newtons, German and Russian customers favored
red apples. As a symbol of their successes, valley exhibitors won the
grand prize for their fruit display at the St. Louis Exposition in 1903.

The Republican Party's rapid rise to power and influence in Oregon dates from the onset of the Civil War. The state legislature
ratified the 13th Amendment (prohibiting slavery) in 1865 and the 14th
Amendment (guaranteeing citizenship to all American-born people)
the following year. A revived Democratic Party, however, made a futile
gesture to withdraw its support for the 14th Amendment when the
Oregon senate passed a resolution to that effect in 1868. Although the
Republican Party, arguably the state's more progressive political organization, carried every presidential election between 1872 and 1908, the
two major parties traded gubernatorial elections and contests for the
U.S. Senate and House of Representatives for much of the 19th century. Beginning in 1880, however, Republicans began a long period of
dominating the state legislature, controlling the house of representatives until 1935 and the senate until 1957. But Oregon's political culture
was always more than simple electoral contests between Democrats
and Republicans, especially in periods when the state's economy went
into a tailspin.

When the national and regional economy floundered in 1873, again
in the mid-1880s, and then descended into even greater turmoil during the banking and industrial collapse of the 1890s, agrarian and urban protesters and reformers challenged conventional politics. With
the completion of the O&C Railroad to Roseburg in 1872, charges of
corporate monopoly and extortionate railroad rates became part of
Oregon's political rhetoric. Farmers were especially vocal, accusing local merchants and the railroad of acting in collusion to unfairly raise
shipping rates. Rural interests organized chapters of the Grange (Patrons of Husbandry) in Oregon's western valleys to push their issues to
the forefront, and newspapers joined the largely rural-urban debate.
Willamette and Umpqua valley farmers called for an independent
congressional candidate who would promote Oregon's agricultural

interests. Finally, with the rural economy suffering through the mid-1870s, farmers were successful in electing county officials who spoke to their concerns. Temperance societies also proliferated during the 1870s, occasionally joining forces with anti-monopoly organizations to push for the prohibition of alcoholic beverage sales, restructured tax policies, railroad regulations, and similar reform programs. With another economic downturn in the mid-1880s, those diverse reform factions eventually coalesced into a powerful statewide insurgency movement.

The social and political turmoil in Oregon during the 1890s was linked directly to events, circumstances, and economic conditions elsewhere in the United States. Portland's Knights of Labor affiliate followed the precepts of the national organization: "To secure the toilers a proper share of the wealth they create." Although Grange membership had declined nationally, Oregon had 86 vibrant chapters, with 3,140 members in 1890. Farmers Alliance chapters, active in the state during the 1880s, provided a continuing forum for rural discontent. Although the Oregon and Washington Alliances differed in their ideological approaches, they both found the power of trusts and corporations intolerable and sharply criticized the unfolding land-fraud cases. High railroad rates, heavy taxes on farmland, and a short money supply filled out their list of grievances. Because the Alliances represented a broad spectrum of Oregon's male voters, the always opportunistic prohibitionists cleverly used the reform agenda to promote their own ends.

When Grangers, prohibitionists, the Union Labor Party members, and Oregon affiliates of the Knights of Labor convened in Salem in 1889, they were answering a call to address common grievances:

> The power of the saloon in politics is continually increasing. . . . The power of the trusts and corporations has become an intolerable tyranny, the encroachments of landgrabbers have almost exhausted the public domain, and the corruption of the ballot box has rendered our elections little less than a disgraceful force.

The Salem convention and subsequent meetings led to the formation of the Union Party, the erstwhile predecessor to the People's Party of Oregon. Always gifted at reading political tea leaves, Democratic Governor Sylvester Pennoyer gained the backing of the Union Party when he supported the secret ballot—a key reform measure—and an investigation of the Oregon Land Board during his second successful campaign for governor in 1890. By the time of the emergence of the Peoples, or Populist, Party in Omaha, Nebraska, in the summer of 1892, Pennoyer had converted to Populism. But the most influential voice behind Oregon Populism—and the early 20th-century reforms known as the Oregon System—was William S. U'Ren, who served only one term in the state legislature. U'Ren and his People's Power League, deeply involved in politics at the turn of the century, pushed through a remarkable series of measures designed to remove corruption and to reform the political process.

The Populists' much-acclaimed Omaha platform served as a catalyst for Oregon reformers who found much to like in the People's Party platform: (1) the free and unlimited coinage of silver; (2) government ownership of railroads; (3) the return of all railroad and other land grants to the public domain; and (4) the enactment of the secret ballot, the initiative and referendum, and the direct election of U.S. senators. Populists formed organizations across Oregon, and in the fall of 1892 Kansas firebrand Mary Ellen (Elizabeth) Lease ("raise less corn and more hell") campaigned for the national ticket in Portland with Abigail Scott Duniway. Despite the Populist insurgency in the state, however, the party elected only four members to the Oregon legislature in 1893 and ten in 1895 in the wake of the industrial depression. Like the rest of the nation, the great strength of the Oregon People's Party was in rural areas.

There were moral and ethical dimensions to the state's insurgent politics, especially the emergence of the women's suffrage movement under the leadership of influential writer and reformer Abigail Scott Duniway. Beginning in the early 1870s and for the next 40 years, Duniway worked with local and national suffrage leaders in women's struggles to achieve rights to property and the right to vote. For much of that time, she battled with her powerful brother, Harvey W. Scott, editor and publisher of the widely circulated Portland Oregonian. Scott's editorials against enfranchising women in Oregon contributed to the defeat of suffrage measures in 1884, 1900, 1906, 1908, and 1910.

With little formal education, Duniway had ambitions to achieve literary distinction, publishing her first novel, *Captain Gray's Company, or Crossing the Plains and Living in Oregon*, at the age of 25. She was also a contributor to two of the state's more progressive publications, the Oregon City *Argus* and the *Oregon Farmer*. But it is Duniway's work for feminist causes—tinged with a heady sense of pragmatism—that

OHS neg., OrHi 4715

OHS neg. OrHi 10258

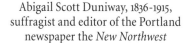

Abigail Scott Duniway, 1836-1915, suffragist and editor of the Portland newspaper the *New Northwest*

Harvey Scott, 1838-1910, editor of the *Oregonian* from 1865 to 1910 (except between 1872 and 1877)

makes her the state's foremost woman reformer. Beginning in 1871 and continuing for 16 years, Duniway's highly regarded eight-page *New Northwest* championed the suffrage cause in the region. She was a tireless speaker, delivering more than 200 lectures a year during the peak of her influence.

Aware that tying prohibition with the vote for women would incur the wrath of brewery interests, Duniway gained the enmity of the conservative Woman's Christian Temperance Union (WCTU) when she also opposed linking temperance with the suffrage cause. When the Oregon chapter of the WCTU had called for enfranchising women as part of a strategy to ban the sale of whiskey, brewery interests had vilified the suffrage measure. After casting derogatory remarks at Oregon's temperance organization, Duniway revived the Oregon State Equal Suffrage Association in 1894. The WCTU retaliated, accusing Duniway of selling out to the whisky and brewery interests. In the eastern United States, the Massachusetts Woman's Christian Prohibitory League charged Oregon's woman's suffrage leader with bringing "disgrace on the Woman Suffrage cause."

An active Republican, Duniway's political activities during the 1890s were at one with the Populists who sought to infuse and en-ergize the nation's politics with Jeffersonian democratic principles and opposition to monopolies. She fully supported U'Ren's Oregon System reforms. When Oregon's male voters narrowly approved the women's suffrage amendment in 1912 (which her influential brother Harvey Scott opposed), all sections of the state supported the measure. In a sense, the suffrage amendment served as the capstone to Oregon's Progressive Era reforms. As many writers have argued, there was nothing revolutionary about Duniway's campaign: men were potential allies rather than antagonists; granting woman the right to vote did not revolutionize relations between the sexes; and women's suffrage did not remove corruption from politics.

With a still declining population, a diminished land base, and access denied to traditional gathering, hunting, and fishing grounds, Indians continued to find their way amidst harsh and inhumane federal and state policies. The Wada Toka band of Northern Paiute, who lived in the vast expanses of the Harney Basin at the time of Euroamerican contact, were one of the last groups to be forced onto a reservation when President Ulysses Grant established the executive-order 1.8 million-acre Malheur Reservation in 1872. The new Paiute homeland, however, proved to be a fleeting enterprise as white settlers continued to pressure the government for more grazing land. Some of the hungry and destitute Paiutes finally joined the Bannocks in their running skirmishes with the U.S. Army across eastern Oregon and south-central Idaho in 1878. Even though most Paiutes did not unite with the Bannocks, federal troops attacked the noncombatants, killing many Indians in their temporary camps. When the Paiutes surrendered in the winter of 1879, the army moved the small bands to Fort Simcoe on the Yakama Reservation where they continued to suffer indignities.

The Paiute survivors were eventually relocated to the Warm Springs, Fort McDermitt, and Owyhee reservations. The relocation to confederated tribal reservations, with limited means of support, created tensions among the tribes. Despite federal prohibitions against leaving the reservations, many Paiutes and other Indians continued to leave in considerable numbers to seek work in eastern Oregon's wheat fields and in the Yakima and Hood River valley fruit orchards. With congressional passage of the General Allotment Act in 1887, the federal government granted several Paiute heads of households (involving more than 100 individuals) 160-acre allotments of alkali sagebrush land on the fringes of the Harney Basin. Without access to water, Paiute families hired out on local ranches and as domestic help in the town of Burns. Through such means, the Paiutes and other reservation people were able to survive and achieve a degree of autonomy.

The federal government began carving huge slices of land from the executive-order coastal reservation in 1865 when it opened to white settlement the tract between the Yaquina and Alsea watersheds. Ten years later, two additional areas were opened to homestead entry—from Cape Lookout south to the Salmon River and from the Alsea River south to the Umpqua drainage. Congress furthered those assaults on the Indian land base when it passed the Dawes General Allotment Act in 1887, a measure ostensibly designed to encourage farming and to assimilate Indians into the larger, white society. The new policy promoted the idea that the true route to civilization involved an incentive to work that was possible only through individual ownership of property. The Dawes Act was a direct attack on traditional communal practices, and it reduced the reservation land base in the United States by approximately 90 million acres before Congress rescinded the policy in 1934.

Of Oregon's Indian reservations, the Siletz and Grand Ronde suffered the most through the allotment process, with large acreages of valuable timberland transferred to non-Indian ownership. The allotment process was uneven, with agents awarding valuable tracts of land to some Indians and worthless acreage to others. Although some agents attempted to carry out selections fairly, Indians often competed over the more valuable parcels. Historian Stephen Dow Beckham points to the "almost circus-like atmosphere" that surrounded the allotment of the Siletz Reservation in 1892. With timber speculators keeping track of the proceedings, more than 75 percent of the rich coastal forest (191,798 "surplus" acres) was sold on the speculative market to non-Indians. Allotment also sharply diminished the size of the Umatilla Reservation, with valuable grazing and farmland winding up in non-Indian ownership. The allotment process eventually left the Umatilla Reservation with a checkerboard ownership pattern with reservation land, individual trust properties, and non-Indian ownerships spread across the landscape.

There were still other aggressions against Indian cultures during the later decades of the 19th century, with President Ulysses Grant's Peace Policy being one of the more egregious. The reform program originated in the early 1870s when the Grant administration turned

reservation control over to various Christian denominations—Protestant and Catholic—that would procure "competent, upright, faith-
ful, moral, and religious agents, to distribute the goods and to aid
in uplifting the Indians' culture." Because rampant corruption had
characterized previous Indian policy, the Grant administration reasoned that turning to religious groups would remove the evil-doers.
The Indian Bureau granted the Methodist Episcopal Church control
of the Siletz Reservation. The five church-nominated agents who
served at Siletz while the Peace Policy was in effect were less corrupt,
according to historian E.A. Schwartz, but they were no more effective
than their predecessors had been. The Methodists also warred among
themselves over management of the reservation, and they singled out
their first agent, Joel Palmer (the architect of the coast reservation),
for special criticism, prompting his resignation.

The state of Oregon was home to yet another late 19th-century Indian Bureau initiative to advance assimilation—the off-reservation
boarding school. The objective of the new educational policy was to
establish schools hundreds of miles from reservations, where Indian
children would be far removed from their parents and tribal affilia-
tions. The overriding purpose of the "civilization" policy was to transform Indian youth into a new, assimilated generation of Indian leaders. School discipline was rigid and severe, and children were ridiculed
for their Native languages, manners, myths, dress, and long hair. Run-
aways were whipped, parents were sometimes denied the right to visit
their children, and in some cases students were not allowed to return
home for vacations.

The first off-reservation boarding school in the American West was
the Forest Grove Indian Industrial and Training School established at
Pacific University in 1880. The initial student enrollees at the school
—from Washington Territory's Puyallup Reservation—were immediately put to work helping to construct buildings for the institution.
Despite efforts to increase the number of students, including forcible
recruitment, a high mortality rate and suspicious tribal elders limited
enrollment. To make matters worse, local citizens objected to the large
number of Indian children in town. Finally, when the Forest Grove
academy suffered a major fire during the winter of 1885, the Indian
Bureau directed the building of a new school north of Salem. During
the five troubled years of its existence, the Forest Grove school strived
mightily to strip Indian children of their cultural identity.

Officially designated the Salem Industrial Indian Training School,
the new boarding school eventually took the name of the local post

OHS neg., OrHi 26558

Forest Grove Indian Industrial and Training School (Chemawa) students, 1881

office, Chemawa, where it still operates today as the nation's oldest off-reservation educational institution. The Chemawa school functioned much like the Forest Grove facility, with students, including the first "carpenter boys," performing most of the manual labor. As more students began to arrive, school officials sent them to work for local farmers, with their wages used to purchase additional land for the school. When the facilities were fully operational in 1887, the school enrolled Indian children from across the American West and Alaska. Some of the enrollees never left, the names on the local cemetery's metal plates providing graphic testimony to illness and personal tragedy. The effort at forced assimilation ultimately was a failure, and the attempt to break tribal attachments continued to prove elusive. Despite the harsh environment, by bringing Indian youth together from around the nation Chemawa and the other boarding schools eventually laid the groundwork for the pan-Indian movements of the 20th century.

Congressional passage of the Newlands Reclamation Act in 1902 heightened expectations in Oregon that federal monies would be available to develop irrigation projects in the arid reaches of the state. In quick order, the newly established Reclamation Service carried out a series of surveys and investigations: the Malheur, Willow Creek, and

Owyhee area in the eastern part of the state; the Umatilla district in the northeast; and, most significant of all, the sprawling marshlands and shallow lakes in south-central Oregon's Klamath Basin. Under the Newlands Act the interior secretary could designate irrigation projects and establish a reclamation fund from public-land sales to finance the construction of reservoirs, canals, laterals, and the like. The Reclamation Service was interested in the Klamath Basin's potential, because privately financed projects already watered about 10,000 acres of cropland.

The Klamath Irrigation Project (1905) was the most significant early federal reclamation undertaking in Oregon. The basin's irregular valleys, shallow lakes, and tule-choked swamps were also home to one of North America's most prolific waterfowl breeding areas, including some 600 fish-eating osprey. The basin supported a productive sucker fishery, an important food source for Klamath and Modoc Indians. At the onset of the 20th century, southern Oregon's lake district also provided profitable killing fields for "plume hunters" who were after egrets, terns, grebes, herons, and pelicans to supply urban milliners who used the feathers as trim for fashionable women's hats. William Finley, a field representative for the National Audubon Societies, reported that the Klamath region supported "the most extensive breeding ground in the West for all kinds of water birds."

The Reclamation Service remade this vast water world in the early years of the 20th century into an irrigated, highly productive agricultural district. From a technical and engineering perspective, the Klamath Project presented a series of complex problems, especially keeping spring runoff from flooding Tule Lake (an internal drainage) and Lower Klamath Lake, which is part of the Klamath River system. The trick for reclamation engineers was to build a reservoir to prevent the annual watering of Tule Lake and to construct a system of dikes to keep the Klamath River from overflowing into Lower Klamath Lake. When the system of dams, dikes, canals, ditches, and drainage arterials east and south of Klamath Falls was completed, it created 233,000 acres of potentially irrigable land and eliminated approximately 60 percent of the original 185,000 acres of wetlands. The extensive engineering feat also involved the cooperation of both Oregon and California because the Lower Klamath Lake and Tule Lake water systems crossed state boundaries.

Another early Reclamation Service effort focused on the semi-arid lower Umatilla Valley, where the federal government funded the construction of a 100-foot-high, earth-fill dam to provide irrigation water to an area east of the Columbia River. Even though canals were operational by 1910, the project never prospered, in part due to the poor quality of the soil. In the early 1920s, however, the larger Umatilla area became the setting for more ambitious plans with the formation of an aggressive promotional organization, the Umatilla Rapids Association. The association developed an ambitious lobbying campaign to build a big dam on the Columbia River that would serve both irrigation and navigation interests. Although the promoters did not realize their dreams until McNary Dam was completed in 1954, the proposal to build a dam at Umatilla Rapids gained momentum during the 1930s when its supporters began to emphasize the project's multiple benefits.

Of Oregon's pre-Depression reclamation works, the Vale-Owyhee undertaking in the arid southeastern part of the state was unquestionably the largest and the most ambitious. Although the Reclamation Service had surveyed the lower Malheur and Owyhee valleys in 1903, the agency did not gain funding for the project until 1927. Ranking second only to Arizona's Salt River and Colorado's North Platte projects, Vale-Owyhee was part of larger ambitious reclamation enterprises being planned for the Snake River. Vale-Owyhee was a vast engineering scheme that ultimately would reconfigure both the Malheur and Owyhee valleys through a series of tunnels, huge siphons, and distribution canals. The project included the construction of 360-foot-high Owyhee Dam, a 3.5 mile-long diversion tunnel, five miles of additional tunnel, a steel siphon 2.5 miles long, and 200 miles of canals.

The completed project would have the potential to irrigate 105,000 acres and provide supplemental water for another 63,000 acres. Vale-Owyhee was similar to the Klamath project in combining the use of public and private lands. When engineers finished building the infrastructure for the water transfer system in the late 1930s, changes were set in motion that would transform eastern Oregon's sage lands into rectangular, row-crop agricultural fields. The project's settlement proceeded slowly as the canal and lateral system was extended across the arid countryside. The Vale-Owyhee and adjacent Snake River projects would eventually deliver inexpensive water to some of the largest agribusiness corporations in the region.

Promoters and dreamers also had ambitions for promoting agriculture in areas with little potential for reclamation development. Railroads, land companies, and an assortment of boosters engaged in an active marketing campaign to promote dryland agriculture in Oregon's high desert country, especially in the area around Fort Rock, Christmas Valley, and Silver Lake. Led by James J. Hill's Great Northern Railroad, booster literature, and congressional passage of the Enlarged Homestead Act of 1909, promoters gulled hundreds of people into taking up homestead claims between 1910 and 1915, effectively selling the idea that Oregon's high desert was suited to wheat production. Barbara Allen's study of the effort to carry on agriculture around Fort Rock during those years concludes that settlement "receded almost as abruptly, leaving the inevitable debris in its ebb." Only half of the homesteaders remained long enough to gain title to their land; most moved on to other enterprises, many to the booming sawmill town of Bend.

Abigail Scott Duniway bridged the period between Oregon's first generation of white immigrants and the passage of the state's women's suffrage amendment in 1912. During her lifetime, the state extended railroad lines through central Oregon and added another major extractive industry—salmon canning—to further emphasize its dependence on nature's wealth. The federal government aided in this effort through its subsidies to reclaim arid lands and to turn those dry acres into productive agricultural enterprises. In all of those ventures, rivers and their surrounding landscapes were treated solely for the benefits they would bring in the marketplace. It would have seemed a crazy idea at that time to leave wetlands untouched or water in streams to support indigenous plant and animal communities. And, of course, there were few restrictions or regulations to restrain such activities. Railroad builders, the farming community, fishers, and other developers operated in unrestrictive and largely unregulated business environments. As the nation moved into the 20th century, however, there were citizen stirrings in Oregon and elsewhere that would challenge the preeminence of uninhibited development.

CHAPTER FIVE

Into the New Century

British-born John Minto, who immigrated to the Northwest in 1844 and died in 1915, is a fitting person to profile turn-of-the-century Oregon. Minto's life spanned dramatic demographic, technological, and environmental changes in the state, beginning in the 1840s when human and animal power supplied the energy to accomplish most physical work. Minto first helped build a water-powered sawmill 30 miles west of Astoria and then did the very slow work of "rolling logs by hand to the saw." When he moved to the Willamette Valley near Salem, he did "the severest kind of field labor—that of binding wheat in its own straw." During his long life, he witnessed spectacular changes to the valley's landscape: the end of the Indians' autumnal burnings and the expansion of Douglas fir on the rolling oak savannahs; the elimination of wolves, large bears, and cougars as a threat to domestic stock; and the ditching and draining of valley bottomlands to make way for field crops and fruit orchards. Toward the end of his life, Minto remarked that the valley's new agricultural landscape no longer provided good breeding places for waterfowl and animals.

In addition to his observations about the physical alterations to the valley landscape, Minto was a tireless promoter of modern agricultural practices. He served as editor of *Willamette Farmer*, a progressive agricultural weekly that promoted scientific farming, railroad development into the interior, and improved navigation on the Columbia River. A highly successful breeder of sheep, he wrote a report in 1892 for the secretary of agriculture on the sheep industry in Oregon. Minto was a renowned orchardist, conducting widely praised and original horticultural research. He also observed a literal revolution in transportation, arriving at his Salem-area land claim on horseback via a narrow trail and living 40 years into the railroad age, which included the opening of the Oregon Electric Railway that ran the length of the Willamette Valley.

Minto was alive to the region's bright prospects for timber production, reasoning that eastern investment in Pacific coastal forests would redound to the benefit of the Douglas-fir region. But there was a problem with such investors—their seeming inability to act with honesty and as good citizens. In a 1908 article in the *Oregon Historical Quarterly*, Minto reported that eastern capitalists were working through "hired cruisers and purchasing agents to secure large bodies of timber." Because "land fraud" had become a household word in Oregon, Minto regretted the timberland frauds that had put the state's reputation in "the columns of ten-cent-monthlies." Minto, who died at the age of 93, lived through the public revelations and criminal prosecutions surrounding the state's celebrated land-fraud trials.

Oregon was at the center of a national *cause célèbre* in the winter of 1904-1905 when special U.S. prosecutor Francis J. Heney tried and convicted 33 prominent individuals on various counts of fraud involving federal lands. The infamous land-fraud trials challenge the notion that Oregon's historical experience has been unique, that the state has been above the struggles, corruption, and host of evils that have afflicted its neighboring states, and that its political leadership established a progressive system that worked to protect the state's natural resources. Much of the land-fraud investigation centered on the manner in which the Oregon legislature disposed of the state's land grant. Beginning in the 1880s and continuing into the early 20th century, the legislature directed the State Land Board to dispose of its "school lands" for $1.25 an acre. Because the state chose its school lands from the unsurveyed Public Domain, and because state and federal land offices were overburdened with work, selection practices were left to speculators and timber locators. It was a system that invited wholesale fraud.

There were early and repeated warnings about the faulty disposal of state lands. Legislative committees reported that speculators were manipulating school land sales, Governor Sylvester Pennoyer worried in the mid-1890s that speculators were obtaining some of the state's choicest timberland for a song, and State Land Agent Timothy Davenport disclosed in 1896 that the system of selecting lands was "pro-lific of abuses and complications." There were repeated signals that something was badly amiss with Oregon's system of disposing of its school lands. The state had sold approximately one-third of its grant lands—1,381,327 acres—between 1898 and 1905; and when the scandals broke in 1903, the most valuable of the state's timberlands had already passed into private ownership. Governors William Lord (1895-1899) and T.T. Greer (1899-1903) were aware of the fraudulent practices but argued that legislative policy hampered the State Land Board in prop-erly managing the grant.

The looming land-fraud debacle helped elect reform-minded Democrat George Chamberlain to the governorship in 1902. The new governor appointed Oswald "Os" West as state land agent. West com-pleted an investigation of the land ring in 1904, and it was his report that led to the federal trials and the conviction of several perpetrators on charges of fraud and conspiracy. The guilty included Congressman John Williamson from eastern Oregon and the state's colorful and pe-rennial U.S. senator, John H. Mitchell. Binger Hermann, an Oregon native and former head of the General Land Office, was indicted twice but managed to stay out of prison on a legal technicality. Still others escaped indictment by turning state's evidence. What surprised the public was not the evils the trials revealed but the scope and magni-tude of corruption. Williamson, Mitchell, Hermann, and other prom-inent citizens had clearly violated the public trust.

Oregon's politics differed only slightly from Washington's and Idaho's. When the Democratic-fusionist candidate, William Jen-nings Bryan, faced off against the eastern establishment and Republi-can William McKinley in the watershed election of 1896, Washington and Idaho voters supported Bryan by wide margins, while McKinley gained a narrow plurality of 1,972 votes in Oregon. In the run-up to the election, the *Oregonian,* the region's most widely circulated news-paper, vilified Bryan for supporting the free and unlimited coinage of silver. In its effort to educate voters in what it considered the falsities of the silver movement, the newspaper charged that free silver would pauperize working people and lower their standard of living. Just be-fore election day, the *Oregonian* issued a dire warning about the pos-sibility of a Bryan presidency: "the bare and remote possibility of his election sends the chill through the social body like the fatal rigor of a fever patient."

Despite Bryan's success across the western states, McKinley easily won the national vote and, with the exception of Woodrow Wilson's two terms in office, established a precedent of placing Republicans in the presidency until Franklin D. Roosevelt's election in 1932. With the support of slightly more than 50 percent of Oregon's voters in 1896, McKinley extended his margin of victory in 1900 to more than 55 percent of the vote. Theodore Roosevelt, who ascended to the presidency after McKinley's assassination in 1901, garnered nearly 67 percent of Oregon's votes in 1904; his successor, the dour William Howard Taft, won 56 percent of the statewide vote in 1908. Woodrow Wilson, who won Oregon's popular vote in 1912, did so only because Theodore Roosevelt ran as a third-party candidate, challenging the incumbent, Taft. Although Wilson won with 34 percent of Oregon's vote, Roosevelt (27.44 percent) and Taft (25.27 percent) polled 52 percent between them.

George Chamberlain's election as governor and the emergence of Oswald West as a reformer established a new mood, a fresh and innovative direction in early 20th-century Oregon politics. Both Democrats, Chamberlain and West were widely respected for their integrity and their activism; in brief, they were at one with the reform spirit of the Progressive Era. Chamberlain supported the Oregon System political reforms and backed the conservation policies of President Roosevelt and his activist chief forester, Gifford Pinchot. Chamberlain pushed other Progressive Era measures through the state legislature: carrying out prison reform, establishing state railway and library commissions, and enacting a child labor law. Unlike his predecessors who seldom used the veto, Chamberlain willingly turned back legislation that he considered foolish or poorly written.

After Chamberlain's election to the U.S. Senate and a brief interim period, voters elevated Oswald West to the governor's office in 1910. With the exception of Tom McCall, no Oregon governor has enjoyed a more favorable historical reputation. West was a progressive reformer to the core, courageous, and seemingly willing to take on all comers. During the 1911 legislative session, he faced off against a Republican-dominated legislature and vetoed 63 bills. Even though Republicans also controlled the 1913 session, he was far more successful in advancing his own legislation. West's legacy was impressive: tougher banking regulations; a measure to protect people from purchasing fraudulent securities; a reformed railroad commission with expanded responsibilities; modernized budgeting policies for the state; a minimum wage law; and a workmen's compensation system and Industrial Accident Commission (approved by voters). West is best remembered today for insisting in 1911 that Oregon's beaches were public highways and should be accessible to everyone.

Reformers also had their way in predominantly conservative and Republican Portland when the city's voters elected Democratic candidate Harry Lane as mayor in June 1905. In the midst of the despair and gloom of the land-fraud trials, the local Republican establishment—accustomed to having its way in city politics—persuaded 82-year-old incumbent George H. Williams to run again. An old party wheelhorse and former U.S. senator (1865-1871), Williams was not a bad mayor, according to Democratic lawyer John Gearin, "he's not been a mayor at all." The Williams administration, which epitomized the close ties between corporate profits and government influence, had come under attack for fraud and corruption, especially for letting bid-free contracts to a clique of insiders. Such cronyism between business and elected officials was accepted as routine in Portland, historian E. Kimbark E. MacColl argues: "Politics, after all, provided the machinery for promoting private economic interest; using political influence was part of the game."

Harry Lane's election to the mayor's office set a different tone for Portland politics. A scrupulously honest man, Lane ended the close and intimate ties between the city's social and business establishment and its elected leaders. "The old days had come to an end," MacColl writes, "a period in Portland's history when business and politics were usually close, intimate activities, connected by long-established family and social ties." Lane was closely allied with Portland's reform movement and represented the city's progressive mood, especially the fast-growing areas east of the Willamette River. Lane, the first east-side resident to serve as mayor, brought decency and civic integrity to the office.

If there was a fabled beginning to the Northwest's lumber industry, the legendary Paul Bunyan's trek from the cutover Minnesota pine country to the great Douglas-fir forests would mark the symbolic moment. First came the timber speculators, rolling across the Plains and Rockies in elegant Pullman cars, accompanied by an entourage of timber cruisers and locators. In the wake of the timber barons came millwrights, blacksmiths, iron and machinery workers, and carpenters who put up state-of-the-art mills in such places as Everett and

Grays Harbor in Washington and in Coos Bay on the southern Oregon Coast. The expansion of the lumber industry in the Pacific Northwest is largely a 20th-century story, with the primary center of production the Douglas-fir bioregion that extends from northern California to British Columbia. Although two-thirds of the timberland in the western states is in public ownership, in California, Oregon, and Washington the forest industry owns a sizable percentage of the most productive land. Because of this ownership pattern, large timber holders and forest products corporations have exercised a powerful influence in the regional economy.

At the onset of the Progressive Era, timber production was clearly the centerpiece of the Pacific Northwest economy, with Washington and Oregon leading the nation in lumber manufacturing. The accelerating harvests along the lower Columbia River during the 1880s and 1890s made the extensive tidewater district the center of lumbering activity on the Oregon side of the river. Other areas in the state also contributed to the increased output of wood products, including the Powder River Valley pine district on the far eastern edge of the state. The completion of the Oregon Short Line through the Blue Mountains in 1884 invited speculation in the area's timberlands, especially in the person of Utah investor David Eccles, who was on the prowl for virgin pine timber. Through ruse and subterfuge and dummy entrymen, Eccles began blocking up large acreages of timber during the 1880s; and at the close of the decade, he and a group of associates incorporated the Oregon Lumber Company.

To gain access to its timber stands, the company formed a subsidiary partner, the Sumpter Valley Railroad, and built a narrow-gauge line for 19 miles along the winding Powder River canyon. The first logs that rolled down the rail line to the new Oregon Lumber Company mill in the small town of Baker City set in motion a production system of harvesting, transporting, and milling timber that lasted through the Second World War. Like the pine operations in Bend, the Powder River logging system followed production-driven business practices, removing only the most marketable timber ("high-grading") and leaving great volumes of debris on the ground.

Similar developments took place on Oregon's isolated southern coast where Minnesota lumberman Charles Axel Smith opened a huge state-of-the-art mill on Coos Bay in 1908. The Big Mill, as it was known, became a significant player in the Pacific lumber trade and provided a great boost to the region's lumber output. The fully inte-

OHS neg., OrHi 6365

Shevlin-Hixon Mill, Bend, Oregon, 1930

grated C.A. Smith production system included logging railroads and camps, extensive booming and rafting facilities, waterfront cranes for loading lumber, and vessels to haul the rough-cut lumber to the company's finishing mill in Bay Point, California. Until the Weyerhaeuser Company opened a new manufactory on Coos Bay in 1951, the Big Mill and its extensive timberlands served as the largest employer on Oregon's southern coast. When the Big Mill and its supporting facilities were working at full capacity, the operation consumed a huge volume of logs. The system involved more than 40 steam-powered donkey engines to haul the huge logs out of the woods and difficult and dangerous work for logging crews.

There is a parallel story that suggests the dinosaur-like appetite of highly productive operations such as the Big Mill. When the company began to run short of logs adjacent to the Coos estuary, it moved deeper into its extensive holdings, especially the tremendous timber stands in the Coquille River drainage southeast of Coos Bay. To facilitate the movement of logs to the Big Mill, the firm constructed a railroad along the South Fork of the Coquille River and put up a company town, Powers, named for boss-logger Al Powers. Beginning in 1914 and continuing into the 1960s, tortuous and winding logging railroads radiated from Powers in a series of long switchbacks and steep grades to provide access to the company's timber. Because the Smith Company dominated timberland ownership in the region, the new railroad system meant that Coos Bay would remain the lumber manufacturing and shipping center on the south coast.

Although writers have given the most attention to the tremendous timber stands and incredible production records in the Douglas-fir district, significant milling centers were scattered throughout the interior ponderosa-pine regions of the West. Because Oregon's interior pine districts were remote and distant from markets, cutting was limited until railroads penetrated the Blue Mountains and central Oregon between 1880 and 1910. Perhaps the most anticipated and celebrated of Oregon's new timber frontiers was what the Portland Chamber of Commerce called the "opening" of central Oregon's great ponderosa district to lumber production. When James J. Hill's Great Northern Railway and Edward R. Harriman's Union Pacific Railroad waged their infamous construction battle through the Deschutes gorge in 1909, timber speculators were already at work blocking up valuable ponderosa-pine stands in the magnificent forested belt that stretched from Bend south to Klamath Falls. Among the largest timberland holders to emerge in the Bend/Klamath pine district were Great Lakes lumber firms Brooks-Scanlon and Shevlin-Hixon in the Bend area and Weyerhaeuser in the Klamath country.

The magazine *Pacific Monthly* spoke for the developers when it declared that completing the railroad to Bend would "tap the rich Central Oregon country" and provide access to the "visible natural wealth" of its forests. With the transportation system in place, Shevlin-Hixon and Brooks-Scanlon began building two large sawmills on opposite sides of the Deschutes upriver from Bend. Shevlin-Hixon began milling lumber from its 200,000 acres of timberland in March 1916, and a month later Brooks-Scanlon opened a facility with a similar capacity. The two large-volume pine manufacturers pursued a strategy of liquidating the old-growth ponderosa forests as quickly as markets and the technical limits on production permitted. The cutting capacity of the two plants was colossal, eventually reaching 200 million board feet a year. For more than three decades Bend and its hinterland were the center of bustling activity, with only market conditions and the constraints of sales from the national forests restricting production. A Forest Service report in the mid-1930s proclaimed: "The history of the economic development of Deschutes County is largely the history of the lumber industry."

Similar conditions prevailed in the Klamath and Harney basins, although on a more limited scale. The extension of the Southern Pacific Railroad from California to Klamath Falls in 1909 created another frenzy of timber speculation, with the Weyerhaeuser Timber Company emerging as the dominant property holder in the region. At the southern fringe of the extensive ponderosa-pine stands, Klamath County's timber grew on relatively even terrain, easily accessible to railroad and, later, truck-road transportation. The greatest volume of that timber was within a 30-mile radius of the big sawmills in Klamath Falls.

The forests of the Blue Mountains on the northern rim of the Harney Basin offer up a more complex and different story involving the aspirations of local people who wanted rail access to the outside and the ambitions of the Forest Service to sell timber. The Forest Service offered a huge volume of timber in Bear Valley for sale at rock-bottom prices in 1922, with the idea that the successful bidder would construct a rail line from Ontario to Burns and then north into the Blue Mountains. After several false starts, the Edward Hines Lumber Company of Chicago emerged as the successful bidder and the big Hines mill opened just outside Burns in 1930. The enormous investments in railroad construction and the company's need to meet its bonded debt meant timber cutting that far exceeded sustainable harvest practices. To keep the Hines operation afloat, the Forest Service sold timber quickly and far above a sustainable rate in the watersheds of the Silvies River, the Middle Fork of the John Day, and the Malheur River.

The great river systems of the Pacific Northwest—the Columbia, the Snake, the Fraser, and many lesser streams that drain the Pacific Slope—once produced enormous salmon runs that provided an abundant food source for Native peoples. Salmon were also physical representations of nature's bounty for the new Euroamerican immigrants who settled the region in the 19th century. To understand something about the prodigious salmon runs that once swarmed up northwestern rivers and streams, it is necessary to begin with the first people to make use of the abundant anadromous fishes. Archaeological finds throughout the North Pacific Slope reveal protracted and sustained fish harvesting as early as 9,000 years ago. For the Columbia system, it is fair to say that geology and the specific timing of the runs provided one of the most productive fisheries in the world.

In truth, Pacific Northwest waterways provided a veritable corridor of foodstuffs for Native peoples, funneling salmon and steelhead through highly productive fishing sites such as Celilo Falls and Kettle

OHS neg. OrHi 11338, Benjamin A. Gifford, photographer

Fishermen working at Celilo Falls, 1899

Falls. The incoming settler and merchant class, however, brought a different set of cultural values to the region's natural wealth, including its anadromous fishes. But the salmon business remained a commercial sideshow in the region until the development of efficient technologies for processing and preserving salmon, improvements in shipping and speed of travel, and the opening of markets in the industrializing Atlantic world. William Hume of Hapgood, Hume, and Company established the first cannery at Eagle Cliff on the north bank of the lower Columbia River in 1866 and put up 4,000 cases of salmon (48 one-pound cans per case). Within three years, other shippers were beginning to open markets in British industrial centers and in working-class areas on the East Coast of the United States.

From those modest beginnings, the salmon business developed quickly into a major regional industry. Canned salmon proved to be especially well-adapted for shipment over long distances, and the sheer abundance of the fish meant they could be suitably priced for eastern U.S. and European markets. From the very beginning, the Columbia River salmon business was a tremendously productive enterprise, with 55 canneries operating on the lower Columbia by 1883. At the front end of the industry—taking fish from the river—operators developed highly efficient technologies: gill nets, stationary fish traps, horse seines on the lower Columbia, and fishwheels—stationary and scow-mounted devices powered by the current that literally pumped salmon from the water.

Although there were canneries on virtually all of Oregon's coastal rivers, there is more statistical information for the Columbia than any other waterway. The catch for all salmon species on the Great River of the West reached a record high in 1911, but the take of the more valuable Chinook salmon had already peaked in 1883, circumstances that prompted some to worry about the industry's future. An astute observer of the salmon business, Frances Fuller Victor remarked: "Nature does not provide against such greed. . . . there is a prospect that the salmon, like the buffalo, may become extinct." Between 1880 and 1920, canneries packed more than 300,000 cases a year, reaching a peak of 579,000 cases in 1885. Columbia River salmon production fluctuated widely for more than two decades and then began a steady but appreciable decline after 1925. State legislatures in Oregon and Washington took small steps to restrict harvests and the type of gear used, but enforcement was weak or nonexistent. In reality, the salmon industry's behavior paralleled similar practices in the lumber industry: too many producers, unlimited entry to a seemingly limitless resource, and too many fish on the market. Such conditions encouraged waste and drove prices down.

A few perceptive individuals were also aware that environmental factors might explain the declining salmon runs. Mining operations, increasingly mechanized agricultural and logging activities, and severe disturbances to riparian areas through destructive grazing practices were all detrimental to salmon breeding habitat. Moreover, growing cities and towns along the region's major streams were dumping domestic sewage and untreated industrial wastes directly into waterways. In the long run, it was the sheer volume of those activities that proved so harmful to anadromous fish. As historian Joseph Taylor and others have indicated, salmon numbers were in serious decline long before the building of big hydroelectric dams on the Columbia and other northwestern rivers. Before Bonneville Dam was completed in 1938, the numerous small dams on the Columbia River system had already made nearly half the basin inaccessible to migrating salmon. In retrospect, the genesis of the seemingly recent salmon crisis is really a century-old phenomenon.

Similar to developments elsewhere in the United States, a literal technological revolution in natural-resource extraction and processing took place in the Pacific Northwest during the decades between the 1880s and the 1920s. Farmers, who had used wooden and metal moldboard plows and rudimentary mowing machines, threshers, and wheat separators, slowly began to adopt a wide array of improved plows, seed drills, mowers, and reapers. Unquestionably the greatest technological breakthrough involved the shift from human and animal power to steam power in agricultural and logging operations. Although the great continental railroads were visible symbols of the new steam technology, during the last quarter of the 19th century steam-driven machines were moving far beyond the region's railroads and waterways, powering combines in eastern Oregon's wheat country and steam-donkey yarders in coastal logging operations.

Steam energy was first used to power stationary threshing machines in eastern Oregon in the 1880s. Within a few years, farmers were using steam-powered combines on the gentler slopes in the Umatilla area. By the turn of the 20th century, a few operators had purchased steam-powered tractors to haul reapers and combines across moderate terrain. With the development of increasingly efficient internal combustion engines after the First World War, gasoline-powered tractors began to replace the old steam-driven machines. Horses, however, were still in widespread use to haul combines on the steeper slopes in eastern Oregon and in Washington's Palouse hills. Still, those technological advances created a growing number of displaced workers who sought jobs in newly emerging industries.

The adaptation of steam to logging operations was even more revolutionary in terms of its productive potential. Although steam energy had been used to power northwestern sawmills since about 1850, its technical adaptation for use in the woods took another 30 years. In the early 1880s, loggers in the California redwoods and around Puget Sound began using improved steam-powered engines to haul timber to waterways or railroad sidings. The increasing use of steam donkeys greatly speeded the movement of logs out of the woods. The transition from animal to steam power was gradual, with steam donkeys in widespread use by the turn of the century. In place of the slow-moving and laborious "bull" teams, steam was fast and made it possible for loggers to work through seasonal rain and snow.

By about 1910, enterprising loggers had developed an aerial twist to their steam-donkey yarding activities. The new technique—the "high

OHS neg., CN 002852

Lumber workers, logs, and a donkey engine by a log pond,
Tillamook County, in about 1900

lead"—allowed operators to haul logs to water's edge or a railroad
siding with one end suspended in the air, thereby avoiding stumps,
smaller trees, and other obstructions. There were human and environmental costs involved in steam-donkey logging—sharp increases
in the accident rate and accelerating disturbances to the ecology of
the forest—but high-lead logging vastly speeded production and increased the efficiency with which loggers could work through the winter. Where oxen would become mired in mud, donkey engines hauled
logs clear of mud, underbrush, and debris. In Oregon's Coast Range
and Cascade Mountains, steam-powered donkey engines remained in
use until the Second World War, when labor shortages accelerated the
shift to new and improved gasoline and diesel-powered yarding machines.

Until the wholesale mechanization of most work processes following the Second World War, the Pacific Northwest's extractive industries were labor-intensive, with a workforce comprised largely of
young single males who formed what historian Carlos Schwantes has
called "an informal commonwealth of toil." In the midst of the super-
charged development of the early 20th century, the 1910 federal census estimated that 90 percent of the lumber industry workforce was
single males, a characteristic that continued well into the automobile

age. The region also had a higher ratio of rank-and-file workers to craftsmen than elsewhere in the nation. It is fair to say that the Pacific Northwest was a place with many workers and few bosses.

Most people sold their labor for daily wages or for some form of piecework production, and many jobs were seasonal—especially in agriculture, logging, and the fish and vegetable canneries. Orchardists, for example, required intense labor for relatively limited periods of time. Winter was the slack season, with the workload picking up for spring pruning, slacking off while fruits were ripening on vine and branch, and then galvanizing into feverish activity during the harvest. The U.S. Commission on Industrial Relations reported in 1910 that there was a heavy seasonal demand for labor on Oregon's 45,000 farms, with the peak occurring during the harvest period in late summer and early fall. Unlike eastern industrial centers, few of Oregon's extractive industries employed workers throughout the year. Racialized occupational categories also characterized the workforce in extractive industries such as fish and vegetable canneries, where certain racial and ethnic groups were relegated to specific tasks. Salmon canneries, which for a time employed large numbers of Chinese workers, are probably the best example.

The boom-and-bust nature of the region's extractive economy invited worker mobility and encouraged union-organizing activity. Working-class people dominated life in labor-intensive logging communities, where a high rate of job turnover characterized employment. Itinerant laborers, continually on the move from one job to the next or to the "slave market" (hiring hall), were the norm in all extractive industries. During the first decade of the 20th century, wheat harvesting and railroad maintenance required thousands of laborers. Some workers dealt with difficult bosses and harsh working conditions by simply walking away from the job. Even after unions had made inroads with many logging outfits in the late 1940s, a lively job market continued to create considerable mobility in the workforce.

The fruit orchards around Medford and in the Hood River Valley employed a large, itinerant labor force during the fall season to pick and pack fruit for shipment to market. Thousands of harvest hands were also on the move across the wheat fields in Sherman and Umatilla counties during the late summer, a literal mobile army shifting from one field to the next until the wheat was loaded aboard rail cars and ready for shipment. In the days when horses and mules pulled the cumbersome reapers and combines, one eyewitness estimates that it took 75 horses and 30 workers to harvest 1,000 bushels of wheat. With the development of mechanized equipment during the 1930s, however, horses and mules disappeared along with much of the migrant labor force. Today, huge air-conditioned combines piloted by a single driver are capable of harvesting up to 3,500 bushels a day.

Employment opportunities for all classes of women expanded during the first two decades of the 20th century when female workers began to move away from traditional labor in agriculture and domestic service to jobs in the retail trades, telecommunications, clerical work, and education. Women increasingly sought positions in state and federal government offices and as factory workers, telephone operators, and office jobs. Although the percentage of women employees increased in every occupational cohort between 1900 and 1920, the sharpest rise occurred in manufacturing, retail, and transportation. During the First World War, women moved into new employment opportunities, especially after the federal government's 1918 draft sent large numbers of men into military service. Women in agriculture and domestic employment took advantage of a lively job market to seek better wages and to improve their working environments as they seized opportunities in formerly male-dominated occupations. While the return to a peacetime economy proved women's vulnerability in the job market, historian Maurice Greenwald contends that the wartime wage-labor experience gave women a new sense of confidence and self-respect.

Women encountered similar experiences in Oregon's logging camps, where they occasionally took jobs as "flunkies" (waiting tables), cooks, and laundresses. In Powers, a small company town in southwestern Oregon, men ran the Smith-Powers Logging Company cookhouses at first, but by the 1920s women began to fill the position. During the First World War, women also took important production positions in some of the specialty wood products companies on Coos Bay. Marguerette Therrien—whose father was a millwright in the big Coos Bay Lumber Company mill—was hired by the Coos Veneer and Box Company in 1928 at the age of 16. Eleanor Anderson, a Finnish immigrant, worked as a domestic, took a job with a wealthy family in San Francisco for a brief period, and then returned to Coos Bay to do assembly piecework in a local veneer plant. Beyond the lumber towns, women also worked in salmon and vegetable canneries, as schoolteachers, and in the nursing profession. In large cities such as Portland, Eugene, and Salem, a few found employment in skilled

Lewis and Clark Exposition, Portland, 1905

trades such as telephone and Linotype operators. The Second World War, of course, would mark the real watershed period for women entering the workforce as wage laborers.

Until Seattle's explosive growth during the 1890s, Portland was by far the most significant urban center in the Pacific Northwest. The building of the Northern Pacific Railroad to Portland and Puget Sound in 1883 and the extension of the Great Northern to Everett and Seattle a decade later, however, altered the region's urban dynamics, boosting Seattle to a preeminent position. Seattle's emergence as a major urban center did not diminish the aspirations of Portland promoters. The city's boosters were at one with the *Oregonian*, which referred to Portland as the "Railroad Cross-Roads" of the Pacific Northwest, a place where great transportation routes developed as naturally as "the physical law which makes water run down hill." Because of its "great natural channels," the newspaper declared in 1890, every productive section of the Columbia region enjoyed a level route to Portland. To further the city's economic interests, local boosters lobbied for improvements to the Columbia River to provide "a deep and safe channel to the Sea."

Developing Portland's transportation infrastructure involved more than railroad connections. After much procrastination, the city completed the Morrison Bridge in 1887, the first structure to span the lower Willamette River and reduce reliance on the numerous ferries that plied the waterway. During the 1890s, the city funded the construction of an electric transmission line from the falls at Oregon City to Portland to power electric streetcars. Portland also invested $6 million to build its first Bull Run Reservoir to bring clear waters from the western slopes of the Cascades to the Willamette metropolis. Beginning in the early 1870s, the city began acquiring lands in its western hills that would eventually become Washington and Forest parks, the largest urban park system in the United States. And in the true spirit of civic promotion, Portland citizens initiated the first of its annual Rose Festivals, a June celebration that developed into the city's signature celebratory event.

At the onset of the 20th century, however, the new urban rival on Puget Sound made the Portland business community nervous. To counter Seattle's ascendancy, the Portland Board of Trade and local bankers moved aggressively to reassert Portland's position as the Northwest's preeminent metropolis. Their effort led in 1905 to the elaborately planned Lewis and Clark Centennial Exposition, which ran from June 1 to October 15, an event that was a striking civic and commercial success. At the city's Guild's Lake area, columned buildings sheltered exhibits from every American state and several foreign countries. The federal government appropriated $1.7 million for the United States Government building, located at the center of pools and fountains and outward-radiating streets and walkways lined with roses. When the attendance figures were tallied, more than 1.5 million people had entered the Exposition through paid admissions and another 900,000 through courtesy passes. The *Oregonian* praised the exposition for its "great financial success" and for surpassing its planners' expectations. A year after the event, the newspaper offered a final perspective: "The Lewis and Clark Exposition officially marked the end of the old and the beginning of the new Oregon." The Exposition also helped boost the state's population by 70 percent and Portland's numbers from 90,000 to 207,000 between 1900 and 1910.

Following the Lewis and Clark Exposition, the Portland Board of Trade and its successors continued to push railroad extensions to Oregon's outback, proposals the business community believed would benefit the city. When rumors surfaced that the Southern Pacific Railroad planned to build a line north to Klamath Falls, the *Oregonian* worried that the route would "drain away to California the rich and rapidly growing traffic of the Klamath country." The newspaper took a different view a few years later when Southern Pacific announced that it would construct a railroad from Eugene to Coos Bay, a prospect that would enable Portland to benefit from trade that otherwise would be lost to San Francisco. Chamber of Commerce publications also promoted efforts to improve navigation on the Columbia River; the projects included deepening the river and the shipping channel to Portland Harbor and building a canal between The Dalles and Celilo Falls. The Portland business community and upriver shippers argued that improving navigation on the Great River would develop the hinterland and advance the city's prospects as a trading center.

The Portland business community's ambitions were expansive, with its publications regularly alluding to "unoccupied" districts, "untapped" wealth, and hightlighting the benefits of "opening up" new country. The city's overweening designs had long been an integral part of state politics, producing tensions that were manifested in legislative debates and statewide political contests. Politicians beyond the state's major metropolis—and especially outside the Willamette Valley—have always distrusted Portland's power brokers. Because Oregon farmers were more isolated from major metropolitan areas than their counterparts in California, historian Earl Pomeroy contends, they were more likely to resent Portland's business and political influences. The tensions between urban and rural Oregon existed, he argues, because "Portland was large enough to stimulate and arouse its neighbors, but not large enough to stifle them." Those characteristics would persist into the 21st century.

The Progressive reform movement of the early 20th century provides some insight into the differences between Oregon's urban and rural voters. Portland and Multnomah County, especially the wealthiest precincts, provided the strongest support for the Oregon System's direct legislation proposals. In the more conservative Willamette Valley's small towns and farming communities and in rural southern and eastern Oregon, direct legislation was less popular. Urban and rural Oregon also divided over support for workplace regulations such as the eight-hour day, child labor laws, and other restrictions on employers. Multnomah County gave full support to such legislation, but beyond the Portland area voters were lukewarm. The state also divided over social conformity issues, with Prohibition more popular in rural areas of the state than in Multnomah County. Rural voters would continue to support social legislation that upheld traditional white, Anglo-Saxon cultural values. Such tendencies placed the state at the center of nativist sentiments during the 1920s with the rise of the Ku Klux Klan. On those occasions when rural voters prevailed at the ballot box, the initiative measures they supported often discriminated against racial and religious minorities, but in that sense Oregon was similar to other states where resistance to social and cultural change was strongest in the countryside.

The First World War marked a turnaround for the Pacific Northwest in what had been a prolonged period of depressed prices for lumber and agricultural products. When Germany sent its armies marching through Belgium, British and French purchases of wheat and lumber sent prices soaring to three and four times their prewar marks. Like growers elsewhere in wheat-producing sections of the country, Sherman and Umatilla county farmers planted more acres to wheat and increased harvests during the war years. The lumber trade also expanded, especially in producing wood structural materials for building army cantonments and milling spruce for use in airplane construction. The tough, lightweight, and straight-grained Sitka spruce was especially well-suited for building aircraft wings. Spruce production ultimately became one of the more interesting stories to emerge from the war, involving for the first time federal intervention in the Northwest economy to produce an essential war commodity. With the creation of the United States Spruce Production Corporation, the government became directly involved in controlling all aspects of the manufacturing process from logging and milling to labor relations.

Because Sitka spruce grows only a short distance from the Pacific Ocean, most timber cutting in Oregon took place adjacent to Toledo, where the Spruce Production Corporation harvested nearly 54 million board feet. During the summer of 1918, 27,000 soldiers were working in the camps and mills of western Oregon and Washington, producing spruce as well as other lumber materials. By the time the European war was nearing its bloody end, the Spruce Corporation was an extensive undertaking: operating a Vancouver mill to manufacture wing beams to exact specifications; directing logging railroads and truck traffic; managing timberlands; and controlling other miscellaneous inventory—all valued at approximately $24 million. When the war ended, the corporation liquidated its assets and its properties and equipment passed into the private sector. The C.D. Johnson Lumber Company, taking advantage of the government's generous terms, assumed ownership of the corporation's nearly completed mill in Toledo.

The war's most significant influence in the Pacific Northwest, however, was reflected in the region's changing labor relations. Shortly after the United States joined the Allies (England, France, and Russia) in their struggle against the Central Powers (Germany, Austria-Hungary, and Turkey), Northwest loggers and millworkers began striking for better wages, a shorter workday, and improved living conditions in the logging camps. The rapidly expanding strike was spectacular. It spread quickly through the region's camps and mills until the industry was operating at only about 15 percent of capacity. On Oregon's southern coast, Coos Bay Lumber Company millworkers struck briefly for higher wages, demands that management agreed to because it feared that the strike would spread to logging operations. Although the American Federation of Labor (AFL) had established a few locals before 1917, the union organizing drive gained momentum in the spring and summer of that year when both the AFL and the radical Industrial Workers of the World (IWW) stepped up recruiting activities in the region. Disgruntled loggers and millworkers found the industry-wide organizing principles of the Wobblies attractive and joined the wide-ranging regional strike in increasing numbers.

At that point, the federal government intervened when Brig. Gen. Brice Disque of the Spruce Production Corporation ordered lumber employers to institute the eight-hour day and to improve conditions in the logging camps. With the full cooperation of the region's timber companies, Disque then set up an industry-wide company union, the Loyal Legion of Loggers and Lumbermen (4-L). The federal government played a cooperative and aggressive part in that effort when it ordered a series of nationwide raids to round up IWW leaders on trumped-up charges of espionage and sedition. As for the 4-L, it took full advantage of the wartime emergency and patriotic demands to ban boycotts and strikes, mandating that workers sign loyalty pledges as a condition of employment. But it is important to point out—as workers who lived through those years have testified—that the achievement of the eight-hour day, higher wages, and improved living conditions was a victory for militant unionism and not the Loyal Legion. Victor Stevens, who worked for the Smith-Powers Logging Company in southwestern Oregon, remembers that the "IWW scare" meant clean bedsheets, warmer and bug-free bunkhouses, and improved medical care for injured workers.

OHS neg., OrHi 7730

Industrial Workers of the World (IWW) Poster, "Education-Organization-Emancipation," 1905-1930

The war also gave a great boost to the Northwest's shipbuilding industry, primarily in the Seattle-Tacoma area but also in Oregon, where a significant number of wooden ships were constructed. By the close of the war, the Emergency Fleet Corporation was operating 28 yards, including plants in Coos Bay, Tillamook, Astoria, Columbia City, and Portland. Because of war-related labor shortages, Idaho and Montana workers journeyed west to take jobs in the shipyards and other such industries. In their efforts to recruit an adequate workforce, companies offered higher wages and raided competitors for skilled employees. On Oregon's Coos Bay, Emergency Fleet Corporation yards in Marshfield and North Bend dominated construction activity, operating with a full complement of carpenters and shipwrights, skills that were in high demand throughout the war. With the signing of the Armistice in November 1918, however, that frantic pace of activity ended and a literal army of the unemployed took to the rails looking for work. The fallout from wage conflicts in Puget Sound shipyards led to the four-day Seattle General Strike in February 1919 in which 60,000 workers walked off the job in solidarity with shipyard workers. The city's mayor, Ole Hanson, briefly became a national celebrity, claiming that the general strike threatened the very fiber of civilization and warning that the day of revolution was at hand.

The First World War took domestic casualties beyond the government's roundup of the IWW's leadership, especially those who questioned America's involvement in the European conflict. Oregon's Democratic Senator Harry Lane provides a striking illustration of a political figure who fell from grace because of his vote against the American declaration of war in April 1917. The Oregon legislature elected Lane—a physician, former mayor of Portland, and progressive reformer—to the U.S. Senate in 1912, where he supported most of President Woodrow Wilson's New Freedom reforms during his first term in office. Lane also backed the president's reelection effort in 1916 but broke with Wilson early in 1917 as the administration moved toward war with Germany. When Lane joined five other senators in opposing the declaration of war measure, the national and local press vilified the group as traitors and betrayers of their nation, politicians who deserved to be driven from public office. Lane's death on May 23, 1917, marked the close of a remarkable reform interlude in the state's political life, one that it would not witness again until Tom McCall became governor in 1966.

Through periods of war and peace, the federal government continued to vigorously pursue its "civilization" policies on northwestern Indian reservations. While the off-reservation boarding schools were the most obvious symbols of this effort, the Bureau of Indian Affairs implemented other programs that were equally intrusive into Native cultural practices. The Bureau deemed Indian reservations as laboratories of sorts, isolated settings where appropriate assimilation strategies would lead to cultural and linguistic change. As part of this policy, reservation day schools prohibited children from speaking their Native languages or wearing Native dress and they often required students to wear uniforms. At the Siletz agency, the Indian Bureau operated both boarding and day schools until the boarding school was closed in 1908. The reservation day school continued for another ten years, when it also closed and children were directed to attend public schools. In reality, coastal reservation Indians went through a period of adaptation that had little relationship to federal policy. Siletz people continued to work in local sawmills, in logging camps, and for a time took seasonal cannery jobs at a salmon-processing plant on the lower Siletz River.

As Siletz agricultural efforts continued to decline after 1900, people drifted away from the reservation in search of wage-earning employment. At the Grand Ronde agency, the allotment policy had literally obliterated the old reservation land base and only remnant plots of land remained—the tribal cemetery, lots for the Catholic church, and agency buildings. When the Indian Bureau opened a short-lived agency in Roseburg, the office reported 3,000 Indians living in southern Oregon in 1910; some had taken allotments on the public domain while still others were pursuing seasonal wage work.

During the First World War, 17 Siletz men enlisted in the army; 2 of them died in battle. In the meantime, the persisting effects of allotment policy continued to diminish the size of the Siltez Reservation. A Lincoln County agricultural agent reported to a congressional committee in 1931 that land patents issued to individual Indians usually found their way into non-Indian hands: "a great deal of land was mortgaged and the mortgage sold, either foreclosed or directly sold. So from that time to the present time the better lands on the Siletz have passed out of the hands of the Indians." The *coup de grâce* to the government's policies was the Indian Bureau's decision to close the Siletz agency offices in 1925. Despite the closure, the Siletz continued to live and adapt as they always had, irrespective of federal directives.

Elsewhere in Oregon, the allotment program continued to add to checkerboard ownership patterns on the confederated tribal reservations at Umatilla and Warm Springs, with non-Indian lands intermixed with tribal and individual trust lands. Over the years, many individual allotments were lost to non-Indian owners when the allottees failed to pay taxes on their property. Counties would then foreclose on the allotments, which were sold at public auction. Thousands of successful allottees also became landowners and citizens and assimilated into the dominant culture. It is also important to know that until Congress passed the Indian Citizenship Act in 1924, Native people had not been considered "citizens" unless they were individual property holders and paid taxes. In retrospect, the 1920s marked a period of transition in federal Indian policy, from the aggressive assimilation efforts of the 19th century to Franklin D. Roosevelt's more benign New Deal programs.

The First World War marked a watershed of sorts in Oregon and Northwest history. When the United States joined the hostilities in Europe, thousands of young men from the region voluntarily enlisted in the military, with some of them serving on the battlefields of France. The war also unleashed a frenzy of German-hating across the country—an outbreak of bigotry to which Oregon was not immune. The state's politicians turned away from the vibrant reform spirit championed by George Chamberlain, Oswald West, and Harry Lane and passed criminal syndicalist legislation directed at pacifists, socialists, and members of the Industrial Workers of the World. The Bolshevik Revolution in Russia and the Seattle General Strike of February 1919—the first city-wide strike in the nation—encouraged reactionaries such as Seattle Mayor Ole Hanson to embark on patriotic crusades in defense of what was called Americanism. Oregon's move away from its Progressive traditions seemed to make a mockery of Woodrow Wilson's 1911 comment that Oregon's remarkable early 20th-century reforms should serve as a model for other states. Historian Earl Pomeroy provided a pointed critique of the shifting politics of Oregon, Washington, and California: "The Far West became less famous for reform than for repression as the people used direct legislation to discriminate against religious, racial, and political minorities." With the emergence of the Ku Klux Klan as a force in state politics in the 1920s, Oregon stood at the forefront of those newly emergent reactionary politics.

CHAPTER SIX

Cultural Politics, Depression, and War

Although his long public career spanned the period from the Populist revolt to Franklin Roosevelt's New Deal, Walter Pierce remains a controversial and enigmatic figure in Oregon politics. Elected as Oregon's 16th governor in 1922 with the active support of the Ku Klux Klan, Democrat Pierce was a notable liberal on issues of gender, class, progressive taxation, and a host of other economic matters. While he could invite Abigail Scott Duniway to speak to his rural northeastern Oregon school in the mid-1880s and supported her long struggle for women's suffrage, with the same enthusiasm he could oppose Asian ownership of property in the state. Pierce may have been the representative Oregonian of his day, a Populist at heart who warred against great concentrations of wealth but who also opposed Japanese ownership of land in the Hood River Valley and Chinese ownership of Portland restaurants. When the Oregon senate considered a memorial in 1919 asking the U.S. Congress to guarantee voting rights for African Americans in southern states, the measure passed with only three dissenting votes, one of them Walter Pierce's.

Among his proudest achievements, Pierce listed his support for Oregon's first graduated income tax and, after his election to Congress in 1932 at age 72, the development of Columbia River hydropower, rural electrification, and federal price supports for wheat. Pierce thought it criminal that Oregon would support aged and dependent people through taxes on liquor sales: "That assistance should be given to the aged as a matter of right." He opposed the sales tax, favored a progressive tax on income, and thought it just to place "the burden of government upon those best able to pay." As an aged New Dealer, he believed that the government had broad responsibilities for the general welfare. His biographer, Arthur Bone, argued that Pierce rejected individualism and "embraced a cooperative, communal view of society."

Oregon's social and cultural life during the 1920s reflected Pierce's fundamentally nativist views, values that fit well with the conventions of a largely homogeneous society and its tendencies toward social, cultural, and religious conformity. Those idiosyncrasies suggest in part the relative geographic isolation of the Pacific Northwest and the welter of changes that followed the European conflict. The First World War, writer Malcolm Clark has argued, marked "a generation of changes . . . compressed into 18 months." Women gained the franchise, the 18th Amendment was added to the U.S. Constitution, and discussions about sex emerged from the closet to become a part of everyday conversation. Added to those issues were anxieties reflecting the triumph of the Bolshevik Revolution in Russia, the emergence of U.S. Attorney General A. Mitchell Palmer and the "Red Scare" of 1919, and the region's faltering agricultural and lumber economy. Many conservative and traditional-minded Oregonians ascribed those disruptions to the growing acceptance of libertarian and licentious behavior, reflected in the growing use of automobiles and the emergence of jazz.

Amid the social and economic turbulence of the immediate postwar years, Oregon's largely homogenous ethnic and religious public served as a ready recruiting ground for groups appealing to white, Anglo-Saxon, Protestant values. The American Protective Association, the American Federation of Patriotic Societies, and the Ku Klux Klan—all purporting to be guardians of traditional American institutions and values—made rapid strides in Oregon during the early 1920s. Klan recruiters arrived in 1921, and within two years the organization was instrumental in electing eastern Oregon's Walter Pierce to the governorship. In this and subsequent elections, Pierce remained notably silent on the Klan issue. Appealing to its own narrow brand of ethnic, racial, and religious bigotry, the Klan dominated the state legislature and helped elect Kaspar K. Kubli (with appropriate initials) speaker of the house.

The Klan was most effective in promoting its nativist social agenda through the direct-legislation process. Its most infamous effort was a 1922 initiative, the Compulsory School Bill, which required all children between the ages of eight and 16 to attend public schools. With prejudice against private (especially parochial) schools deeply rooted in Oregon's history, the Compulsory School Bill reflected nativist thinking and the efforts of the Federation of Patriotic Societies to strengthen public schools. The Klan opportunistically took advantage of a social climate broadly representative among the state's largely white, Protestant voting public. With the exception of the Portland *Telegram*, George Putnam's Salem *Capitol Journal*, and a few small-town newspapers, the state's press largely ignored the school bill and the Klan until the *Oregonian* issued a mild series of editorials late in the campaign calling for local school boards to supervise private-school curricula. Although voters approved the measure 115,506 to 103,685, the Oregon Supreme Court declared the law unconstitutional, a decision upheld by the U.S. Supreme Court in 1925.

Under the Klan's influence and with the support of agricultural organizations and the American Legion, the Oregon legislature passed an Alien Property Act in 1923, a measure directed at immigrant Japanese in Portland and the Hood River Valley. The measure was a response to Walter Pierce's request that the legislature enact a law prohibiting the sale or lease of land to Asians. Similar to laws passed in Washington and California (and upheld in the courts), the Oregon statute prohibited aliens from owning or leasing land. The same Klan-influenced legislature, again with Pierce's support, banned sectarian clothing in public schools and petitioned Congress to restrict Asian immigration to the United States. Although the sentiments the Klan appealed to continued to be part of Oregon's political fabric, its national and state membership declined as precipitously as it had risen in the late 1820s. As for Walter Pierce, he went on to serve five terms in the U.S. House of Representatives as a public-power advocate and supporter of Franklin Roosevelt's New Deal.

Oregon's most renowned national political figure during the first half of the 20th century was Salem-born Charles McNary, a Republican with legitimate Progressive credentials. McNary's political ideology bridged the period from William U'Ren's direct legislation reform measures to Roosevelt's New Deal policies. Educated at Stanford University, McNary served briefly as dean of Willamette University's law school and was appointed to the Oregon Supreme Court, where he gained a reputation for writing legal opinions upholding the state's Progressive reform measures. When Harry Lane died in the spring of 1917, Governor James Withycombe appointed McNary to the U.S. Senate. After surviving a tough primary campaign against a conservative Republican, McNary defeated his Democratic opponent—and friend—Oswald West in the general election, garnering 54 percent of the votes. Labor unions, the Farmer's Union, the Grange, and remnants of the Progressive Party provided important support for his successful campaign. McNary served in the Senate until his death in 1944, a remarkably productive 26 years in which he practiced a nonpartisan politics that earned him great popularity in his home state.

Charles McNary also spoke for prominent political and corporate business groups in the Pacific Northwest, especially the region's powerful lumber industry. Although he billed himself as a Teddy Roosevelt conservationist, McNary effectively opposed the efforts of Gifford Pinchot and others who wanted to impose federal regulations on private forestry practices. With New York Congressman John D. Clarke, McNary cosponsored the most significant piece of federal forestry legislation in the first half of the 20th century. Passed in 1924 and signed into law by President Calvin Coolidge, the Clarke-McNary Act provided federal aid to states for fire protection on all classes of land. The measure also included provisions for reforestation work and funds to purchase cutover lands for the national forest system. The lumber industry praised the act for its cooperative principles and for avoiding the federal regulation of harvesting practices.

McNary also sponsored farm-relief legislation during the 1920s, congressional bills designed to alleviate the prolonged period of depressed prices in the agricultural sector. Known as the McNary-Haugen bills, the measures called for the federal purchase of surplus agricultural commodities and price supports for domestic and international sales. McNary biographer Steve Neal has called the McNary-Haugen bills "the chief ideological debate of the Twenties." The *Wall Street Journal* dubbed McNary-Haugenism "an unwise experiment in socialism and government price-fixing." When the issue became a factor in the Republican presidential primaries in 1924, California Senator Hiram Johnson backed the McNary-Haugen principle in an effort to unseat President Coolidge. Coolidge, who opposed the bills, won the primary and the general elections and then appointed an agriculture secretary—William Jardine—who shared his opposition to McNary-

OHS neg., OrHi 74272

OHS neg., OrHi 89968

Charles McNary, 1874-1944, Oregon
senator from 1917 to 1944

Walter Pierce, 1861-1954, Oregon
governor and U.S. representative

Haugenism. Congress passed McNary-Haugen bills in 1926, 1927, and 1928 only to have President Coolidge veto the measures in sharply worded messages. The principle of government price support would surface again during the Great Depression in the form of several New Deal reform proposals.

Along with the rest of the nation, Oregon fell on hard times during the 1930s. Bank failures, bankruptcies, business foreclosures, and high unemployment worsened the region's already struggling agricultural and lumber industries. The Oregon and Washington economies had floundered after the First World War because of defunct shipyards, glutted agricultural markets, and weakness in the construction industry. Dependent on California sales for its livelihood, Oregon's lumber industry suffered greatly when prices and demand in the Golden State continued their downward spiral. The region's major trade organization, the West Coast Lumbermen's Association, announced in August 1931 that its mills were operating at only 38 percent of capacity. Evidence of delinquent county and local taxes meant financial collapse, the inability of businesses to meet payrolls, and sharply curtailed revenue for schools and other community services.

Private relief efforts, job clearinghouses, donations of food and clothing, and meal tickets for the destitute were quickly overwhelmed everywhere in Oregon. Desperation, protests, and, in some cases, direct action were the order of the day. On the southern Oregon Coast, service clubs and civic groups around Coos Bay organized a central clearinghouse to provide information about employment and to investigate the needs of those seeking relief. Sharp increases in unemployment ultimately overwhelmed voluntary relief efforts and deepened the poverty and hunger that settled over Oregon and the Pacific Northwest. To compound those difficulties, migrants arriving from the Dust Bowl and the impoverished South added to the numbers of unemployed and destitute people, placing even more burdens on private relief agencies for food, housing, and employment.

In the Portland metropolitan area, where construction activity had slowed sharply after 1925, depressed lumber prices forced many local sawmills to close operations long before the stock market crash in October 1929. Because of the high unemployment and the increased number of destitute in the city, local officials had exhausted all local emergency funds by mid-1930. At the time of Franklin Roosevelt's inauguration in March 1933, 40,000 Portlanders were on relief and 24,000 householders were registered with the local employment bureau. The collapsing economy worsened conditions in Portland's poorer neighborhoods. Shanty-town "Hoovervilles" appeared: 100 people lived under the west end of the Ross Island Bridge; more than 300 bivouacked in Sullivan's Gulch on the near east side; and another large group of homeless congregated at the filled-in Guild's Lake on the west side. Fearful of social disruption in the summer of 1932, Governor Julius Meier, elected as an independent, asked President Hoover for assistance: "We must have help from the federal government if we are to avert suffering and possible uprisings."

Although Portland participated in several New Deal programs, the city's political leadership was unenthusiastic about most federal initiatives. Shortly after his election in 1932, Mayor Joseph Carson told local business groups that his administration would not be looking for federal handouts. Through his long tenure in office, from 1934 to 1941, Carson strongly opposed all public power proposals; and during the Portland dock strike of 1934, the mayor fully supported waterfront employers by authorizing police to attack strikers. Carson's language became more inflammatory in opposing Roosevelt's Works Progress Administration (WPA) initiative of 1935, the New Deal's best-known work-relief program. With a majority of the city council, Carson successfully fought local efforts to establish a city housing authority in 1938, arguing that public housing was akin to "unadulterated Communism" and would depress property values.

Oregon Senator Charles McNary and Congressman Walter Pierce, who both enjoyed cordial relations with President Roosevelt, did not share the views of Portland's political leadership. Both men were full participants in pushing through the most famous schedule of reform legislation in American history—the creation of the Civil Works Administration, the Civilian Conservation Corps, and the Farm Credit Administration. McNary and Pierce got along well with key Roosevelt officials, including Agriculture Secretary Henry Wallace and Interior Secretary Harold Ickes, and both were key supporters of the New Deal's most enduring legacy, the Social Security Act of 1935. Pierce was disappointed only with the measure's inadequate provisions for the aged, urging the president to increase the program's benefits. Along with equally influential senators from the state of Washington, McNary and Pierce consistently supported the big Columbia River hydropower projects. But on the home front, McNary was in trouble. He barely survived a challenge by radical Democrat Willis E. Mahoney in the 1936 election, squeaking through with a plurality of 5,510 votes. It was clear that the Roosevelt landslide of 1936 made it difficult to elect *any* Republican to national office.

Beyond Portland's conservative political establishment, New Deal programs were immensely popular in Oregon. The Civilian Conservation Corps (CCC), perhaps the most celebrated of the reform initiatives, operated camps across the state, providing modest wages, food and shelter, and constructive outdoor work for young men. Congressman Pierce especially favored the CCC because the agency's purpose dovetailed nicely with his interests in forest conservation and the need to put unemployed youth to work. Before it was disbanded in 1942, the CCC employed nearly 87,000 "boys" in Oregon who were housed in 49 camps across the state. The young men labored at a variety of forestry and conservation jobs, building roads, trails, shelters, and lookouts and providing foot soldiers for a vastly expanded workforce for fighting forest fires. The Coos Bay *Times* gave the CCC unstinting praise on its fifth anniversary on March 31, 1938:

> The CCC experiment has been so much of a success that it is being continued. Anything that prevents soil erosion, builds new forest highways, opens new park projects, sets out new trees, saves the old ones from

CCC workers fight fire in the Willamette National Forest in about 1934

fire–anything that does such things is of lasting value to the country. Coos County has been fortunate in having her share of the camps, varying from two, as at present, to five or six.

Among the more notable public venues constructed with CCC labor were Silver Falls State Park east of Salem and Jessie M. Honeyman State Park on the central coast. CCC and WPA workers also helped build Timberline Lodge high on the southern slopes of Mt. Hood and the Oregon Department of Forestry headquarters in Salem.

During the late 1930s, the Oregon highway department used state and federal monies to put people to work building bridges over coastal bays and estuaries. Designed by the famous engineer Conde Mc-Cullough, the still-standing and aesthetically pleasing McCullough bridges offer visual testimony to his engineering expertise. When it was completed in 1936, the 1,700-foot cantilever bridge spanning Coos Bay was the longest in the Pacific Northwest. Because of its vaulting height, which permitted ocean-going vessels to pass underneath, the engineering blueprint for the bridge involved complicated planning, lay-out, and design. The completed bridge network vastly quickened travel along Oregon's Highway 101 and eliminated the need for the slow, laborious ferry systems that operated on coastal streams and estuaries.

When the Roosevelt administration used the Emergency Relief Appropriations Act of 1935 to establish the WPA (including several other relief divisions), it introduced the largest and one of the more controversial of all New Deal initiatives. Until the Second World War made the WPA redundant, the agency was the most visible of all federal relief efforts in the nation, employing more than 3 million people in its first year and a total of 8.5 million nationwide before it was disbanded in 1942. WPA labor was used to build the McCullough bridges and to work on a variety of city projects, including the construction of local parks, sewage facilities, and small airports. The WPA's chief utility, however, was to provide people with pride and a small income when there were few employment prospects available. The agency's larger achievement was to lessen the potential for social disorder and to ensure that the basic framework of the American economy would transcend the Depression.

In Portland, the WPA put 25,000 people on the federal payroll, employing citizens to work on projects large and small, including Rocky Butte Scenic Drive and the Portland Municipal Airport. To maximize its potential for direct relief, the WPA shied away from mechanized equipment and relied on hand tools for most of its work tasks. The construction of the Portland airport, which regularly employed more than 1,000 people, was the most significant WPA activity in Multnomah County, but it was the less glamorous smaller projects that put the greatest number of people to work. The agency was responsible for hundreds of small-scale projects in Portland, including the construction and improvement of local parks, building roads, and installing street drainage systems. One of its most significant efforts involved improvements at Macleay Park in the West Hills, where workers cleared brush and built an extensive trail system.

The WPA also hired large numbers of Portland residents to build the Wolf Creek and Wilson River highways, which greatly speeded travel to the coast. Because of the lengthy commute, the agency used an old CCC camp on the Wolf Creek section to house workers. The WPA also hired skilled Portland-area artisans to produce ornamental wrought iron for projects across the state; the ornaments included straps, hinges, handles, and other items made specifically for Timberline Lodge on Mount Hood. The agency supported Portland musicians who performed in public places around the city and in venues such as the Portland Art Museum and Marylhurst and Reed colleges. The Federal Arts' Theater and Writers' projects were other WPA activities that attracted a great deal of attention and controversy, because critics considered them frivolous and a waste of taxpayers' money. The Writers' Project produced the *Oregon Guide*, a descriptive narrative of the state's history, its physical landscape, and cultural heritage. Public buildings, such as post offices and schools, still display WPA-funded artwork, murals, and other creative works.

Although the WPA included women in its service-project jobs, females made up only a small percentage of overall agency employment. Federal, state, and local administrators operated on the assumption that useful and productive work primarily involved construction jobs, traditionally the province of males. While Eleanor Roosevelt and a few others spoke out on behalf of WPA employment for women, "institutionalized sexism in the WPA guidelines," writer Neil Barker argues, "made most women ineligible for work relief." Moreover, the few women who did obtain relief work were placed in jobs that required sewing, housekeeping, or serving school lunches to needy children. Portland-area women also found WPA jobs through the household service-training program, a closely supervised, class-based plan that provided domestic labor for the city's elite families.

In Portland and other urban centers, people muddled through the Depression years, birthing fewer children, living in multiple-family households, surviving on sporadic and part-time employment, and doing occasional work-relief jobs. In Oregon's outback, where families still practiced semi-subsistence lifestyles, barter, labor exchanges, and the timeworn practice of poaching fish and game usually meant that people had enough food on the table. Individual family members frequently exchanged labor on neighboring farms and ranches for fruits, vegetables, and dairy products. Wood for cooking and heating was readily accessible, and wild fruits, especially blackberries, were seasonally abundant and easy to preserve. Along the coastal settlements, the ocean troll-fishery thrived, although the daily catch was usually at the mercy of a very weak market. One woman remembers that while food was plentiful, neither her family nor her neighbors had "new clothes to speak of for several years."

New Deal reforms also ushered in dramatic new directions for the nation's Indian policy, terminating the allotment program, fostering Indian arts and crafts, and ending the prosecution of Indi-

Ben Jones Bridge at Depoe Bay, designed by Conde McCullough

ans for exercising Native religious beliefs. The new policy initiatives also encouraged tribes to draft their own written constitutions and to form business corporations. John Collier, President Roosevelt's dynamic commissioner of Indian affairs, attempted to reverse decades of mismanagement, corruption, and failures in the nation's Indian programs. His chief vehicle for launching the new direction was the Indian Reorganization Act (IRA) of 1934. Although Congress dramatically modified and weakened the final measure, Collier set out to convince Indian tribes to organize under the provisions of the act. Over the next few years, 172 tribes agreed to adopt the IRA and 73 refused. Even in its watered-down version, the new law repealed allotment, restored "surplus" land to tribal ownership, and provided funds to purchase additional land for reservations. What happened in the ensuing years was a mix of misunderstandings that further exacerbated existing tribal factions and worsened tensions between mixed and full-blood Indians. Nevertheless, in the end, Collier's policies empowered Indians and marked a progressive shift in federal programs.

Oregon tribes greeted Collier's initiatives with mixed sentiments. The Grand Ronde and Warm Springs peoples voted to come under the

provisions of the IRA. At Warm Springs, the three tribal groups organized as the Confederated Tribes of the Warm Springs Reservation in
1937 and adopted a constitution and bylaws to guide their daily affairs.
The next year they elected a tribal council and set up a corporate charter to conduct business activities. Today, the Warm Springs view their
business charter as the beginning of a move toward self-sufficiency.
The most notable among the Oregon groups to reject the IRA were
the Klamath, who were riven by tribal factions, each suspicious of the
other's motives. The background to those divisions can be traced to
the 1920s when two groups emerged, each seeking greater autonomy
for the tribal economy. Those differences persisted into the future and
were important factors in the move toward termination in the early
1950s.

The Great Depression remained a fact of life in Oregon for a full decade and began to ease only when war orders slowly began to en-
ergize the American economy in late 1940 and 1941. Despite improved
conditions in the late 1930s, the WPA continued to provide employment
for a large number of workers in the state's more heavily populated
counties. Other public works projects employed an even larger number of people at marginal wages. Throughout the 1930s the number of
people receiving some form of direct relief remained high; the categories of welfare included support for dependent children and seniors,
surplus food, and general assistance. Despite the variety of New Deal
work-relief programs, the economy moved unevenly through partial
recoveries and slumps for the remainder of the decade. At the outset of
1940, the Coos Bay *Times* expressed concern because the southwestern
Oregon economy continued to struggle:

> This area suffers, as does much of the United States, from almost chronic
> unemployment of some needy citizens. Youth particularly is finding it
> hard to gain steady employment. Relief loads are heavy but by the com-
> bined efforts of federal, state and county governments, are being met.

Urban historian Carl Abbott aptly describes Portland at the end
of the Depression decade: "The census of 1940 described a city that
had ceased to grow." Although Portland's population had inched
slightly upward, its demographic profile had changed: the city had
fewer skilled and more unskilled and domestic laborers at the close
of the 1930s. Portland had also grown older during the decade, a trait

reflected in the declining number of school-age children by 1940 (23 percent of the city's population compared to 35 percent nationally). But those population characteristics were temporary, subject to watershed events such as the Second World War, a profoundly dramatic and transforming period in modern American history. The wars in Europe and Asia brought an abrupt end to years of unemployment and stagnation, and workers accustomed to long periods of unemployment suddenly found themselves sellers in a buyers market.

Although Charles McNary's key legislative achievements were well behind him by the early 1940s, his later life provides an interesting transition from the Great Depression to the Second World War. Despite his near election loss to radical Democrat Willis Mahoney in 1936, Oregon's senior senator remained at the center of national Republican politics through the remainder of the decade. Although he sought the Republican presidential nomination in 1940, he accepted the vice-presidential nomination on the Wendell Willkie ticket. McNary's reputation as an isolationist hurt his prospects in the face of the growing international crisis, and Franklin Roosevelt easily prevailed in his unprecedented third run for the presidency. In the ensuing months, McNary supported most of the administration's war preparation measures; and when President Roosevelt signed the declaration of war following the Japanese attack on Pearl Harbor, photos show the Senate minority leader standing directly behind the president. When Roosevelt offered McNary a Supreme Court seat early in the war, the Oregon senator turned it down. Although he worked with the administration to shape a strategy for the postwar era, McNary's work was cut short when he became ill from a brain tumor in the fall of 1943. After an operation and his release from the hospital, McNary left for Florida, where he lapsed into a coma and died in February 1944.

Historian James Patterson has called the Second World War the "central convulsion" of the 20th century. It was a time of beginnings and endings; it signaled the end to the Great Depression, and for thousands of people who moved from farm and ranch to urban settings, it brought to a close the steady pace of life and the intimate associations with the seasonal rhythms of summer and winter. For Oregonians, the war meant new beginnings in the sharp increase in demand for the state's natural resources, market conditions that continued to accelerate when peacetime returned. War-related industries

OHS neg., OrHi 96949. Ray Atkeson, photographer

Night shift workers at the Oregon Shipbuilding Corporation in about 1943

brought new ideas and new and more ethnically diverse people to Oregon and the Northwest, the seeds of a population influx that in time would change the region's demographic makeup.

The war had the same effect in Oregon as it did elsewhere in the United States. The years between 1941 and 1945 revolutionized the Oregon population, scrambling communities and reshaping virtually every corner of the state. The war uprooted people from home and sent them to distant defense industries or into the armed forces. As many personal stories attest, at the national level the most prominent movement of people was from east to west. "It was as if someone had tilted the country," writes historian Richard White, and "people, money, and soldiers all spilled west."

Wartime conditions severely disrupted rural communities, creating dire labor shortages in agricultural and natural resource industries such as logging and lumbering. Thousands of Oregonians left farms, ranches, and logging towns for military production centers such as Portland's Kaiser shipyards or defense plants in Seattle and San Francisco. What had been a glutted job market before the war suddenly became one of labor scarcity after 1941. Those new conditions were heady experiences for families who had suffered through more than a decade without steady work. Although many defense workers came from beyond the Northwest, residents within the region made up the largest percentage of the wartime labor force. The exodus of people from the countryside to urban centers contributed to a dramatic reshuffling of the region's population, with many of Oregon's rural counties, especially those east of the Cascade Range, losing people during the war.

The most visible signs of change in the Pacific Northwest involved two principal centers of war manufacturing, the Portland-Vancouver and Seattle-Tacoma areas. In Seattle, the Boeing Company employed 50,000 people during 1944, its peak production year. Equally renowned were the three big Kaiser shipyards in Portland and Vancouver: the Oregon Shipbuilding Corporation on the Willamette River near Portland's St. John's Bridge; another upriver at Swan Island; and a third shipyard in Vancouver near the Columbia River Bridge. The huge federally subsidized operations employed as many as 120,000 workers at peak production, with another 40,000 people employed in related jobs. The state and the region were literally on the move, with the daily train arrivals packed with immigrant workers and departing coaches filled with enlistees and draftees headed for the armed services.

To alleviate the housing crisis caused by the sudden influx of people, industrialist and ship-building magnate Henry J. Kaiser acquired federal loans to purchase 650 acres of floodplain land along the Oregon shore of the Columbia River north of Portland. Kaiser's company eventually constructed housing for 35,000 residents, making Vanport City Oregon's second largest "city." Supported on wooden blocks and with fiberboard walls, the instant residential community was the nation's largest wartime housing project. Because women as well as men worked in the shipyards, the community provided new social services, including year-round schools, nurseries, and day-care programs. Vanport also became an instant anomaly in Oregon, home to the first sizable immigrant non-white population in the state's history. Vanport's floodplain location, however, made the settlement vulnerable to nature's sometimes volatile and unpredictable forces.

Vanport's special mix of people, especially the sizable numbers of African Americans who made the move west to work in the shipyards, underscores another reality that linked race and class to place of residence. By war's end, African Americans made up 35 percent of Vanport's population, a much larger concentration than anywhere else in the state of Oregon. Moreover, real-estate covenants prohibiting

Blacks from living in certain sections of Portland would eventually place both African Americans (and their white working-class neighbors) in harm's way, subject to the Columbia River's fluctuating waters when the great flood of 1948 breached a railroad dike and pounded Vanport to kindling.

Long-time Portland residents greeted the new people who flocked to the wartime city with open skepticism. The 1940 census listed fewer than 2,000 African Americans out of a total population of 340,000 people in the Portland area. When the Kaiser shipyards and other local defense industries began to bring in significant numbers of Blacks in 1943, the new migrants encountered a wall of deeply ingrained suspicions—discrimination in housing, public transportation, union membership, access to recreational facilities, and openly offensive eating establishments such as the infamous Coon-Chicken Inn on Northeast Sandy Boulevard. Even before the large African American influx, a former Portland city commissioner urged local officials to discourage shipyards from recruiting minority workers, and Mayor Earl Riley worried that the incoming groups would threaten the city's "regular way of life," code words for segregated communities. Although only a few Blacks had arrived in Portland by September 1942, the *Oregonian* printed a front-page article under the bold headline: "New Negro Migrants Worry City." Historian Rudy Pearson accurately describes the relationship between the city and the new ethnic groups who arrived during the Second World War: "By any measure, Portland responded with prejudice and insensitivity to the wartime immigration of African Americans."

The earliest arrivals of the new African American families moved into cramped quarters in Portland's Guild's Lake district and after 1943 into the new wartime housing project at Vanport. Because of the extreme housing shortage, newly arriving Black workers found temporary shelter with members of the older African American community in north Portland, in local churches, the Black Elks Lodge, and in Black-owned businesses. The completed Vanport project in 1943 and the settlement of Blacks in inner northeast Portland's Albina district, an old immigrant neighborhood, eventually relieved the housing crunch for African Americans. It did nothing, however, to lessen the discriminatory practices of Portland Housing Authority officials or the racially restrictive real-estate covenants. Until it became apparent that realtors would neither sell nor rent property outside north Portland's Albina neighborhood, African Americans had few complaints about the development of Albina as a Black community. Of the more than 10,000 Blacks in the Portland metropolitan area at the end of the war, approximately 5,000 of them lived in Vanport, outside the city's limits. Pearson argues that Vanport's destruction in the 1948 flood marked a turning point in Portland's race relations. By the time homeless African Americans were searching for housing in the city proper, Portland's Black population had doubled. Moreover, the self-confident African American community, especially through local members of the National Association for the Advancement of Colored People and the Urban League, was also becoming more active in its fight for equal rights.

As many writers have indicated, the Second World War transformed the gender mix of the nation's workforce, with thousands of women taking wage-earning jobs for the first time. Nationwide, female wage-earners increased by 57 percent between 1941 and 1945. At the peak of Seattle-based Boeing's wartime production effort, 46 percent of its 50,000 employees were women. Comparable figures for Portland's big Kaiser shipyards in 1944 indicate that women made up 30 percent of the firm's 28,000 workers, with countless others scattered in smaller shipyards along the Columbia River. Women who lacked out-of-home work experience could earn $200 to $250 a month at Boeing or in the shipyards. To accommodate families with children, day-care centers became important features of urban life for the first time.

The Kaiser shipyards made an early commitment to hire women to fill a variety of construction positions at its Portland and Vancouver facilities. When the Oregon Shipbuilding Company hired two women welders in April 1942, the occasion marked the first time a U.S. Maritime Commission yard employed females to carry out production work. As news circulated about the shipyard's willingness to hire women, welding schools began training more women for the work; and by early 1943, all the major shipyards operated paid trainee-welding programs in an effort to meet the critical need for labor. Sociologist Karen Skold, who has studied the activities of women workers in the Portland shipyards, points out that the yards hired women earlier and in greater numbers than elsewhere in the nation. Reflecting the region's dire labor shortage, women shipyard employees earned good wages, gained equal pay with men for the same kind of work, and labored at jobs that had formerly been prohibited to them.

Kaiser shipyard and federal officials both recognized the importance of government-funded child-care accommodations for women
shipyard workers. Federal money eventually funded community-based
facilities in Portland, Vanport, and Vancouver. Two Kaiser child-care
centers, strategically located at shipyard entrances and operating for
all three work shifts, provided excellent care for working mothers.
Staffed by professionally trained child-development experts, the innovative centers provided nutritionally balanced diets and became
national showcases. At their peak, the two Portland yards—Oregon
Shipbuilding and Swan Island—employed 16,000 women and the two
child-care centers housed approximately 700 children. These figures
also suggest that thousands of women sought care for their children
from relatives, neighbors, and friends.

Employing women in the shipyards was an uneven process, with females over-represented as welders but making little headway in those
crafts where there was a sufficient supply of male workers. For unskilled "help" tasks, women dominated the labor force. The mere fact
that the shipyards hired women, however, challenged conventional
notions about appropriate work and ideals about feminine identity.
The employment of women in the Portland shipyards may have been
less revolutionary than the figures indicate. As the war was winding
down and orders for ships began to decline, female employees were
the first to be handed "quit-slips" at the end of the workday. "Women
were temporary substitutes for men in a labor shortage," Karen Skold
concludes. Although a few unskilled females held onto their jobs after the war, the Oregon Shipyard Corporation laid off its last three
women welders in October 1945. Real gains and full equality between
men and women in the workplace lay in the future.

Similar conditions prevailed at the Evans Products plant on Coos
Bay, where women made up 800 of the 1,200 employees and job turnover remained high. Because producing battery separators "wasn't
that glamorous," Dorotha Richardson recalled that women regularly
quit for higher paying jobs in Portland or San Francisco. She also remembered that the local union forced the company to pay the same
wages for people doing the same job, irrespective of gender. With the
Japanese surrender in August 1945, however, Evans Products laid off
much of its workforce, in part because plastic was replacing wood as
the principal material used in making battery separators. Although
Richardson's union negotiated token employment for women in
the plywood plant, there were only 20 women working in the Coos

Bay division when the company began to phase out its operations in 1959.

Oregon's labor shortage in natural resource industries accelerated the transition to mechanized processes, with gasoline-and-diesel-powered tractors replacing horses, mules, and oxen on farms and ranches. Even greater manpower deficiencies in woods operations speeded the mechanization of timber harvesting, as logging bosses began placing a premium on labor-saving devices such as the chain saw. Western Oregon loggers also began replacing steam-powered donkey engines with gasoline and diesel-powered machines to yard and load logs, a savings of several workers for every operation. By the end of the war, steam power was relegated to gyppo operations, small outfits that functioned with little capital and used outdated, surplus equipment.

Studs Terkel and others have described United States involvement in the European and Asian struggles as the "good war," with the nation's citizens united in a broad front to contend against the fascist threat to Western traditions and values. But even as the Allied forces engaged in the titanic struggle against evil, 40,000 men across the nation refused—for religious, philosophical, or political reasons—to commit violence against other humans. These conscientious objectors included men associated with traditional peace groups—Quakers, Mennonites, Church of the Brethren—and Catholics, Methodists, Muslims, Jehovah's Witnesses, and Jews. Because of their refusal to take part in combat, conscientious objectors either joined the military service as noncombatant medics or were placed in Civilian Public Service camps such as those located in Waldport and Cascade Locks. Private churches, under the supervision of the federal government, ran the individual camps, with the Church of the Brethren managing the Waldport and Cascade Locks operations. The camps served two purposes—to keep the conscientious objectors out of sight and to engage them in tasks "of national purpose." In actual practice, however, many of the men complained that they labored on make-work projects.

The Second World War also produced one of the most notable violations of civil rights in American history. As historian Roger Daniels points out, the removal of more than 100,000 Japanese Americans from the Pacific Coast and their resettlement in the interior West brought about "one of the grossest violations of the constitutional rights of American citizens in our history." The United States and the Canadian province of British Columbia evacuated all persons of Japanese descent from the Pacific Coast within three months after the bombing of Pearl Harbor. The relocation that followed remains to this day the central reference point for modern Japanese American history. Congressman Walter Pierce wholeheartedly supported relocation, and after his defeat for reelection in November 1942 declared that the war in the Pacific was an "attempt to beat back oncoming hordes and swarms of the yellow race." He also called for all Japanese Americans to be returned to their homeland at the end of the war.

While military security was the ostensible rationale for relocation, the documented record shows that the directive was political and that it came from the highest office in the land. When President Franklin Roosevelt signed Executive Order 9066 on February 19, 1942, he set in motion policies that forced the evacuation of Japanese-American citizens and resident aliens to inland internment camps. Gen. John L. De-Witt of the Wartime Civil Control Administration directed the relocation process beginning in early March, ordering Japanese along the Pacific Coast to report to temporary assembly points to await transfer to interior camps. It is important to recognize two significant issues about relocation: nearly two-thirds of the Japanese were American-born citizens, and several highly placed military figures (but not De-Witt) assured civilian authorities that Japanese Americans were loyal citizens and posed no threat to the nation's internal security.

Even before the federal government issued the relocation order, it had already restricted the movement of all people of Japanese descent. City of Portland officials prohibited Japanese from being outside their homes between 6 PM and 8 AM and from traveling more than a few miles from their residences. When authorities ordered Oregon's Japanese to assemble at Portland's Pacific International Livestock Exposition Center in March 1942, families had only a brief period of time to gather a few personal belongings and leave their homes. The Portland assembly center, now home to the Multnomah County Fair, sheltered approximately 4,500 Japanese during the spring and summer of 1942. Families were housed in whitewashed, 200-square-foot livestock stalls with straw mattresses, a single lightbulb, and uninsulated wooden walls and floors. Open cafeterias and communal showers compounded the lack of comfort and privacy. George Azumano, a Portland native, remembered that the stench of animal dung was heavy in the air.

The War Relocation Authority and its director Dillon S. Myer eventually operated ten relocation camps. Tule Lake and Pinedale in the California interior and Minidoka on the sweeping Snake River plain in Idaho housed most of the Japanese Americans from the Pacific

Japanese being escorted to the assembly center in Portland before being shipped to internment camps

Northwest. Although Japanese American internees could attend college or work as farm laborers in the interior West, most remained in the camps until the war in the Pacific began to wind down in late 1944. The relocation centers were, in effect, concentration camps, surrounded with barbed wire and guarded by army troops. As for the interned Japanese American-born citizens, three challenges to the evacuation order went to the U.S. Supreme Court, with the justices upholding the federal directive in each instance. Hood River's Minoru Yasui, an attorney and reserve army officer, was one of those who deliberately challenged Portland's curfew. Yasui lost in the federal district court, and his appeals eventually gave way to other cases, especially that of Gordon Hirabayashi who challenged the evacuation order's constitutionality.

When the war ended, about 8,000 Japanese Americans—known as "renunciants" because they reputedly had renounced their citizenship during their stay in the camps—were sent to Japan. In many instances, they were individuals under tremendous pressure in the relocation centers who were reduced to pleading for any favors; in exchange, some of them renounced their citizenship or signed away the citizenship rights of their children. From 1944 until 1959, the U.S. Department of State and the Department of Justice fought the renunciants' efforts to regain their citizenship rights.

When the federal government permitted the internees to leave for their homes in December 1944, most remained in the camps for another year because of the rampant anti-Japanese sentiment in their hometowns. A few regional political figures, including Washington's senator Warren Magnuson, called for tough restrictions against Japanese Americans when they began to return from the relocation centers. Former Congressman Walter Pierce continued his hate-mongering, urging rural audiences around Oregon to protest the return of Japanese to their properties in the Hood River Valley and in Malheur County. Addressing a large audience in Gresham in February 1945, Pierce told the Oregon Property Owners' Protective Association that the state legislature should act to remove illegal land titles held by the Oregon-born children of Japanese aliens. Pierce charged that those who tolerated the Japanese were "appeasers" and ill-informed church-going people.

Before the Oregon legislature concluded its 1945 session, it amended the 1923 Alien Land Law, declaring that it was a crime for Japanese aliens to hold land purchased in a relative's name. Although Governor Earl Snell signed the bill into law, the Oregon Supreme Court declared the measure unconstitutional, and legislators repealed the measure in 1949. Such hate legislation, however, encouraged others to action. In Hood River, where many shopkeepers displayed signs that read, "No Jap Trade Wanted," returning Japanese farmer Ray Yasui was forced to travel 25 miles to The Dalles to purchase supplies. Local newspapers published a "No Japs Wanted" petition signed by dozens of Hood River Valley residents. In the most egregious case of ethnic hatred, the Hood River American Legion removed the names of 16 Japanese American servicemen from the local honor role, a move that unleashed a critical reaction elsewhere in the United States. Still other Japanese Americans returned to hostile receptions and loss of property, with the latter especially conspicuous in the Portland metropolitan area.

In the years following the war, the Japanese-American Citizens League (JACL) made a major effort to seek justice for the internees. One of the JACL's most important achievements was congressional passage of the Japanese American Claims Act in 1948, a federal measure designed to help Japanese people recover lost property. In its statement supporting the bill, the JACL argued that "principles of justice and responsible government require that there should be compensation for such losses." As it worked its way through Congress, the bill enjoyed broad support and received high praise from Cabinet members and the former leadership of the War Relocation Authority. Although the JACL initiated 17 years of litigation, the legislation provided only limited redress for wartime losses. As Roger Daniels indicates, however, the 1948 law "was an important symbol of the improved image of the Japanese American people." It was not until 1990 that Congress provided across-the-board payments to the surviving internees, appropriating $17.2 million for Japanese American survivors and their dependents.

During the Second World War, Portland and its suburbs (including Vancouver, Washington) gained more than 250,000 residents and Oregon's growth rate for the 1940s was nearly 40 percent (432,000 people). At the peak of wartime production in early 1944, approximately 140,000 defense workers lived in the Portland metropolitan area. The state's population was becoming increasingly skewed toward urban settings, especially towns and cities in the Willamette Valley. Whereas every western Oregon county gained population during the 1940s, four eastern Oregon counties—Baker, Gilliam, Sherman, and Wallowa—experienced net losses. Nearly half the state's population lived in the greater Portland metropolitan area by 1950, a trend that would accelerate in the coming decades.

The Second World War had far-reaching effects on the region's forest products trade and its dependent communities. After years of seasonal and market-induced unemployment, Northwest timber districts—especially those with large stands of old-growth timber—entered a period of sustained expansion, full employment, and regular paydays. With self-sacrifice as their rallying cry, lumber trade officials told the U.S. Forest Service that trees were less important than human lives and that the United States should forego "future needs for immediate demands." Appeals to sustainable forestry practices and community stability, they argued, should be sacrificed for increased production. During the peak of wartime lumber manufacturing, the labor shortage was the only factor that limited the output of wood products. Forest Service chief Lyle Watts, who once headed Region Six (the Pacific Northwest), noted in his annual report for 1944 that national forests were now supplying 10 percent of the nation's timber harvests. If that trend continued in the heavily forested sections of Oregon and Washington, Watts feared that regional foresters would "exceed sustained-yield cutting budgets." He warned: "There must be no yielding to such pressures."

The changes that took place during the Second World War would have lasting effects on Northwest forests. The shortage of workers placed a premium on labor-saving equipment such as the chain saw and other devices to speed production. The increasing use of diesel-powered yarding machines placed a priority on clear-cutting practices, harvesting methods that became standard everywhere across the region's timber districts following the war. The new and more powerful technologies, including the dramatic expansion of logging roads into western Oregon forests, compounded erosion and landslide problems and accelerated the spread of a root fungi in southern Oregon's Port Orford (white) cedar district. And when domestic savings accumulated during the war precipitated two decades of booming construction activity, the new technological advances enabled the industry to meet the increased demand for structural materials. Few in that time and place questioned the essential rightness of the massive clear-cutting, road-building, and stream-channeling that helped sustain the boom.

CHAPTER SEVEN

The Postwar Boom

As the wars in Europe and Asia slogged toward their bloody ends, federal and state officials turned their attention toward the shape of the postwar economy. With the Depression crisis still foremost in everyone's thinking, "reconversion" became the popular buzzword for public officials, journalists, and especially development groups in the Pacific Northwest that stood to benefit from the shift to a peacetime economy. Oregon's Postwar Readjustment and Development Commission, first appointed in 1944, published monthly findings to suggest a blueprint for the state's future. Similar to advisory agencies in other western states, the commission focused much of its attention on federal water projects, especially the huge dams planned for the Columbia and Snake rivers and the lesser but still significant Willamette Valley Project. Although it praised the benefits of private enterprise, the Oregon commission also reflected some of the New Deal's passion for planning, applauding reclamation plans for the middle Deschutes, the Klamath Basin, and the Ontario and Umatilla districts of far eastern Oregon.

The most impressive development in the postwar era, however, was the booming home-construction industry, reflecting wartime savings and deferred home purchases. In the autumn of 1945, when returning veterans began placing greater strains on available living spaces, Oregon newspapers confirmed the critical housing shortage. In central Oregon, city officials in Bend held September hearings shortly af-

ter the Japanese surrender to discuss the local construction program
with special emphasis on the housing crisis. The community's immediate postwar problems were similar to those experienced by cities and towns elsewhere in the state. Medford, Salem, Coos Bay, and
Pendleton all reported housing shortages as their community's most
pressing problem.

Beyond those urban settings, the Oregon countryside was experiencing its own version of suburbia, a dramatic demographic and
technological transformation in the way people lived. The state's
farm population declined from 258,751 in 1940 to 221,399 in 1945, and
rural farm families were taking full advantage of modern technological devices. By war's end, more than 75 percent of Oregon farms had
electricity, 40 percent had telephone service, 90 percent owned at least
one motor vehicle, and 89 percent owned radios. As electrical power
was extended to rural areas, farmers and ranchers purchased electrical pumps, cream separators, and milk coolers, and they wired their
homes and barns with electrical lights. Both urban and farm dwellers
also were purchasing refrigerators, vacuum cleaners, toasters, wash-
ing machines, irons, radios, and other domestic electrical appliances.
The new gadgets coming on the market were popular in a region with
cheap power rates. Oregon's domestic and commercial energy consumption would soar in the next two decades, as the Bonneville Power
Administration and public and private utilities promoted the use of
electricity for virtually every purpose imaginable.

The most significant moment marking the onset of the modern
age occurred at 8:16 on the morning of August 6, 1945, the day an
American B-29, the Enola Gay, dropped the five-ton uranium bomb
known as "Little Boy" on the Japanese port city of Hiroshima. The
United States government released the news later in the day that an
American airplane had dropped an atomic bomb on Hiroshima with
the explosive power of more than 20,000 tons of TNT. The government's statement ended with a terse announcement: "It is a harnessing
of the basic powers of the universe." The Medford *Mail-Tribune* judged
that the day belonged to other watershed events in human history—"a
date for school boys to remember, as marking the end of one great
epoch and the start of another." The Hiroshima bomb and "Fat Boy,"
made with plutonium from the Hanford nuclear facility and dropped
on Nagasaki, Japan, three days later, brought the quick surrender of
the Japanese. When the news reached the American people, there was

riotous celebrating everywhere, including the small towns and cities in Oregon.

Because of its proximity to the Pacific theater of military operations, the surrender held special meaning for Oregonians who were celebrating an end to "their" war. On the day following the Japanese surrender, the Coos Bay *Times* reported that local communities were calm, "like a ship at sea after the storm." Farther north along the coast, the *Astorian Evening-Budget* reported that business and industry were at a standstill as people recovered from the previous day's revelry. In the far northeastern corner of the state, the Pendleton *East Oregonian* declared: "The war is over and a new era is at hand." A few days after the battleship U.S.S. *Missouri* sailed into Tokyo Bay to formalize the Japanese surrender, the Labor-Day issue of the *Mail-Tribune* praised the American free-enterprise system for its ability to produce "in conflict as well as tranquility" and for its contributions to winning "the greatest war in history."

While Hiroshima and the bomb suggested a path to doomsday, there was a widespread belief across the nation that the wondrous scientific advances made during the war would redound to human benefit. One of the most extensive of those developments, the Hanford nuclear complex on the Columbia River, seemed to promise a bright future for Oregon and the Northwest with inexpensive, clean electrical energy. Elsewhere, new wonder chemicals such as 2-4D and DDT, "the atomic bomb of insecticides," provided conclusive evidence that the future would also be free of destructive and annoying pests and weeds. Those postwar technical advances included the promise of a push-button paradise: LP records, Polaroid cameras, automatic transmissions, and—in a region with inexpensive hydropower—electric clothes dryers, refrigerators, garbage disposals, and vacuum cleaners. Writing for the *New York Times Magazine* in late 1945, Richard Neuberger, Oregon's popular and influential journalist, referred to the Northwest as "The Land of New Horizons," a place where people were "buoyant and cheerful." The future U.S. senator praised the region for its "treasure-trove of hydroelectricity," its expanding acres of irrigated land, and its scenic majesty. With good stewardship and care for its fields and forests, Neuberger believed, the Pacific Northwest promised a bright future.

For five years, the Oregon legislature's Postwar Readjustment and Development Commission issued regular monthly reports suggesting a variety of policy options for the state to pursue. From today's vantage, the bulletins read like a prescription for the massive reordering of the Oregon landscape: building dams on the Columbia, Snake, and Willamette rivers; developing the irrigation potential of the middle Deschutes, the Klamath Basin, and the Ontario and Umatilla districts in eastern Oregon; expanding the state's highways; "straightening" rivers; building jetties and deepening harbors; and funding agricultural and forestry research. The commission occasionally addressed potential problems, such as deforestation, declining salmon runs, and water pollution; and in a scathing report in early 1946, it referred to the Willamette River as "a State shame." Polluted waterways and the fishery question would loom larger in the coming decades.

The most ambitious postwar development plans for the Pacific Northwest centered on the region's waterways, especially the Columbia River and its major tributaries, the Snake and the Willamette. Chambers of commerce and development groups aggressively lobbied Oregon's congressional delegation to promote their pet projects on the Columbia and Willamette. It is mistaken, however, to assume that the river developers had no opposition, that dam-building proponents simply steamrolled those who wanted to proceed more cautiously. Indian tribes, sports and commercial fishers, conservation groups, and organizations interested in protecting scenic waterways fought tenaciously against specific dam proposals. At least through 1947, it was not apparent that the river developers would have their way. There were other options, other alternatives, and opponents raised stiff opposition to McNary, The Dalles, the lower Snake River dams, and some of the projects proposed for the multipurpose Willamette Valley Project.

Dam-building opponents forced a series of public hearings that placed the outcome of some of the Columbia River and Willamette projects in doubt. Columbia Basin development reached a critical juncture in the fall of 1946 when the U.S. Fish and Wildlife Service suggested a ten-year moratorium against building more dams on the Columbia and lower Snake rivers. At the most notable of the "fish versus dams" hearings in Walla Walla in June 1947, the Columbia Basin Interagency Committee (CBIAC) took two days of conflicting testimony. After sifting through thousands of pages of testimony, CBIAC advised against the moratorium and passed that recommendation to its parent committee in Washington, D.C. The Federal Interagency River Basins Committee then voted unanimously against the mora-

OHS neg., OrHi 105530

McNary Dam, built 1947 to 1956

torium. Following those regional and federal decisions, nature con-
spired to create conditions that placed powerful propaganda tools in
the hands of the river developers. The great Columbia River flood in
the spring of 1948 and the destruction of the wartime housing project at
Vanport marked the coup de grâce for river development proponents.
The destructive 1948 flood speeded financing for McNary (on the Columbia River) and Hungry Horse (on the Flathead River in Montana)
dams and persuaded Congress to authorize new dams. Between 1952
and 1958, one to three dams were completed every year.

In the years immediately following the war, the U.S. Army Corps of
Engineers designed and directed the construction of the Willamette
River's multipurpose dam system. Fishery interests who opposed the
Willamette Valley Project directed much of their criticism at high dams
that would block the upstream movement of migrating salmon. The
construction of Detroit and Lookout Point dams suggests that most
of those objections fell on deaf ears, but the Army Corps modified its
plans for a huge dam that would have flooded much of the McKenzie
River Valley and opted instead for dams on tributary streams (Blue
River and Cougar Creek). Opposition from fishery interests, espe-

cially those that cited the McKenzie River as a world-famous trout stream, played a significant part in persuading the agency to modify its original draft. Testimony at hearings in Portland revealed that famous writers, movie actors, and a former president of the United States, Herbert Hoover, regularly fished the McKenzie.

Oregon's politics from the Great Depression through the 1960s reflected the state's mix of conservative and progressive traditions. Nan Wood Honeyman—born in West Point, New York, and daughter of lawyer, artist, and nationally known writer Charles Erskine Scott Wood—was Oregon's first elected woman representative to Congress. Honeyman, who earned her political stripes as a Portland activist, served in Oregon's House of Representatives for one term from 1935 to 1937 before she was elected to represent Oregon's Third Congressional District for one term, from 1937 to 1939. With Walter Pierce, she was the only other Democrat in the state's congressional delegation during the Depression decade. A left-leaning progressive, Honeyman ran afoul of labor politics when she supported the newly reconstituted International Woodworkers of America when it broke with its American Federation of Labor (AFL) affiliate, the Lumber and Sawmill Worker's Union. Despite the support of the new Congress of Industrial Organizations (CIO) union and Harry Bridges's International Longshoremen and Warehousemen's Union (ILWU), Honeyman narrowly lost her reelection bid in 1939. Not until Edith Green polled a majority of votes in the 1954 election against Tom McCall would Oregon voters elect another woman to Congress.

Nan Honeyman's contemporary, Oregon governor and newspaper publisher Charles Sprague, led a courageous effort to protect the civil liberties of returning Japanese internees as American forces advanced toward Japan in the winter of 1944-1945. Biographer Floyd McKay argues that through Sprague's role as publisher of the *Oregon Statesman*, he became Oregon's leading champion of civil liberties once he left the governor's office in 1943. In an effort to atone for his early wartime support for Japanese relocation, the Presbyterian and ecumenical Sprague called former Governor Walter Pierce's racist comments about the Japanese "blind prejudice and unwarranted hatred." First-and-second-generation Japanese should be allowed to return peacefully to their homes, he declared, because they had committed no acts of sabotage or terrorism against the United States. When Governor Earl Snell signed a rabidly anti-Japanese legislative measure in the spring of 1945, Sprague called the bill malevolent and vicious and warned that it would fasten an "almost insensate prejudice within the white mind."

In addition to his bold efforts on behalf of Japanese Americans, Sprague opposed a Cold War-inspired loyalty oath for public school-teachers and generally stood with civil libertarians in their opposition to the anti-Communist witch hunts that emerged in the late 1940s. He regularly and persistently criticized Wisconsin's U.S. Senator Joseph McCarthy, fearing that the Republican Party would become captive to right-wing intolerance and malevolence. When the Multnomah Republican Club invited McCarthy to speak in August 1951, Sprague wrote in the pages of the *Statesman* that the Wisconsin senator was mendacious and should not be identified with the Republican Party. The former governor was far less assertive, however, when it came to standing up to the House Committee on UnAmerican Activities. When the witch-hunting committee went after Reed College and forced the firing of philosophy professor Stanley Moore, Sprague and other newspaper editors remained mute. Sprague closed out his notable public career with a brief stint as an alternate delegate to the United Nations, where he worked with American ambassador Eleanor Roosevelt.

Oregon's most dazzling political figure of the immediate postwar years was brilliant, controversial, and outspoken Wayne Morse, dean of the University of Oregon Law School from 1931 to 1944. A Wisconsin native, the progressive-minded Morse was elected to the U.S. Senate under the Republican banner in 1944, his first try for elective office. Reelected in 1950, the fiery and impetuous Morse split with President Dwight D. Eisenhower's administration over domestic and foreign-policy issues, became an independent, and then migrated across the Senate aisle to the Democratic Party for two successful election campaigns in 1956 and 1962. Morse first gained statewide notice during the Depression, when he led the successful opposition to the Oregon legislature's effort to merge the University of Oregon and Oregon State College, referring to the scheme as a "Rotten Plot." While dean of the law school, the ambitious Morse gained a national reputation as a fair and impartial labor arbitrator, especially for his handling of volatile longshoremen's strikes beginning in 1934. Because organized labor gave Morse its wholehearted support during his run for the Senate in 1944, conservative Republicans referred to him as a "New Dealer masquerading as a Republican." Rank-and-file ILWU members, however, continued to trust Morse and supported him in each of his Senate campaigns.

When he took his U.S. Senate seat in 1945, Morse proved to be independently minded from the outset, often arguing against Republican policy proposals and voting with his party only 30 percent of the time. A renowned orator, the Oregon senator willingly engaged in lengthy filibusters on the Senate floor on issues that he strongly opposed. When the controversial Taft-Hartley bill was making its way through Congress in 1947, Morse spoke unsuccessfully—but without interruption—for nine and a half hours against the union-busting measure. A staunch advocate of public power, Morse also worked diligently to gain congressional appropriations for Pacific Northwest water projects. But Morse is best remembered for his long opposition to the Vietnam War, especially his lonely stand with Alaska's Senator Ernest Gruening opposing the Gulf of Tonkin Resolution in August 1964. Morse responded with characteristic bluntness to a constituent's criticism:

> It is one thing for politicians . . . safe in the security of their political offices to vote to send young American draftees to die in an unconscionable war in Vietnam, but it is another thing to be one of those boys. I do not intend to put their blood on my hands.

Another product of the University of Oregon, Richard Neuberger—an undergraduate at the university during Morse's tenure—was one of "the master reporters of the 20th century," according to his biographer, Steve Neal. Supreme Court Justice William O. Douglas praised Neuberger for doing more than anyone else to place the Pacific Northwest at the forefront of national attention; and *Oregonian* reporter Tom McCall predicted that Neuberger's writings about the Northwest would prove to be his most enduring legacy. Neuberger first gained national attention in October 1933, at the age of 20, when he published an article in *The Nation* condemning Adolf Hitler's Nazi Germany for its brutal police-state tactics and its persecution of Jews. Neuberger continued in the same vein for more than 25 years, publishing articles in *Collier's*, *The Nation*, *Harper's*, *The Progressive*, and the *New York Times Magazine*. "With the zest of a crusader," Neal writes, "Neuberger fought the good fight," exposing Francis E. Townsend's Depression-era pension plan as the work of a con man, for example, and attacking Senator Joseph McCarthy in 1950 for his assaults on civil liberties.

For a time, Richard and Maurine Neuberger were at the center of Oregon's liberal politics. Elected to the Oregon legislature in 1940,

OHS neg., OrHi 5727

Maurine and Richard Neuberger at the capitol in Salem

Richard Neuberger served in only one session before enlisting in the army as a second lieutenant in the late spring of 1942. After mustering out of the army in 1945, he made an abortive run for the Oregon senate in 1946 before his successful election in 1948. Two years later, Maurine Neuberger was elected as the only woman in the Oregon House, distinguishing the Neubergers as the nation's first married couple to occupy legislative offices. Richard Neuberger's celebrity status as a journalist and his influential contacts with powerful Democratic leaders nationwide vaulted him to the U.S. Senate when he narrowly defeated incumbent Guy Cordon in 1954. When Neuberger was sworn into office the following January, he became the first Oregon Democrat to serve in the U.S. Senate in 40 years, placing the national party back in control of the Senate and reversing the fortunes of the state's Democratic Party. Neuberger exercised considerable influence during his single term in the Senate, opposing the Eisenhower administration's natural-resource policies, especially those associated with public-power development. Oregon's junior senator was an outspoken proponent of civil rights for minorities and encouraged the Eisenhower administration to move more aggressively against racial discrimination.

When Richard Neuberger died in March 1960 of a cerebral hemor-
rhage after a bout with cancer, the Democratic Party chose Maurine
Neuberger to run for the Senate in the fall election. After Republican
Governor Mark Hatfield refused to offer her an interim appointment
to fill her husband's seat, she easily defeated former Republican governor Elmo Smith in the general election, with more than 54 percent
of the vote. Tall, highly intelligent, and with a keen sense of humor,
Maurine Brown Neuberger was only the third woman to serve in the
U.S. Senate (and the first from Oregon). Unlike her husband, who was
interested in natural-resource and public-power questions, Maurine
Neuberger focused on consumer issues, denouncing the meat-pack-
ing industry for watering hams, criticizing bedding manufacturers
for selling flammable material, censuring cosmetic firms for deceptive
packaging practices, and calling for restrictions on automobile emis-
sions. Neuberger questioned the efficacy of industrial self-regulation
and sought greater federal oversight to protect the interests of consum-
ers. Troubled by the need to fund an expensive reelection campaign
and the likelihood that Republican Governor Mark Hatfield would
run for her Senate seat, Neuberger decided against a second run for
office in 1966. Hatfield defeated Congressman Robert Duncan in the
November election, adding a second strident Oregon voice to the Senate in opposition to the Vietnam War.

Until the development and expansion of the high-tech industry
in the 1980s, Oregon's economy remained heavily dependent on
exporting forest products and agricultural goods. Despite occasional
downturns in the lumber market, the state's timber-dependent communities prospered for more than two decades following the Second
World War. Towns such as Bend, Coos Bay, Roseburg, and Grants Pass
experienced mini-housing booms, merchants carried on a lively retail
trade, and newspapers across the state praised Oregon for being the
nation's top lumber producer. With a heavy demand for lumber, especially in California, and an incredibly productive technology, timber
harvests increased dramatically through the 1950s and 1960s. Oregon
increased its cut from 5.2 billion board feet in 1940 to a postwar high of
9.1 billion board feet in 1955. Local newspapers heralded the production
figures and made frequent references to the industry's permanence.
    In keeping with the technological optimism of the postwar period,
the lumber industry boasted that it was practicing scientific forestry
and treating timber as a crop. Trade association officials touted their

Lumber Production, 1940-1979 (in million board feet)								
	1940	*1945*	*1950*	*1955*	*1960*	*1965*	*1970*	*1975*	*1979*
Oregon	5,202	5,003	5,239	9,181	7,401	8,206	6,680	6,342	7,312
Washington	4,541	3,257	3,606	3,118	3,377	3,958	3,189	3,104	3,841
Idaho	773	780	1,126	1,413	1,654	1,750	1,631	1,635	1,893
California	1,054	2,260	4,262	5,319	5,160	5,032	4,979	4,153	4,639

intensive forest-management practices, the new buzzwords of the day. If there was an ideological center to postwar forestry practices, it was vested in sustained-yield management, a fuzzy concept subject to endless interpretation. Several pieces of federal legislation referred to the term, Oregon newspapers frequently published articles praising the benefits of sustained-yield management, and the Bureau of Land Management administered the re-vested Oregon and California railroad grant (O&C lands) under the Oregon and California Sustained-Yield Management Act (1937). The O&C legislation, according to its supporters, would protect local communities from timber exhaustion and provide for a stable and settled economy. In the heart of the timber-rich Umpqua district, interspersed with numerous sections of O&C timber, the city of Roseburg stood at the threshold of a production boom in the postwar era. "On a sustained yield basis," the *News-Review*'s Charles Stanton enthused, "Douglas County had a most outstanding advantage."

Although the heaviest timber harvesting took place in the Douglas-fir region west of the Cascade Range, there were sizable pine-milling centers in central and eastern Oregon, especially in the great ponderosa district extending from Bend to Klamath Falls. With the Brooks-Scanlon and Shevlin-Hixon mills operating two shifts a day at the end of the war, timber harvesting boomed in the greater Bend area. Brooks-Scanlon extended its logging railroad past the town of Sisters to Black Butte to speed the movement of logs to Bend. To upgrade the efficiency of its operation, the company resettled its large mobile logging camp in the same vicinity. Shevlin-Hixon also moved its huge portable logging camp of some 350 people to a new location in the huge timber stands about ten miles southeast of Chemult in Klamath County. Pine production neared record levels, and central Oregon's economy prospered as discharged servicemen and women flocked to the area. As the 1940s came to a close, however, rumors began to circulate that the Shevlin-Hixon mill would close because of dwindling log supplies. The *Bend Bulletin* confirmed those suspicions with bold headlines on November 21, 1950: "Shevlin-Hixon Sells to Brooks-Scanlon." The sale included the firm's timber, its production facilities, and its logging equipment.

There were immediate social costs and hardships associated with the Shevlin-Hixon sale, as 850 people lost their jobs (225 in northern Klamath County and 625 in the Bend vicinity). The huge ponderosa harvests had come to an end. Ferdinand Silcox, the chief of the U.S. Forest Service, had warned as early as 1934 that the two Bend mills were cutting their timberland far beyond a sustainable capacity. Shevlin-Hixon's closing, however, did little to slow harvests of the remaining stands of old-growth pine. With a hot market for pine lumber, production at the sprawling Brooks-Scanlon complex along the Deschutes River continued at record levels despite the diminishing volume of private timber. Beginning in the 1950s, company loggers began cutting commercially less valuable lodgepole pine to extend its log supplies. At the same time, the firm reported increased operating expenses because of the costs of hauling timber over such long distances. It was obvious to many observers that the heavy cutting of company timber had a limited future.

The Bend story is especially interesting, because it provides a striking example of a community's transition from an extractive and processing economy to a new world of outdoor recreation—selling central Oregon's natural beauty to visitors, second-home buyers, and retirees. A small but thriving town in 1960 with a population of about 12,000, Bend and its one remaining mill continued to churn out a large volume of pine lumber for more than two decades. In parallel developments, however, winter sports venues and destination resorts were rapidly becoming the centerpiece to a new central Oregon economy.

Not all former lumber towns have made successful transitions to new forms of economic endeavor, with the Coos Bay area on Oregon's southern coast perhaps the most striking example. For more than 30 years following the end of the Second World War, the booming California lumber market brought prosperity to southwestern Oregon as new mills opened, small operations multiplied, and people looking for work flocked to the Coos district. Two years after the Japanese surrender in 1945, the *Oregonian* proclaimed Coos Bay the "Lumber Capital of the World." Locals referred to those years as "the great boom," a period filled with heady optimism and abundant jobs. Even during the winter season, when companies cut back their crews, workers expected the slackening spring rains to bring a return to good-paying jobs. In the midst of the record-setting production, however, there were warning signs as forest-products employment began to decline after 1960. Improvements in mechanization, corporate mergers, and an increase in capital investment explain the declining number of loggers and millworkers in the Pacific Northwest. Although economic conditions remained relatively stable on the south coast through the 1960s and early 1970s, there were worries about depleted timber inventories, especially on private holdings, with loggers spending up to four hours a day traveling to and from work.

People who lived through those years remember that jobs were becoming harder to get by the mid-1970s. And then came the whirlwind, a rash of layoffs and mill closures in 1979 led by the Georgia-Pacific Corporation's plywood operation, one of the largest employers on Coos Bay. What followed in the next few years was a hemorrhaging of well-paid industrial jobs and a downward spiraling economy as one mill closure followed another. Coos Bay gained a new reputation as the state's most depressed area. In truth, the bay communities were pacesetters for mill closures everywhere across the Northwest during the 1980s; and even when a few mills reopened, they did so with new automated equipment and sharply reduced workforces. A stagnant forest-products market, mechanization, and sharply diminished timber stands continued to erode Coos Bay's industrial base.

Economists and state bureaucrats coined a new expression, "economic restructuring," to describe the malaise that settled over the Northwest's timber-dependent communities. The phrase was little more than a bloodless term that cloaked the suffering and hardships that people were experiencing in the region's smaller communities. Mill closures—many of them permanent—struck places as far removed from each other as Willamina, Burns, and the tiny community of Kinzua in Wheeler County. In the face of shuttered mills and a glutted forest-products market, Oregon's unemployment rate rose above 8 percent in 1981. Newly minted high-school graduates and a good number of working people from lumber towns left for college or went where job prospects were more promising. The region's heavy timber harvests since the Second World War and an expanding forest products industry in the southeast part of the United States pointed to continuing hardships for Oregon's timber-dependent communities.

Like other western states, Oregon has a sizable public-land base, with approximately 53 percent of its 61 million acres in federal lands, most of it managed by the Bureau of Land Management (BLM) and the U.S. Forest Service. Other important federal holdings include Crater Lake National Park, national monuments, and the recently created Steens Mountain Cooperative Management area. State and local governments control another 3 percent of the land base. President Theodore Roosevelt created one of the nation's crown jewels, Crater Lake National Park in 1902—the sixth park established following Yellowstone in 1872 and the first of the 20th century. One of Oregon's major tourist attractions, the park has different meanings for Native people than it does for outdoor enthusiasts, photographers, and visitors. For millennia, the Klamaths, Modocs, Cow Creeks, and other Indian peoples traveled to the Crater Lake area to visit sacred sites and as part of their seasonal rounds of food gathering. For non-Indians, the park represents something much different. As National Park Service historian David Louter puts it, Crater Lake is a reservoir "of what we value in nature and ourselves."

Crater Lake, Oregon's only national park, represents the successful efforts of William Gladstone Steel and the Portland-based climbing group, the Oregon Alpine Club (subsequently renamed the Mazamas). Steel, who first visited Crater Lake in 1885, worked tirelessly for 17 years to gain protected status for the spectacular caldera and the nearly 2,000-foot-deep lake. His promotional genius was to link the preservation of spectacular scenic places such as Crater Lake with public access. Although his advocacy for the park was sprinkled with notions of science and nationalism, Steel insisted that such areas should remain in public ownership with limited commercial development. The Portland activist also promoted interest in Oregon's Cascade Range and its scenic splendors, such as Mount Hood and Three Sisters.

In addition to Crater Lake, Oregon's other federal lands have been a significant force in shaping the state's history, especially in the 20th century. Oregon ranks fifth behind Alaska, Nevada, Utah, and Idaho in its percentage of federally owned land. An Oregon legislative committee reported in 1966 that more than 34 million acres, or 55.8 percent of state land, is tax exempt because of federal, state, or Indian ownership. These extensive public lands have been important to the Pacific Northwest economy because of their forested wealth and the forage they provide for livestock. Federally owned lands have played a significant role in sustaining the state's preeminent lumber industry and

Oregon's beef production. Income from these activities have provided state and local governments with payments in lieu of taxes.

The Forest Service manages 15.6 million and the BLM 15.7 million acres of Oregon's federal lands. Although the state's most productive, low-elevation forest lands are in private ownership, national forest timber harvests have been important to many local economies. In addition to its vast rangelands in southeastern Oregon, the BLM also manages 2.2 million acres of productive timberland in western Oregon. Those acres are remnants of the 19th-century Oregon and California Railroad lands that reverted to the federal government when a successor company—the Southern Pacific—violated the terms of the original grant. Because of Oregon's sizable federal lands and their importance to local economies, management decisions have always been politically volatile. Before the onset of the environmental age in the 1970s, most controversies over the national forests involved access to remote areas, roadbuilding, fire prevention, and, by the early 1960s, wilderness set-asides.

With the emergence of the environmental movement, however, growing public criticism emerged over clear-cutting, an industrial forestry harvest practice that was especially popular in the Douglas-fir districts. Environmental groups, congressional committees, and a few foresters began to question the ecological soundness of the practice. Forest industry groups responded aggressively in defense of clear-cutting, urging the public to "think of the forest as a crop" that should be managed for maximum productivity. Jerry Franklin, a young scientist who would become well-known for his progressive understanding of forest ecology, made the first in a series of scientific challenges to clear-cutting, suggesting that the biological requirements for good forestry required a variety of harvesting practices. But Oregon governors Tom McCall (1967-1975) and Robert Straub (1975-1979), both praised for their environmental activism, never openly criticized clear-cut harvesting. McCall's biographer, Brent Walth, contends that the governor's environmentalism had limits, especially when it might run counter to the state's economic health. Although Straub agreed that clear-cuts should be limited in size to reduce their visual impact, he firmly supported the practice.

For the first time since logging and lumbering emerged as a powerful component of Oregon's economy, the industry's forestry practices were being criticized from seemingly every direction. Before court orders invoking the Endangered Species Act—known as the spotted owl decrees—began to curtail national forest harvests in the late 1980s, public debate focused on the size of proposed wilderness areas and the use of chemical herbicides and insecticides on public and private forestlands. Although the application of DDT had come under increasing criticism after the publication of Rachel Carson's *Silent Spring* in 1962, the chemical remained the spray of choice for most foresters until the federal government banned its use in 1972. But the debates involving DDT were only the opening volleys in the fight over the use of chemicals in forest environments. The most significant controversy during the 1970s centered on the application of the herbicide 2,4,5-T, a component of Agent Orange that produces highly toxic trace elements of dioxin (TCDD). The Forest Service continued to spray with 2,4,5-T in western Oregon to control brush until the federal government removed it from the list of authorized herbicides in 1979. The environmental struggles over the management of the national forests, however, would continue into the 21st century.

Oregon's Indian tribes were also involved in federal decisions relating to jurisdiction over tribal reservation lands. In a sharp reversal of policies established under Indian commissioner John Collier during the 1930s, postwar administrators initiated aggressive efforts to "get out of the Indian business," that is, to terminate the special relationships between tribes and the federal government. The idea of termination gathered momentum in the years after 1945 and became formal policy with the passage of House Concurrent Resolution 108 in 1953, a measure announcing that the federal government should terminate its special trusteeship responsibility for Indians "at the earliest possible time." The resolution further directed the "Secretary of the Interior to submit legislation putting into effect a policy of termination for certain named tribes." The language of the termination proposals referred to "liberating the Indian," "turning the Indian loose," "emancipating the Indian," and "terminating the trusteeship restrictions"—pleasant sounding words suggesting that Indian reservations were segregated and unacceptable ghettos.

Termination legislation was designed to remove federal supervision over reservation lands. While the Collier administration attempted to strengthen tribes as social and legal entities, the Eisenhower administration's new policies were intended to end the Indians' status as wards of the government. Eisenhower's interior secretary was a former Oregon governor, Republican Douglas McKay, who spoke for powerful timber and water-resource developers in the West. There is evidence to suggest that McKay wanted his home state to serve as a showcase for the new direction in Indian policy. For their part, private interests were greatly interested in gaining access to valuable timber and grazing lands on reservations. Historian Stephen Dow Beckham writes that when the interior secretary began the push to terminate the Klamath and other Oregon tribes, none of them had achieved "a measure of readiness for immediate termination of federal services." In the Klamath situation, the attractions of the reservation's extensive ponderosa pine stands were the objective.

Congress passed the Klamath termination act in 1954, authorizing the sale of reservation lands and establishing procedures for terminating all federal relationships with the Klamath Tribe. Enrolled tribal members then voted on whether to receive cash payments or to retain shares in the former reservation and participate in a federal management plan. Approximately 22 percent of enrolled members chose to have their shares managed by the U.S. National Bank of Oregon, an institution that would act as trustee for the remaining tribal members. The other 78 percent of members received lump-sum cash payments of $43,000 in 1961. When the U.S. National Bank wanted out of its trust relationship in 1973, the remaining land was sold and the shareholders received lump-sum payments. After lengthy testimony, Congress passed a bill turning the vast 700,000-acre Klamath timberlands into the Winema National Forest. In addition to the Klamath, termination legislation was directed at several smaller Oregon tribes west of the Cascade Mountains (the Siletz, Grand Ronde, Cow Creek, Coos, Lower Umpqua, Siuslaw, and Coquille).

The federal government's grand experiment with termination proved to be an abysmal failure everywhere. Many Klamath people were ill prepared to manage the windfall payments, and Klamath County subsequently developed some of the highest unemployment rates in the state. Alcoholism increased, welfare rolls expanded, health conditions spiraled downward, people died at a younger age than before, and few Klamaths had access to educational opportunities. In its report on terminated tribes to the American Indian Policy Review Commission in 1976, a Klamath tribal survey reported that few people owned land or were otherwise economically independent: "In general the Klamaths lost their land and have nothing to show for that loss."

By the time of Jimmy Carter's presidency (1977-1981), Oregon's congressional delegation was well aware that termination was a bankrupt

Automobiles dumped along the Willamette River west of Salem in the hopes of
slowing bank erosion, 1939

policy. Congress began to reverse termination when it passed legislation granting Wisconsin's Menominee Tribe federal recognition in
1973. In the following years, lawmakers granted federal status to Oregon's terminated tribes, including the Klamath, Siletz, Grand Ronde,
Cow Creek, Coos, Lower Umpqua, Siuslaw, and the Coquille tribes.
Of those groups, only the Siletz has a sizable land base.

Although Oregon gained national attention as a progressive environmental pacesetter during the early 1970s, the state has a long
history of using its waterways as municipal and industrial dumping
grounds. The postwar condition of its major stream, the Willamette
River, belies Oregon's late 20th-century reputation for clean water. As
early as 1907, the newly created Oregon Board of Health referred to the
Willamette River as "an open sewer," a characterization that would fit
the waterway for the several decades. A Portland City Club study in
1927 called the river "filthy and ugly," a widely popularized reference
that eventually led to an initiative measure in 1938 that established the
Oregon Sanitary Authority. Despite the new enforcement agency, state
legislators dragged their feet, municipal governments put off installing primary sewage treatment facilities, and industries continued in-
discriminately to dump toxic wastes into the river. While all bets were

off during the Second World War, a major flood in 1948 spurred the construction of several multipurpose dams under the auspices of the Willamette Valley Project. It was not until 1950, however, that the Oregon Sanitary Authority set its first deadline requiring pulp mills to cease dumping waste liquors into the river.

The Willamette River had become the center of increasingly intense politicking by the 1960s, especially with the emergence of two progressive political figures, Democrat Robert Straub, the state treasurer, and Republican Tom McCall, a journalist with KGW-TV who was elected Oregon's secretary of state in 1964. During his years as a television reporter and evening television commentator, McCall began giving greater attention to pollution issues, especially those affecting the Willamette River. After nearly a year in preparation, KGW aired McCall's famous documentary, *Pollution in Paradise*, on November 12, 1962, which sharply criticized the condition of Oregon's principal waterway. In making the documentary, McCall firmly staked out a moral position in the pollution debate that pushed questions of livability to the forefront of public attention. *Pollution in Paradise* was a *tour de force*, pressing home the powerful idea that there was no contradiction between jobs and Oregon's quality of living.

More than any elected official in Oregon since the Second World War, the charismatic and flamboyant Tom McCall helped forge a unique and modern identity for the state. Those who influenced him as a young man included an older generation that was already shaping Oregon's political identity. As a student at the University of Oregon during the Depression, McCall became acquainted with Richard Neuberger, who would become one of the region's most prominent journalists. The dean of the university's law school was Wayne Morse, soon to make his mark in national politics. As McCall worked his way into Republican Party politics, he served a stint as executive secretary to Governor Douglas McKay in the late 1940s and made a failed attempt in 1954 to win the third congressional district seat. Democrat Edith Green defeated McCall by a narrow margin in that election and went on to serve ten terms in the House of Representatives. McCall's popularity as a statewide television commentator, however, helped elevate him to the secretary of state's office in 1964 and then to the pinnacle of Oregon politics when he was elected governor in 1966 in a campaign against Bob Straub, his political friend.

Time has not diminished the significance of Tom McCall's election to Oregon's highest office. It would be an understatement to say that he brought a different style, a flair for imaginative expression to the governorship. While he shares credit with other policymakers for several wide-ranging environmental achievements in the late 1960s and early 1970s, it was the Willamette River that brought the governor to national attention. In truth, McCall's two terms in the governor's office were fortuitous, paralleling significant improvements in the water quality of the Willamette River and the completion of the last Willamette Valley Project dams. But McCall also acted forcefully on several fronts, appointing himself interim chair of the State Sanitary Authority, threatening to shut down pulp and paper mills unless they cleaned up their operations, and creating the Oregon Department of Environmental Quality (DEQ) with expanded statutory responsibilities. Even with the vantage of hindsight, events seemed to move at a dizzying pace during those years.

If "livability" has descriptive meaning to modern Oregon, it is linked closely to the reforms of the McCall administration. The Bottle Bill, passed by the state legislature in 1971 and requiring minimum deposits on glass and aluminum beer and soft-drink containers, brought national recognition to the state. During McCall's governorship—and with the full support of Secretary of State Robert Straub—the legislature also enacted the Beach Bill, a measure that reasserted public ownership of Oregon's coastal beaches. One point to be made about Oregon's environmental reputation during the McCall years is that he was no Lone Ranger acting without significant political support. Mark Hatfield, who was elected to the U.S. Senate in 1966 after two terms as governor, initiated what became a statewide dialogue about livability when he began to speak against thoughtless speculators who were befouling Oregon's landscape with uncontrolled development projects. When the Lincoln County Chamber of Commerce began touting its ticky-tacky stretch of U.S. Highway 101 as the "Twenty Miracle Miles," Hatfield remarked that "Twenty Miserable Miles" would be a more fitting description.

The capstone to Oregon's environmental reform agenda during the McCall years was Senate Bill 100, the nation's most progressive land-use legislation, signed into law in 1973. Two state senators, liberal Democrat Ted Hallock from Portland and Republican dairy farmer Hector Macpherson from rural Linn County, joined Tom McCall in the legislative battle to pass Oregon's pioneering land-use law. An educated and articulate agrarian, Macpherson earned a reputation during the 1960s as a proponent of stiffer land-use regulations to protect farm and forest lands. "Visualize the alternative," he warned in 1967, "a valley where neighbor encroaches upon neighbor, a land unproductive agriculturally where hunger and want must surely follow, a land defiled and unsightly, a monument to man's greed and shortsightedness." Elected to the Oregon senate in 1970, Macpherson was a lone voice in the legislature until he found kindred spirits in the governor's office and in the person of Ted Hallock. With McCall skillfully working the Oregon public and Macpherson and Hallock cultivating legislative support, the senate passed the bill by a vote of 18 to 10 and the house approved the measure without amendment.

Late 20th-century historians agree that Senate Bill 100, which established the Department of Land Conservation and Development (DLCD), is Tom McCall's most lasting legacy. Fly the length of the Willamette Valley, across the rich irrigated lands in central and eastern Oregon, or the great reclamation district in the Klamath Basin and you will see contiguous agricultural lands and an absence of urban sprawl. Although there have been problems implementing statewide land-use goals and there has been some attrition, the LCDC has mandated urban-growth boundaries, protected farm and forest land, and preserved recreational and natural areas. The effects of Senate Bill 100 are visually scripted across Oregon's landscape. The measure survived three initiative challenges—in 1976, 1978, and 1982—and a more recent measure in 2000 that would have required state and local jurisdictions to compensate owners for land-use policies restricting property use. The Oregon Supreme Court declared the latter initiative unconstitutional on technical grounds. But with McCall's passing from the scene on January 13, 1983, defenders of land-use planning lost a powerful and influential voice. By the early 21st century, opponents to land-use planning were becoming more successful at the ballot box.

For more than three decades following the Second World War, Oregon's economy was heavily dependent on agriculture and forest products. California's burgeoning population and booming home and industrial construction provided a lively market for Oregon's logging and saw-milling producers. But the lifeblood to Oregon's postwar prosperity suffered a severe setback when increases in mechanization, corporate mergers, depleted timber inventories, and high interest rates plunged the woods-products industry into recession in the early

1980s. For the next decade the Northwest's timber-dependent communities experienced painful adjustments, with some towns successfully diversifying with new enterprises and others languishing with high unemployment rates and persisting social problems. The emergence of a vibrant environmental movement in the 1970s increased tensions between resource-dependent rural communities and Oregon's urban centers, adding an increasingly bitter and partisan tone to Oregon politics.

The postwar years also witnessed the reemergence of progressive political traditions in the state. Voters elected to national office Wayne Morse and Mark Hatfield, senators who gained national reputations as critics of American foreign policy, especially for their opposition to the Vietnam War. Richard Neuberger, already a renowned national journalist, was elected to the Senate in 1954, where he established legitimate credentials as a conservationist. Hatfield, who served two terms as governor beginning in 1958, marked a progressive turn in those elected to the state's top office. Tom McCall and Robert Straub, who followed Hatfield, accelerated Oregon's reputation as an environmental innovator, overseeing a remarkably activist period in state government that embraced issues of livability—clean rivers, publicly owned beaches, the Bottle Bill, and the state's pioneering land-use legislation. Oregon's politicians did not act alone in establishing the state's environmental distinctiveness. Federal initiatives such as clear air and water legislation, the Endangered Species and Environmental Protection acts, and wild-and-scenic river initiatives gave regulators additional enforcement mechanisms to work with. Those issues, however, also added to the contentious mix of Oregon politics, providing fuel for developers and others who viewed environmental protection as a threat to the state's livelihood.

CHAPTER EIGHT

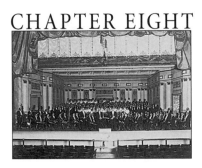

Education, the Arts, and Letters

Over generations of time, Oregon boosters have pointed with pride to the state's educational and cultural institutions as symbols of progress and forward thinking, evidence that citizens attended to educational matters as well as to economic development. A humorous and apocryphal story—passed down from the first generation of white immigrants to the Oregon country—tells of wagon trains passing west from Fort Hall on the Oregon Trail only to come to a fork in the road. A glittering pile of quartz veered toward the left, pointing in a southwesterly direction toward California and its goldfields. An old, weathered sign with the word *Oregon* etched into the wood marked the other trail, trending toward the west and northwest. Those who could read took the right-hand fork. While a heavy sprinkling of Oregon chauvinism infuses the story, it also underscores the boosters' pride in the state's literacy and its educational and cultural accomplishments. A closer inquiry into such boasting, however, suggests that those early achievements in culture and education often fell far short of the mark.

In reality, educational and cultural opportunity in Oregon has paralleled similar developments in other western states. Through the 19th and well into the 20th century, the educational infrastructures in many northeastern and midwestern states provided far greater opportunity and surpassed the accomplishments of their western counterparts. Schools in the West may have been sources of community pride, but too often marginally qualified people taught students for limited periods between fall harvest and spring planting. Oregon's experience suggests that educational institutions were underfunded and understaffed, that they struggled with vast distances and difficult terrain, and that they often operated beyond the bounds of professional certification standards. With growing maturity, however, western states slowly achieved educational parity with the East. In an effort to achieve scholastic excellence, Oregon's forward-thinking educators struggled mightily to establish viable publicly supported elementary and high schools, an effort that continues into the 21st century.

The genesis of educational systems in the Pacific Northwest begins with the Hudson's Bay Company, when New Englander John Ball taught the mixed-blood children of fur traders who frequented Fort Vancouver in the mid-1830s. The initial American effort began with the establishment of the first missionary schools during the 1830s. These proselytizing enterprises included the Methodists' Willamette Mission, the ecumenical American Board of Commissioners for Foreign Missions' enterprises in the interior, and more than two dozen Roman Catholic ventures (Franciscans and Jesuits). Collectively, those groups extended educational activity and religious outreach throughout the region. Those early denominational influences also shaped Oregon's educational system, with nearly 30 parochial schools operating across the state by the early 1880s. In addition, many of the region's colleges and universities were rooted in various Christian denominations, with the Oregon Institute, the forerunner to Willamette University, tracing its beginnings to 1842 and the Methodist Mission. Pacific University in Forest Grove dates its founding to 1849 and New England Congregational influences.

Public school systems also owe their inception to missionary influences, especially in the person of Rev. George Atkinson who wrote Oregon Territory's first body of school law in 1849. Reflecting New England educational systems, the territory's organic school legislation included these principles: (1) education should be free; (2) control should be decentralized and local; (3) a permanent school fund should be established; (3) professional standards should be adopted to provide for the certification of teachers; (4) schools should be tax supported; and (5) all educational institutions should practice religious freedom. Except for its inspirational objectives, the legislation had little effect because Oregon's publicly supported educational systems continued to struggle for several decades.

Article VIII of the Oregon Constitution, approved by Congress in the statehood act of 1859, chartered the fundamental body of school law that has guided public education in the state to the present day. Embodying the principle of free public schools, the article declared that the governor should serve as superintendent of public instruction for the first five years the constitution was in effect. After that, the legislature was free to create a position for an elected superintendent with specified powers and responsibilities. The constitutional provisions also required that "the Legislative Assembly shall provide by law for the establishment of a uniform and general system of Common schools." Another provision mandated that all proceeds from the Oregon's school lands—provided by the federal government in the statehood act—be used for educational purposes. The constitution directed that a State Land Board (governor, secretary of state, and state treasurer) "shall manage lands under its jurisdiction with the object of obtaining the greatest benefit for the people of this state." The Board of Commissioners charged with the sale of school lands and the management of the Common School Fund issued an optimistic report in 1868: "If the state school lands are all sold, and the funds carefully managed, in a few years it [the school fund] will fully support a free public school system." That great hope was rent asunder during the land-fraud scam of the 1890s and early 1900s, when the state squandered away its school-grant lands. Thereafter, the school fund was able to provide only minimum support for public education, and local districts had to rely on property taxes to support their schools.

From the very beginning, powerful and influential people acted to obstruct the constitutional provisions that called for free public education for all school-age children. *Oregon Statesman*'s editor Asahel Bush argued that common schools could not be justified, because the state was too sparsely populated. Harvey W. Scott, the influential editor of the *Oregonian* from 1865 until his death in 1910, opposed free public-school textbooks and tax-supported high schools. In editorials, he regularly harangued against the evils of using tax money to fund high schools. In lieu of financing such a "cumbrous and expensive system," he wrote, parents who wanted to educate their children "beyond the common branches of the old fashioned common school should pay for it." Other leading figures also spoke out on educational policy: Governor W.W. Thayer (1878-1882) believed that education beyond elementary school should focus on teaching trades; prominent businessman William S. Ladd argued that public money should

OHS neg., OrHi 94279

Third-grade class at Blachly School in western Lane County, 1952

be used to teach academic subjects; Populist governor Sylvester Pennoyer insisted that public taxes should be used only to teach the three R's; and Simeon Reed, the chief benefactor of Reed College, thought children should be taught "useful industry" and kept in school for fewer hours.

In the face of such political detractors, effective and comprehensive public-school education in Oregon was not achieved until the early 20th century. Establishing high schools was fought out on a district-by-district basis from 1880 until 1901, when the state legislature mandated that all districts provide high-school education. But Oregon was little different from other states with similar geographic and demographic profiles—suffering from vast distances between towns, lack of transportation, insufficient funding, rundown school buildings, abbreviated school terms, and inadequate and shoddy equipment. There were questions about low salaries; the absence of uniform curricular, instructional, and textbook selections; and common standards for teacher certification. There were also matters of equity, providing children in all districts with the same quality of education; and there were no standards for employment, with district superintendents responsible for most of the hiring.

Teachers' organizations and educational institutes in the late 19th century led the move to establish professional certification standards, higher salaries, better textbooks, and improved teaching methods. Although the state legislature established the office of state superintendent of public instruction and a state board of education in 1872, local school districts had done little to improve the livelihoods of lowly paid teachers. On one occasion, the *Oregon Teachers' Monthly* urged its membership to organize unions to push for improved salaries. Teachers' groups also took the initiative to shift high-school curricula from an emphasis on the classics and factual information to more nuanced courses in history, trigonometry, physics, and the practical sciences.

Even with the growth and expansion of publicly supported high schools in the late 19th century, Oregon's private academies and parochial schools continued to flourish. Portland residents supported Roman Catholic, Protestant, Hebrew, and German schools to provide religious or language instruction. The Portland Academy and Female Seminary, originally established in 1854 as a Methodist institution, was a striking success when it reopened in 1889 as the Portland Academy. The school provided an advanced curriculum for the children of Portland's elite, eventually offering courses equivalent to the first two years of college instruction. Portland historian E. Kimbark MacColl lists the academy as one of the limited number of social and cultural opportunities in the community's early life. Patterned after private schools in the East, the Academy boasted that wealth and status were the pathway to success. The school continued to flourish until improvements in Portland's public high schools began to siphon students away during the First World War.

Support for public education in Oregon continued to flounder well into the 20th century. Voters approved a two-mill state property tax (two-tenths of a cent) to support and maintain elementary education in 1920. Thereafter, property taxes provided most of the support for schools until the late 20th century, when property-tax limitation initiatives shifted funding to the state level. After Oregon adopted an income tax in 1929, the state no longer relied on property taxes to support state programs, but exploding population growth during the Second World War placed further strains on the ability of local districts to support schools. A consortium of educators and supporters successfully placed an initiative measure on the November 1946 ballot to establish a program for state school support. Approved by the voters, the Basic School Support Fund was intended to provide stable funding, additional state support, and equalization for all districts. Although the fund was supposed to provide 50 percent state support for public schools, lawmakers never delivered, placing additional burdens on local property taxes.

Governor Tom McCall put a plan before the voters in 1973 to increase state school funding (via a 30 percent increase in the income tax to 90 percent) and to permanently reduce property taxes. The "McCall Plan's" narrow defeat in the November election meant that districts would continue to rely on local property taxes to sustain their schools—and face angry voters when financial exigencies dictated the need for additional revenue. During the 1980s, tax limitation initiatives began appearing on general election ballots and several school districts closed for limited periods when irate voters refused to support local budgets. Although voters approved a "safety net" constitutional amendment in 1987, allowing districts to continue operating with funding levels based on the previous year's rate, the school-funding crisis persisted. Finally, successful property-tax limitation measures in 1990 and 1996 shifted school-funding responsibility to the state—and a continuation of the same problems.

With the Oregon economy and state revenue in free-fall beginning in 2001, the school-funding crisis became acute. With the precipitous drop in corporate and personal income taxes and the state claiming the nation's highest unemployment rate, the governor's office and the legislature went into crisis mode. Schools eliminated curricular and sports programs, laid off teachers, and increased class sizes. Then, in the spring of 2003, the fiscal crisis forced many districts to shorten the school year to balance their budgets. Oregon's school-funding crisis made national news when the popular comic strip *Doonesbury* made antic fun of Portland's school problems. When the city of Hillsboro lopped 17 days from its school year, *New York Times* columnist Bob Herbert reported that Oregon's once proud school system was being dismantled, victim to a bad economy and "the radical anti-tax fever that has gripped so many Americans." Herbert quoted a Hillsboro teacher who pointed out that no schools were closed during the Great Depression or the Second World War. "Are we," the teacher asked, "the most civically irresponsible generation in Oregon in 100 years?" The persistence of the state's revenue problems and popular anti-tax activism continued to bedevil state lawmakers in the 2005 legislative session.

During the last half of the 19th century, Oregon's denominational academies and colleges were obstacles to the establishment of tax-supported institutions of higher learning. Even the distinguished Judge Matthew P. Deady initially opposed publicly supported colleges because of competition from private schools. It was not until the 1870s that the legislature appropriated funds to establish a state university in Eugene. With contributions from local benefactors, the city raised money to begin construction of the University of Oregon's first building, ironically named Deady Hall after the judge who had once opposed public schools and who served as chairman of the university's board of regents. With a limited enrollment, the University of Oregon opened for business in the fall of 1876.

Oregon State University's institutional lineage can be traced to privately funded Corvallis College in 1858. Although the fledgling school was sold to the Methodist-Episcopal Church in 1860, the institution did not enroll its first collegiate-level class until 1867. The following year, the Corvallis school became the Agricultural College of the State of Oregon, the state's officially sanctioned land-grant institution. When the church relinquished control in 1885, the school became Oregon Agricultural College. Western Oregon University had a similar evolution, beginning in 1855 as Bethel Institute operated by the Disciples of Christ north of Rickreall. The institution merged with Christian College in 1864 to become Monmouth University and then a publicly supported teacher-training academy, Oregon State Normal School, in 1883.

Among Oregon's independent colleges and universities, Methodist-sponsored Willamette University is the oldest. One of the earliest coeducational institutions in the United States, Willamette's once extensive landholdings included most of present-day downtown Salem. Beginning in the 1920s, the university's trustees embarked on a major "forward movement" to build the institution's endowment, raise funds for several new buildings, and increase faculty salaries. Lewis and Clark College traces its roots to 1867 and the Presbyterian-sponsored "collegiate institute," which became Albany College in 1892. The college relocated to temporary quarters in Portland in 1938 and moved to its present location when trustees purchased the beautiful 63-acre M. Lloyd Frank estate on Palatine Hill. Nonsectarian Reed College owes its origins to Simeon G. Reed's widow, Amanda Wood Reed, who established a $1.5 million endowment at the urging of her pastor, Unitarian Thomas Lamb Eliot. Originally called Reed Institute, the college opened in temporary quarters in 1911 and moved the following year into two newly constructed Elizabethan Tudor-style halls.

Beyond the state's struggling educational institutions, 19th-century Oregonians had access to a wealth of newspapers and journals. Although many of the newspapers were short-lived enterprises, they served as regional forums for political invective and special causes. Beginning its brief tenure as a biweekly in 1846, the *Oregon Spectator* led the parade as the region's first newspaper. The state's two most venerable publications, the Portland *Oregonian* and the Salem *Statesman Journal*, both appeared in 1850. Except for news articles lifted from the eastern press, local news was unapologetic and presented in dull and uninteresting prose. With the growing professionalism of journalism in the late 19th century, however, the *Oregonian* and *Statesman Journal* developed into first-rate regional newspapers, establishing a conservative ethos that reflected the state's most powerful vested interests.

There were still other monthly and periodical forums for disseminating information, with Abigail Scott Duniway's *New Northwest* among the best-known weekly newspapers. After the *New Northwest* ceased publication, Duniway assumed editorship of its successor, *The Pacific Empire*, an effort that subsequently morphed into the more literary *Pacific Monthly* in 1898. For several decades *Pacific Monthly* was the Northwest's most prominent literary magazine. The Portland-based monthly *West Shore*, published from 1875 to 1891, was the most assertive and widely circulated booster journal in the region, focusing most of its attention on commercial and industrial development, especially building railroads into the interior of the Columbia Basin. Within three years of its publication, *West Shore* was being distributed in 32 states and in England.

In the decades before electronic communication, many citizens mixed social and educational activities with physical labor. Oregonians attended lyceums, debating societies, literary clubs, and discussion groups that served adults' interests. Among the more popular public gatherings were those featuring "extemporaneous discussion," with topics ranging from American foreign policy to temperance. There were history clubs, French and German clubs, and literary organizations—all of them holding regular, well-attended meetings. Portland's leading citizens organized the venerable (and still functioning) Oregon Academy of Sciences to study and discuss the latest scientific developments. The most memorable of all educational enterprises were the Chautauquas, organized gatherings held throughout the state during the 1890s and featuring such well-known national figures as William Jennings Bryan. Beginning in the early 1980s, the Oregon Council for the Humanities renewed the venerable tradition and now sponsors speakers who address a wide variety of topics in large and small communities around the state.

From the beginning of significant white settlement in the Northwest, hotels and social clubs sponsored reading rooms where magazines and newspapers were made available. The Oregon Territorial Act of 1848 included a provision for a territorial library with an appropriation to purchase books and legislative documents from the eastern United States. The Portland Public Library traces its origins to the private and exclusive Portland Library Association in 1863, an organization that became free and open to the public early in the 20th century. Beyond Portland, however, the scattering of people across the state impeded library development until 1901, when the Oregon legislature passed a measure to coordinate school and district libraries. Four years later, lawmakers established the State Library Commission to facilitate the creation of new libraries and to set up traveling book collections. Within a brief period of time, the commission reported the opening of several small libraries around the state.

In addition to its rich educational heritage, Oregon has a long history of flourishing cultural institutions, many of them dating to the 19th century. German, Scandinavian, and numerous other ethnic organizations proliferated in the late 1800s as immigrant groups flocked to communities such as Astoria. As their numbers grew, they formed social and ethnic clubs to provide meeting places for Old World celebrations, dancing, and other social activities. Some of those cultural festivals have changed through time to become some of the state's more popular community celebrations. Junction City's annual four-day Scandinavian Festival is one such event, with each day devoted to celebrating the food ways, fashions, folk music, and dancing of Norway, Finland, Sweden, Denmark, and Iceland. Since its inaugural festival in 1961, Junction City's downtown has been transformed every August with booths, entertainment, glass-blowing demonstrations, and other cultural activities.

In similar fashion, the small town of Mt. Angel has celebrated an annual harvest festival since 1966. With German sausage, Old World music, craft booths, and dancing in a huge biergarten, the Oktoberfest draws more than 300,000 people to the mid-September event, billed by its sponsors as the region's best-attended folk celebration. Other ethnic events include Astoria's annual Finnish gala, Portland's Nordic festival, Mexican fiestas, and Greek and Asian celebrations. Beginning in 1941 and resuming again in 1946, the annual Albany World Championship Timber Carnival attracted competitors from all over the world to participate in logging skills contests. For four days over the Fourth of July weekend, men and women engaged in competitions ranging from climbing and chopping to bucking and burling. Reflecting smaller crowds and the state's declining timber economy, the city of Albany discontinued the carnival in 2002.

Oregon's cultural establishments include long-standing institutions such as the venerable Portland Art Museum and the Oregon Historical Society in Portland, the more recent High Desert Museum in Bend, and two new tribal cultural museums. Collectively, these museums offer multifaceted efforts to publicly document and portray the state's history, to present new topics and interpretations, to house traveling artistic works and exhibits, and, in the case of tribal museums, to offer different voices and perspectives on the state's history. The cultural representations evident in the state's public and private museums contribute to the development and redefinition of Oregon's identity.

Opened to the public in 1993, the Museum at Warm Springs chronicles the Tribes' history and serves as a living tribute to the people of the Confederated Tribes of the Warm Springs Reservation. The museum houses a permanent collection of historic photos, rare and valuable documents, and an impressive collection of Native material culture. The changing gallery exhibits present a variety of explorations into the Native American experience, and the surrounding grounds include an outdoor amphitheater where tribal members put on performances and demonstrations.

Equally striking is the Tamástslikt Cultural Institute of the Confederated Tribes of the Umatilla, which opened in 1998. Located five miles east of Pendleton, the Institute's purpose is to document and protect the culture and history of the Cayuse, Umatilla, and Walla Walla peoples and to present the Tribes' story to the public. The building's 45,000 square feet house valuable archival materials, a research library, and a growing collection of historical photographs. Museum exhibits portray seasonal rounds; hunting, gathering, processing, and manufacturing practices; the extensive trading networks that existed before white contact; and the importance of horses, which were acquired in the 18th century. The permanent exhibit has a tule-reed lodge, the traditional shelter for most Plateau people. Exhibits also tell the story of the coming of non-Indians to the interior Northwest—fur traders, missionaries, and settlers—and the Tribes' subsequent encounters with disease, warfare, forced treaties, boarding schools, and the federal government's erosion of the tribal land base.

The private, nonprofit High Desert Museum, south of Bend, houses significant exhibitions on Indian culture as well as other exhibits that focus on the natural and cultural heritage of the arid high desert. The museum's main building houses 53,000 square feet of historical, cultural, and artistic exhibits, including accurate portrayals of Indian material culture in the pre-contact and post-contact periods. The museum also sponsors writers, artists, and other professionals with expertise on the high desert region. Beyond the building, paved walkways guide visitors through outdoor exhibits and animal habitats. Museum staff also regularly present living-history demonstrations.

Oregon's foremost private cultural institution, and the oldest of its kind in the Pacific Northwest, is the Portland Art Museum. The organization originated in 1888 as the Portland Art Association through efforts of such elite figures as Henry Corbett, Henry Failing, William Ladd, and C.E.S. Wood. The museum became part of the association's mission when members signed incorporation documents in 1892 and opened a modest gallery in 1895. Through the museum's early years, Portland's leading families loaned collections for most of the exhibitions. The association hired Anna Belle Crocker, in 1909, who served as museum curator until her retirement in 1936.

The Portland Art Museum moved to its present location at Southwest Park and Jefferson streets in November 1932, where it opened its new building to the public in the midst of the Great Depression. Designed by young Pietro Belluschi, the new structure was praised for its "simplicity and convenience" and its excellent lighting. The museum opened with an exhibit of 750 Japanese prints, the gift of patron Mary Andrews Ladd. During the Second World War, museum officials operated on a restricted schedule and sent its most valuable art pieces to the interior of the country for safekeeping. Since the war, the museum has moved into the era of big, traveling exhibitions including paintings from the Walter Chrysler collection, a Vincent Van Gogh exhibit, and single-person shows for regional artists. The museum's

board initiated its first capital campaign in 1967 to expand its facilities to include a new wing, classroom and studio space, and a sizable
auditorium. The museum opened the new wing, another Pietro Belluschi creation, and the other amenities in 1970. A few years later the
museum began its long association with Vivian and Gordon Gilkey
and their outstanding collection of print works. The Portland Art
Museum closed out the 20th century with its purchase of the Masonic
Temple, a building that now serves as another wing for the museum's
expanding exhibits.

Music festivals have become a part of Oregon's performance scene
in the 20th century, with Jacksonville's Britt Festivals the longest running of them. The Jacksonville festival had its beginnings in the early
1960s when Portland conductor John Trudeau and his friend Sam
McKinney visited the hillside estate once owned by southern Oregon's
renowned photographer Peter Britt. Attracted by the great acoustics
and ambiance of the setting, Trudeau and a small chamber orchestra
put on a public performance from a makeshift stage in the summer of
1963. The event was off and running. Although the Britt Festivals performed only classical music during its first years, it has since broadened its venue to offer jazz, rock, and country music. The Festivals
completed its first pavilion in 1978 and added bench seats in 1987 to
accommodate crowds of more than 2,200 people. Currently operated
by Jackson County, Britt Park attracts world-class performers.

Several other summer music festivals have surfaced in the last few
decades. One of the more popular has been the Mt. Hood Jazz Festival,
an annual August event held in the city of Gresham. Since its beginnings in 1982, its posters have become collectors' items and the event itself is the largest celebration of jazz music in the state. A classical music
venue, the Oregon Bach Festival originated in a fortuitous partnership
between German organist and conductor Helmuth Rilling and Royce
Saltzman of Eugene. The two men collaborated to put on four concerts
in Eugene in the summer of 1971 under the rubric "Summer Festival of
Music." Late in the 1970s, the annual performances, which originated
in the University of Oregon's School of Music, were renamed the Oregon Bach Festival. Today, the event attracts internationally renowned
artists and annual audiences of more than 30,000 people, all of whom
come to honor a 300-year tradition of Bach's music.

The most distinguished of all of the state's musical institutions—and
the one with the highest artistic standards—is the Oregon Symphony
Orchestra, long associated with the city of Portland. The symphony's

lineage can be traced to the founding of the Portland Symphony Society in 1896, the first of its kind in the American West. Between 1911 and 1918 the symphony made the transition to a modern professional organization and signaled its emergence as Portland's premiere musical organization when it performed its first concert in the new Civic Auditorium in 1918. The Portland Symphony ranked as one of the nation's largest orchestras at the onset of the Great Depression, but the economic collapse of the 1930s forced the suspension of its concerts in 1938 and the city was without an orchestra until 1947, when the Portland Symphony Society was reorganized. Because of its growing commitment to serve communities beyond Portland, the Society changed its name to the Oregon Symphony in 1967, a move that was popular among music lovers beyond the state's largest city.

The appointment in 1980 of James DePriest as music director and conductor, a man widely recognized in the United States and Europe for his symphonic repertoire, elevated the symphony to still higher professional standards. Shortly after he assumed his position, the symphony moved from Portland's Civic Auditorium to the Arlene Schnitzer Concert Hall, where the orchestra could rehearse and perform on the same stage. Under DePriest's leadership, the Symphony achieved advanced levels of performance, stepped up its educational and community programs, and in 1987 began releasing recordings. When DePriest announced that he would not renew his contract as music director when it expired in 2005, the Symphony's board of directors appointed Carlos Kalmar to succeed him.

The city of Ashland is renowned for being home to the highly acclaimed Oregon Shakespeare Festival and its repertory theater company. The festival has its roots in the 1890s, when Ashland opened its first beehive-shaped Chautauqua dome. City entrepreneurs constructed successive domes in 1905 and 1917 and its first outdoor Elizabethan stage in 1935. In that same year, Angus Bowmer produced the first Shakespeare play in a setting that would gain Ashland, Bowmer, and the Oregon Shakespeare Festival a national and international reputation. The outdoor theater, remodeled and expanded several times, seats 1,200 people. The festival directors added the 500-seat Bowmer Theater in 1970 and the smaller, 150-seat Black Swan theater in 1977. Remnant materials from the old Chautauqua beehive now provide the perimeter walls for the festival's outdoor theater. The Oregon Shakespeare Festival has been an enormous success, attracting more than 340,000 visitors a year to its 11 productions performed on three stages.

The festival and Southern Oregon University provide much of the Ashland area's economic base.

While Native American peoples possessed no traditions of written communication, they created elaborate drawings and symbols, with many of them indicating attachment to particular places to illustrate special meaning through depicting animals, humans, and spirit-like beings. Some of the oldest of these visual artifacts are in the form of pictographs (painted images) and petroglyphs (etchings or scratched designs) in Oregon's high-desert rock formations, stone facings in the Cascade Mountains, and basalt rocks along the Columbia River. Referred to as "rock art," the pictographs and petroglyphs have meanings for Native peoples that embody many elements of the past, suggesting such traditions as spiritual reckonings through hunting images, special prayers, obligations, and acknowledgments associated with a successful hunt. Historian William Layman, who has studied Indian drawings and etchings on the mid-Columbia, calls the work "primary to the story of the Columbia River" and "present-day connections [for Native people] to these special riverplaces." For the Great River and beyond, these ancient endeavors provide a memory bridge to cultural meaning that transcends the millennia of time.

The English and French speakers who came to the Pacific Northwest in the early 19th century brought with them experiences with several millennia of written language. The narratives they carried with them also had the capacity to define one people in proximity to others and to vest landscapes with new meanings and purpose. The earliest writing in the Pacific Northwest involved descriptive journal literature, the works of the fur men and explorers who attached new value and importance to fur-bearing animals. The many journal-travel accounts that have been published include the writings of Alexander Ross, Ross Cox, Peter Skene Ogden, Osborn Russell, David Thompson, David Douglas, and, of course, Lewis and Clark. Theirs was a literature that placed in the written record information about climate, topography, vegetative patterns, and river systems. In brief, journal writers established the facts of place in the region. The journals, travel accounts, reconnaissance reports, and the later federal surveys gave the region and the state of Oregon a physical identity. Most of the literary efforts that followed—prose, poetry, memoir, fiction, and history—reflected varied efforts to understand the raw details of those earlier descriptive narratives. At this second level, literary effort moved toward larger interpretive themes that linked events and circumstances over time. When regional literature comes of age, literary historian Harold Simonson contends, "both artist and the region come alive through the transforming power of imagination and spirit. Person and place are wedded to each other." A highly selective survey of a few Oregon writers suggests the degree to which they have crafted a unique regional literature.

William Lysander Adams, a schoolteacher from Ohio with an eccentric, sarcastic wit and a sharp pen, wrote Oregon's first literary piece, *A Melodrame Entitled "Treason, Stratagems, and Spoils" in Five Acts*, under the pen name, Breakspear. First published in five parts in the *Oregonian* in 1852, the play ruthlessly skewered Oregon's Democratic Party, especially its public voice, the *Oregon Statesman* and its editor Asahel Bush. Historian Edwin Bingham has called Adams' play "local literature with a vengeance." As literary art, the play was imitative, but it was also an expression of original and unrestrained political satire. Equally centered in Oregon's newly developing immigrant society is Margaret Jewett Bailey's *The Grains, or Passages in the Life of Ruth Rover* (1854), the region's first novel and the first woman writer to appear in print. A thinly disguised book with autobiographical undertones, *Grains* tells the story of the author's real-life marriage to a drunken missionary, William Bailey. The Oregon press shredded the novel, with most of the venom directed at the author because she was a woman and a divorcee. While the book is not literary art, *Grains* entertained and titillated readers, with some critics suggesting that the novel was equal to contemporary works published in the eastern United States.

The first Oregon writer to emerge as a significant regional and national figure was Joaquin Miller (1837-1913), a colorful person who moved about Oregon through a series of interesting careers—schoolteacher, judge, and defender of the South during the Civil War. Miller eventually moved to Portland and then to California, where he made his reputation as the "Poet of the Sierras." The flamboyant Miller never achieved the acclaim at home that he received in European salons where he dressed in buckskin and portrayed himself as the "Byron of the Rockies." He wrote two interesting histories, *Unwritten History: Life Among the Modocs* (1874) and *An Illustrated History of the State of Montana* (1894), and published an acclaimed book of poetry, *Songs of the Sierras* (1871). Many critics have claimed that Miller's estranged wife, Minnie Myrtle, was a much better poet. An energetic woman with a flair for life, she published a contemptuous "defense" of her wanderlust former husband in the *Oregonian* (reprinted in the *New Northwest*) and assured readers that by virtue of her request for a divorce, Joaquin Miller would "no longer be chained to the annoying cares of a family" and would be free to "give his whole attention to his poems."

More significant was Abigail Scott Duniway, the author of an early novel, *Captain Gray's Company; Or, Crossing the Plains and Living in Oregon* (1859). In addition to editing and publishing the *New Northwest*, Duniway also wrote a best-selling autobiography, *Path-Breaking: An Autobiographical History of the Equal Suffrage Movement in Pacific Coast States* (1914). The *Oregonian*'s Harvey Scott seldom agreed with his sister, who was the leading suffragist and women's rights advocate in the American West. Another Oregon woman, Frances Fuller Victor (1826-1902), a remarkably gifted writer and the author of several of the Hubert Howe Bancroft's histories of the American West, emerged as the region's first significant historian and an important national literary figure. Victor wrote *The River of the West* (1870), a biography of fur-trapper Joe Meek based on interviews with the aging mountain man, and the two-volume *History of Oregon* for Bancroft's multi-volume *History of the Pacific States*. She also wrote for newspapers and published books promoting the development of the Northwest.

Among all of Oregon's literary figures, the long career of Charles Erskine Scott Wood (1852-1944) may be the most fascinating. Wood's active life spanned several decades over two centuries and embraced an eclectic field of human endeavor—the military, the law, writing, painting, and humanitarian work. Wood's conservative background included graduation from the U.S. Military Academy at West Point, service as a young lieutenant in military campaigns against northwestern Indian tribes, and a Columbia University law degree. He accompanied Gen. Oliver O. Howard and the U.S. Army in its running battles with the Nez Perce in 1877 and recorded (and "doctored") Chief Joseph's famous surrender speech. During his military assignment in the Northwest, Wood was detailed to Camp Harney, where he fell in love with the Oregon desert. Before leaving the army, he served a short stint as adjutant in charge of the West Point military academy and then was off to Portland, where he developed a highly successful law practice, representing railroad corporations and some of the community's wealthiest citizens. In his time away from the courtroom, he gained fame for writing radical literature.

C.E.S. Wood's life was a paradox. He defended railroad monopolies by day and wrote radical essays and poetry for publications such as *The Masses* in the evening. The *Oregonian* once called him hypocritical for quietly accepting the largesse of the railroads while publicly espousing anarchist views. A man of immense personal charm and a gifted public speaker, he was a prolific writer, contributing a column for *Pacific Monthly* and writing short stories (under a pseudonym) for several magazines. Wood was also a talented painter, exhibiting his work at the Portland Art Museum and other regional venues. *Poet in the Desert* (1915), published when he was 63 years old, was influenced by his deep affection for eastern Oregon and is his best book of poetry. His most brilliant radical essays, collected in *Heavenly Discourse* (1927), depict a series of dialogues between St. Peter and the Devil. Published when Wood was 75, the book brought him national and international acclaim.

Appealing to nostalgia and romancing the region's heritage, authors of historical fiction have always enjoyed sizable audiences in the Pacific Northwest. The first Oregon writer of this genre to gain a popular readership was Eva Emery Dye (1855-1947), who was enamored with the "pioneer epoch" and who claimed that her work was based on thorough and meticulous research in historical archives. In a series of fictional novels, *McLoughlin and Old Oregon* (1900), *The Conquest* (1902), and *McDonald of Oregon* (1906), Dye wrote highly romanticized tales of Homeric figures struggling to create a civilization in the Northwest wilderness. Although the *Oregonian* and the *Oregon Historical Quarterly* praised Dye's contributions at the time, Frances Fuller Victor panned her work in the pages of the *American Historical Review*, criticizing the McLoughlin book for its literary weaknesses and for "the mingling of fiction with historical truth."

If Eva Emery Dye wrote romantic and frivolous historical novels, her contemporary, John Reed, was quite the opposite. Born to a wealthy Portland family, he became a radical journalist and, like C.E.S. Wood, published in *The Masses*. Reed, who was in Russia and witnessed the outbreak of the Bolshevik Revolution in the fall of 1917, subsequently wrote the classic English-language account of the revolution, *Ten Days that Shook the World* (1919). When Attorney General A. Mitchell Palmer indicted Reed under the Espionage Act later that year, Reed left for Russia, where he died of typhus in the midst of the revolutionary turmoil. Reed remains to this day the only American buried at the Kremlin Wall Necropolis in Moscow's Red Square. He went without honor in the place of his birth until 2001, when the Oregon Cultural

Heritage Commission dedicated a bench to this home-grown radical in Portland's Washington Park.

Two young Oregon writers, Harold Lenore Davis and James Stevens, mark the transition to greater realism in Northwest fiction writing in the early 20th century. In an angry, privately published tract in 1927, Davis and Stevens accused regional writers of provincialism, of avoiding social realism, of writing nothing more than rubbish and "tripe." Under the Latinate title, *Status Rerum*, the authors used wit and sarcasm to ridicule the region's literary figures and to take swipes at the poetry-and-fiction-writing classes offered at the University of Washington and University of Oregon. They assailed a Salem literary monthly for "metrical ineptitude" and for representing the "perverted taste" of an editor who published "the most colossal imbecility." The authors of *Status Rerum* went on to write regional literary gems of their own, with Davis publishing *Honey in the Horn* in 1935 and Stevens publishing *Big Jim Turner* in 1948.

H.L. Davis, a Portland resident, was the first major Northwest novelist to have credentials to literary excellence. Adopting the initials "H.L." after his mentor, H.L. Mencken, the most powerful literary influence in the United States, Davis began publishing short stories in Mencken's *American Mercury* in the late 1920s. There was nothing romantic and syrupy about his first novel, *Honey in the Horn*, which won the Pulitzer Prize for fiction and provided a sharp contrast with the sentimental, melodramatic, and parochial characters that traipsed through earlier novels. *Honey in the Horn* offered stark realism, with its chief protagonists—Clay and Luce—burping, picking their noses, and generally exhibiting unromantic and unsavory behavior. Early reviews in Oregon panned the book for its vulgar and reprehensible language and its failure to portray the region in a more favorable light. Davis went on to write four more novels, including *Buelah Land* (1949), but none approached the level of acclaim achieved by *Honey in the Horn*. He also wrote poetry, including "Mid-September," a moving and melodic commentary on the harvest season and nature's beauty. To this day, Davis remains the only Oregon writer to win the Pulitzer Prize for fiction.

Stewart Holbrook outranked both Davis and Stevens in popularity and sheer volume of literary production. A freelance writer who lived in Portland, Holbrook was a person of many talents—logger, prizefighter, semi-pro baseball player, and watercolorist—and until his death in 1964, he was the acknowledged dean of Northwest writers.

Stewart Holbrook (*left*), 1893-1964, logger, prizefighter, semi-pro baseball player, watercolorist, and popular freelance writer

His popular historical writings were uncritical, informal, often folksy, and filled with an ironic and deft sense of humor. Among those, the best known are *Holy Old Mackinaw: A Natural History of the American Lumberjack* (1938), *Burning an Empire: The Story of American Forest Fires* (1943), and *Far Corner* (1952), a smartly contrived collection of short essays on unconventional characters and small towns in the Northwest. Under the pen name "Mr. Otis," Holbrook painted watercolors that one critic referred to as "wildly imaginative."

Ernest Haycox developed his writing skills at the University of Oregon and while working the "cop beat" at the *Oregonian*. After migrating to New York City, Haycox was a prolific writer of Westerns and is perhaps best known for his short story "The Stage to Lordsburg," which was adapted for the award-winning film *Stagecoach* (1939). More than any other writer of his time, Haycox achieved literary excellence as a writer of classic western fiction. A first-rate literary stylist, he developed larger-than-life characters who maneuvered through epic western backdrops. In an effort to get away from classic Westerns and write serious historical fiction, Haycox completed *The Earthbreakers* (1952) just before his death, a novel whose ending takes place at the end of the Oregon Trail.

The regional literary winds shifted again in the early 1960s with the emergence of Don Berry and Ken Kesey, two talented and gifted writers who brought an engaging style and a different tone to regional literature. Berry, who worked in the Reed College bookstore, published two important books, *Trask, A Novel* (1960) and *Moontrap, A Novel* (1962). Based on careful historical research, the novels confront the Indian-white race issue and describe the fur-trapper period of early Oregon. Berry spent the later years of his life on Puget Sound's Vashon Island, where he gained a reputation as a creative genius—writing music, poetry, and children's literature and designing home computers during their early stages of development. The *Seattle Post-Intelligencer* once described Berry as the "Michelangelo of Puget Sound."

Ken Kesey also gained preeminence as Oregon's most gifted author during the 1960s, writing two best-selling novels, *One Flew Over the Cuckoo's Nest* (1962) and *Sometimes a Great Notion* (1964). Both novels were made into motion pictures, with *Cuckoo's Nest* winning several Academy Awards, including the prize for best motion picture. A gifted athlete at Springfield High School and the University of Oregon, Kesey attended Stanford University's creative writing program, where he studied with Wallace Stegner in a seminar that included Larry McMurtry and Wendell Berry. After Kesey volunteered to participate in U.S. Army-sponsored research involving LSD at Stanford University's medical school, he joined a fun-loving drug-culture group known as the Merry Pranksters. Celebrated in Tom Wolfe's *The Electric Kool-Aid Acid Test* (1968), Kesey and the Pranksters toured the country in a brightly colored school bus. Although he published other novels during the next three decades, none achieved the acclaim of his first two works.

William Stafford was the first Oregon poet to win the National Book Award. Educated in his native state at the University of Kansas and a conscientious objector during the Second World War, Stafford joined the faculty at Lewis & Clark College, where he taught until his retirement. He wrote more than 50 books of poetry, received the National Book Award for *Traveling Through the Dark* (1962), and served as a Consultant in Poetry to the Library of Congress. With a reputation for gentleness and compassion, Stafford was renowned both for his talents as a teacher and his prowess as a poet. At the time of his death in 1993, he was Oregon's Poet-Laureate.

Among Oregon's writers since the Second World War, Ursula Le Guin is preeminent. The author of 18 novels, several collections of short stories and poetry, 12 children's books, and collections of critical essays, she is a writer with truly catholic interests. The daughter of prominent anthropologists Theodora and Alfred Kroeber, Le Guin gained literary fame for science-fiction writing. She won the Newbery Silver Medal Award for *The Tombs of Atuan* and the National Book Award for Children's Books for *The Farthest Shore*, both in 1972, and the Lewis Carroll Shelf Award for *A Wizard of Earthsea* in 1979. Her other works have been shortlisted for the National Book Award and Pulitzer Prize. Among her several honorary degrees are tributes from the University of Oregon, Lewis & Clark College, Portland State University, and Western Oregon University.

Raised in south-central Oregon's remote and sparsely populated Warner Valley, William Kittredge returned to the home ranch after a stint at the University of Oregon and a tour of duty with the U.S. Air Force. After four short years in the valley as one of the bosses on the huge family spread, he tired of being part of an agribusiness empire and left for the graduate writing program at the University of Iowa. From there Kittredge moved west to join Richard Hugo at the University of Montana, where he became a prominent essayist on western American themes and served as director of the creative writing program. His most important books—a collection of personal essays, *Owning It All* (1987), and an autobiographical work, *Hole in the Sky: A Memoir* (1992)—are thoughtful reflections about the variety of ways of inhabiting and living in the West. Seattle-based writer Ivan Doig has called *Hole in the Sky* "the very stuff of epic—of a family that seized its chance to become ducal then suffered the costs of its possessions." One of Kittredge's most recent books, *Balancing Water: Restoring the Klamath Basin* (2000), is a beautifully illustrated and passionately written account of the historical background and persisting water crisis in the Klamath Basin.

Craig Lesley's writings must also be included in this very select review of Oregon writers. Born in the Columbia River town of The Dalles, Lesley was educated at Whitman College, the University of Kansas, and the University of Massachusetts. His first two novels, *Winterkill* (1984) and *River Song* (1989), deal with several generations of Nez Perce who drift through Oregon rodeo towns and the Indian fishery on the Columbia and who are trying to cling to their heritage in a destabilizing world. The Pacific Northwest Booksellers' Association awarded both *Winterkill* and *River Song* its Best Novel of the Year award. Lesley's *The Sky Fisherman* (1995) was a finalist for the Oregon Book Award for fiction and a nominee for a Pulitzer Prize. His most recent book, *Storm Riders* (2000), is a deeply personal novel, filled with heartache, humor, and fear, in which the protagonist struggles to raise a foster son with fetal alcohol syndrome.

If there are significant themes that distinguish Oregon and Pacific Northwest writing from other regions, then it may be its investment in classic descriptive backdrops that embrace the influences of geography, climate, and landscape. From the 19th through the 20th century, Oregon's best fictional writers featured the mood and texture of ocean, rain, snow, thick forested mountains, and the winds of the eastern desert country. This is similar to the way that the Civil War and race questions have influenced southern writers and how the extremes of heat and cold characterize the literature of the Great Plains. When Portland's *Willamette Week* held a prose and poetry contest in 1984, the judges offered the following: "Rain country is good writing country: there is less temptation to stray outdoors away from the work. This year's entries . . . support that theory, and proof that barrels of midnight oil are burning to good effect in this region." Washington writer Tom Robbins, who lives north of Seattle, judged that rain "allows for prolonged periods of intimacy. It's cozy and reduces temptation. It keeps you inside where you can turn inward, rather than scattering yourself about the beach and boulevards. And it makes the little mushrooms grow."

CHAPTER NINE

From Natural Resources to a New Economy

Steve Prefontaine grew up running the hills around the southern Oregon coastal town of Coos Bay, where his father worked in the sprawling Weyerhaeuser complex along the waterfront. Graduating from Marshfield High School in 1969 and then heading off to the University of Oregon, Prefontaine proved himself to be a precocious and gritty athlete who set several national distance running records. A *Life* magazine article published in 1972 remarked that his "racing style reflected the tough, elemental life of Coos Bay, Oregon, the logging town where he grew up." In truth, Prefontaine lacked the prototypical distance runner's graceful stride and slender build. He was a blue-collar runner who worked his shoulders awkwardly and pushed as hard as he could until he reached the finish line. When he died in an automobile accident at the age of 24, Prefontaine had set or broken his own American distance records 14 times and recorded nine sub-four-minute miles. A fan favorite—indeed, the show at the University of Oregon's Hayward Field track and field events—the long-haired, mustachioed "Pre" was impetuous and brash, taking on the imperious Amateur Athletic Union in the United States, which insisted that athletes had patriotic obligations to participate in designated events. Prefontaine preferred to look beyond flag-waving to the enjoyment of pure, international competition.

At the time of Prefontaine's death in May 1975, the Northwest's forest products industry was in the beginning stages of technological changes that would dramatically reduce labor as a factor in production. At the outset of the 1980s, the closure of several labor-intensive, old-growth mills on Coos Bay served as pacesetters for other timber-dependent communities in Oregon, with high unemployment and escalating social problems. Although several highly automated mills reopened in timber districts around the state within the next few years, the new computer-operated plants required far fewer workers and did little to alleviate economic hardship in places such as Coos Bay. A parallel recession in agriculture, followed by a corresponding technological displacement of workers, worsened problems for other rural communities. The governor's office, legislators, and many in the business community pointed to Oregon's lack of diversity and overdependence on lumber and agricultural production as the root of the state's economic woes.

Oregon's struggles with plant closures and business bankruptcies in the early 1980s paralleled similar developments elsewhere in the United States, especially among old-line northeastern industries where changes in the nature of production and work contributed to a precipitous decline in blue-collar manufacturing jobs. People living along Oregon's natural-resource byways, many of them with more than a quarter century in the same line of work, saw their job security disappear in the face of technological innovations that replaced labor-intensive production. Where logging, mill, and cannery employment once defined Oregon's work life, there now ensued a scramble for jobs and an exodus of people to Wyoming's coal fields and other places where jobs were more plentiful. For the Pacific Northwest, the shakeout in the wood products industry brought sharp reductions in the number of jobs. The forest industries employed 171,500 workers in 1972, a figure that dropped to 134,400 in the midst of the recession in 1982. But the relative health of the industry has always been linked to the national economy, and employment climbed back to 152,000 in 1988, a period of record national forest timber sales.

The eastern Oregon town of Burns, much like Coos Bay, provides another poster-town example of the transition to new economic realities. When the local Edward Hines Lumber Company was operating full time in 1980, the firm employed 912 workers in its sawmill and woods operations. Then the Hines Company shut down production and reopened with computerized equipment and laser-guided saws with a combined mill and woods crew of only 272 employees. The town's population dropped from 3,571 to 3,102 that year, and unemployment ranged between 23 and 37 percent. With its sharp increase in shuttered businesses and vacant homes, Burns appeared to be up for sale.

Critics of Oregon's demoralized economy—state bureaucrats, elected officials, business leaders, and academics in university think tanks—pointed to the need for economic diversification as the solution to the struggling natural-resource sector. A semblance of stability existed, they argued, in communities such as Corvallis, McMinnville, and Beaverton, home to major high-tech manufacturing firms. If Oregon followed national trends—away from resource extraction and toward a more diversified economic base centered in high-tech and service industries—it could better protect itself from national recessions. Although the forest products sector had recovered by the mid-1980s and reached new production highs by the end of the decade, overall employment in the industry continued its downward spiral. Greater efficiencies in cutting and milling logs, the closure of antiquated plants, and sharp increases in forest products output in the southeastern United States, *not* environmental restrictions, were the chief culprits in the loss of jobs.

Even as timber-related employment declined, however, an expanding low-wage service sector began to provide an element of stability for many communities. Reflecting the arrival of new urban refugees seeking low-tax, small-town retirement living, places such as North Bend on the southern Oregon coast and Hoquiam on Washington's Grays Harbor slowly began to experience rising property values and a growing tax base. But hard times persisted in other communities— Klamath Falls, Chiloquin, Prineville, Burns, and La Grande—where alternative economic enterprises failed to materialize. Nestled in the North Santiam Canyon, the small community of Detroit was going through a different kind of transition in the late 1980s. The town had once been wholly dependent on the great stands of old-growth timber in the surrounding hills, but it found new opportunities when nearby Detroit Lake slowly emerged as an attractive setting for summer homes. Despite the changes that took place in some towns, environmental issues continued to provoke anger in rural communities.

When the U.S. Fish and Wildlife Service listed the spotted owl as a threatened species early in 1990, the decision set off a prolonged period of wrangling and litigation and increased economic difficulties for communities dependent on federal timber sales. The invocation of the

Endangered Species Act in the 1980s and 1990s to protect the spotted owl, marbled murrelet, and several salmon species divided Oregon's public largely along urban and rural lines. Because federal courts determined that logging, grazing, and certain agricultural activities were harmful to endangered species, natural resource industries and their rural constituents believed they were under siege to policymakers and environmentalists. When the U.S. Fish and Wildlife Service first proposed listing the spotted owl as threatened in June 1989, the announcement triggered a series of lawsuits, sharply curtailed national forest harvests, and brought a torrent of protests from timber-dependent communities. In many respects, the owl was a smokescreen for the sharply diminished national forest timber supplies, highly automated and efficient sawmills that employed only a handful of workers, increasing competition from Canadian imports, and the emergence of a vibrant forest products industry in the southeastern United States.

There were other complicating factors. When Northwest sawmills began to close in the late 1980s and early 1990s, private firms continued to export a large volume of raw logs to Asian buyers. Although federal restrictions banned the overseas export of national forest timber, there were no regulations prohibiting the sale of logs harvested on private lands. Washington and Oregon exported nearly 4 billion board feet of raw logs in 1988, approximately 25 percent of the total cut for the two states. While mills in Coos Bay and elsewhere lay idle, huge stacks of dockside logs awaited shipments to Asian markets. The consequences for many timber-dependent communities were high unemployment, rising social problems, an eroding tax base, and an exodus of young people in search of education or employment elsewhere. President Bill Clinton's famous "Forest Summit" in Portland in 1993 and the adoption of the Northwest Forest Plan were intended to resolve the crisis and provide a balanced program that would satisfy logging communities and environmental groups. The plan did neither. Loggers and their families continued to define the problem as owls versus jobs, environmentalists persisted with lawsuits and protests against federal timber sales, and the stalemate persisted into the 21st century.

Despite the sharply diminished flow of timber from the national forests, the Pacific Northwest continued to lead the nation in wood-products output. Oregon ranked first in 1995, producing 5.7 billion board feet, and Washington ranked second with 4.2 billion board feet. While trade association officials acknowledged the impressive production figures, they cautioned that long-term supplies remained a problem. Although declining federal timber sales contributed to pockets of unemployment by the mid-1990s, job losses were less than one-third of the industry's predictions, with the three Pacific Northwest states losing 16,695 wood products jobs, far below the Northwest Forest Research Council's prediction of more than 65,000 direct job losses. It is fair to say, however, that the new environmental restrictions had their greatest impact away from the Interstate-5 corridor and especially in eastern Oregon's smaller timber-dependent communities.

When Congress passed the Clean Water Act in 1970, Oregon was ahead of other states in its efforts to clean its waterways of pollution. The several dams on the Willamette River system, constructed between 1940 and the 1960s, helped reduce pollution, especially in the Portland Harbor area, and have provided a kind of technological fix to persistent problems. Tributary dams store seasonal precipitation, which is released during the summer and autumn months to maintain a relatively even flow in the main river—a procedure that flushes contaminants downriver and out of sight. The dams have changed the valley in still other ways; the water impounded in the reservoirs keeps most seasonal flooding from farmland and the valley's major cities. A 1972 *National Geographic* article praising Governor Tom McCall for his "cleanup" of the river is well deserved, but an important and seldom mentioned factor in this pollution story has been the regulated flow of the river. The mushrooming growth of Willamette Valley cities and suburbs since the 1970s and the continued introduction of chemicals into the environment, however, have contributed to other problems in the basin. Once again, the Willamette River—perhaps the valley's miner's canary—is speaking back, producing deformed and disfigured fish in the lower stretches of the waterway.

What Oregon had accomplished in its 1970s cleanup of the Willamette River was the elimination of point-source pollution, the most readily identifiable pollutants that flow into the river from sewers and pipes. Nearly two decades would pass before the condition of the river again made headline news, and then reports of troubled waters came with a rush. First, Governor John Kitzhaber's 1997 task force reported findings of petroleum residues, toxic chemicals, and metal by-products in urban areas and pest and nutrient contaminants in rural sections of the waterway. The report emphasized that non-point source pollution entering the stream during months of high precipitation far exceeded point-source contaminants and that urban areas were contributing a far higher pollutant load per acre than rural lands.

The valley's booming economy, its reputation for livability, and a skyrocketing population were all placing greater burdens on the Willamette waterway. The valley's population increased from 1.49 million in 1970 to 1.94 million in 1990 and surpassed the 2 million mark shortly thereafter. Expanding suburbs, parking lots, shopping centers, and the removal of riparian vegetation increased the runoff of petroleum residue, a variety of chemicals, and metal by-products into the Willamette and its smaller tributaries. Pesticides, fertilizers, and nutrient non-point source pollutants entering streams in rural sections of the basin added to this contaminent load. Aided by increasingly sophisticated measuring instruments in the 1990s, scientists were able to assess with greater precision the health of the Willamette system.

"How could this happen?" an *Oregonian* editorial piously asked. After all, it seemed like only yesterday that Oregon was heralded for its clean waters and environmental stewardship. The state's most widely read newspaper acknowledged that the Kitzhaber report should be a "wake-up call" for citizens and businesses to remedy the conditions that were contributing to the river's deterioration. Although the *Oregonian* called for a broad-based strategy to restore the Willamette's health, the Kitzhaber task force had already taken the initiative—recommending the restoration of wetlands, making greater efforts to mimic natural runoff conditions, inventorying pesticide use, and operating Willamette-system dams to maintain minimum flows during the summer and early fall.

While evidence of pollution in the Willamette River seemed to multiply daily, the U.S. Environmental Protection Agency (EPA) was moving on another front to declare significant sections of Portland Harbor a Superfund cleanup site. Waterfront property owners, including the City of Portland and the Port of Portland, asked for voluntary compliance and requested that the Oregon Department of Environmental Quality (DEQ) be responsible for monitoring the cleanup. Portland and DEQ also quarreled over the proper way to solve the city's sewer overflow problems during the rainy season, and city commissioners complained that fixing the sewers would not dramatically improve water quality in the Willamette River. Then, in 1999, the National Marine Fisheries Service invoked the Endangered Species Act and listed nine Northwest salmonid populations as threatened. One year later, the hammer fell again when the EPA designated a large section of Portland Harbor a Superfund cleanup site.

In a sense, the past was coming home to roost. The long history of Portland's industrial connection to the Willamette River was being played out in messy confrontational forums. The city's commissioners dueled with Governor Kitzhaber when he questioned Portland's resolve in dealing with its persisting sewage problems. Fingers were pointed upriver and downriver and between rural and urban politicians. Repeating its time-worn habit, the *Oregonian* defended Portland's efforts and accused the DEQ of sticking it to the city "with what can only be imagined as the governmental equivalent of glee." And planners in the greater Portland metropolitan area continued to battle with property-rights groups who viewed pollution mitigation efforts as too restrictive to private property owners. These struggles would continue into the future, especially as development groups continued to push against environmental restraints.

The gradual emergence of Oregon's vital high-tech industry after 1980 contributed to a booming economy and the manifold problems associated with rapid population growth. Palo Alto's Stanford Research Park, which pioneered science-based research and development, was at the center of the emergence of California's famed Silicon Valley and its high-tech industry. Similar entrepreneurial efforts in Bellevue and Redmond, Washington, and in the Portland metropolitan area contributed to the expansion of electronics manufacturing facilities in the Pacific Northwest. Even the inland city of Boise boomed in the 1980s as a manufacturer of computer hardware and software. Hewlett-Packard, with 4,000 jobs in Boise alone, was Idaho's leading private-sector employer by the late 1980s. Led by Tektronix and Intel, the greater Portland area developed its own "Silicon Forest" with specialities in developing and manufacturing semiconductors and display technologies.

Tektronix, which had its beginnings in the 1940s as a manufacturer of oscilloscopes and related measuring instruments, served as the core of Portland's electronics industry from the 1950s until Intel opened its major plant in 1976. Howard Vollum and Jack Murdock, creators of Tektronix, first expanded their operation to a Hawthorne Boulevard plant on Portland's near east side, where engineers worked on a profit-sharing arrangement, freely exchanged research ideas, and pushed the boundaries of innovation. With the input of its employees, the Tektronix executives purchased land in Washington County and opened a 20,000-square-foot building in 1951 with easy access to Sunset Highway, a convenient transportation arterial. In short order, the firm was employing more than 700 people and looking for additional space, a need the company satisfied when it purchased more than 330 acres to the west of Beaverton. It was there that Tektronix created its campus environment, putting up several well-spaced buildings in an attractive, open setting. By the 1960s, Tektronix possessed impressive international sales accounts and was well known in greater Portland as the largest employer in the metropolitan area.

Location, the availability of open space, a favorable tax climate, an educated workforce, and Oregon's well-known livability were the major factors attracting additional high-tech investors to Portland and its surrounding counties and communities. In addition to Tektronix spin-off start-ups such as C. Norman Winningstad's Floating Point Systems, California's giant Intel opened a branch plant near the community of Aloha in late 1976 with active government assistance in the form of tax breaks and land-use concessions. Within three years, Intel's Oregon operation employed 2,600 workers, and the company expanded to a new industrial park in Hillsboro. In quick order, Hewlett-Packard (1979), Wacker Siltronics (1980), and Japanese companies—SEH, Sharp, Fujitsu, Epson, and NEC—joined greater Portland's rapidly expanding cohort of high-tech firms. These and other spin-off enterprises employed combined workforces of more than 60,000 workers by 1997.

Oregon's booming high-tech industry profoundly affected the state's economy, its land-use planning laws, and, of course, its politics. Nowhere was this more evident than in the lower Willamette Valley, where most of the explosive growth was taking place. Oregon's statewide population increases since the Second World War were phenomenal, paralleling stride for stride spectacular growth in other western states, collectively the fastest growing region in the nation. Although Oregon's late-20th-century population boom never approached the dramatic surge of the 1940s (39.6 percent), the state's growth rate of 20 percent or higher for each decade since 1970 has been consistently among the highest in the United States. While Bend and Deschutes County have been in the midst of a demographic boom for more than two decades, cities and counties in the lower Willamette Valley have experienced the most noticeable population increases. These newcomers were a mixed blessing, according to some critics: they distanced themselves from civic virtues of environmental stewardship, built huge trophy homes, and isolated themselves from community responsibilities.

Population Growth in Oregon, 1950-2000		
Year	*Population*	*Percentage Growth*
1950	1,521,341	39.6
1960	1,768,687	16.3
1970	2,091,385	18.2
1980	2,633,156	25.9
1990	2,842,321	20.3
2000	3,421,399	20.0

The most explosive growth in the Pacific Northwest was taking place in urban counties surrounding the Seattle-Tacoma and Portland-Vancouver metropolitan areas. Portland's urban reach extended across the Columbia River to Clark County, east and south to Clackamas County, and west into Washington and Yamhill counties. The propensity of the electronics companies to seek open spaces in semi-rural settings and the lower Willamette Valley's expanding suburban growth placed increasing strains on Oregon's heralded land-use laws and its ability to control development. The quality of life and livability so attractive to the thriving high-tech sector was proving to be a Catch-22, with new suburbs eating away at the valley's valuable farmland, creating traffic problems where none existed before, and increasing pollution runoff from streets and parking lots. In addition to suburban sprawl, huge rectangular, box-like warehouses began going up at Interstate-5 interchanges until the stretch of highway between Stafford and Wilsonville was a continuous line of commercial buildings.

As the 20th century drew to a close, developers and public officials increasingly battled over contentious land-use questions, most of them centered in the Portland metropolitan area and its urban-growth boundary. Approved in 1979, Portland's urban-growth boundary encompassed Multnomah, Clackamas, and Washington counties and 24 municipalities. The Metropolitan Service District (Metro), the only regional government of its kind in the United States, had jurisdiction over the boundary, reviewed all comprehensive planning issues, and determined if plans met the state's guidelines. While developers attacked Metro's decisions because they restricted home and business construction, environmentalists charged the agency with being too lenient. Despite its problems—rising real-estate costs, the displacement of low-income families, and the gentrification of older sections of the city—Portland gained a reputation as a national laboratory for prudent urban growth. Planners drew distinctions between Portland

and Kansas City, where metropolitan sprawl extended its spatial reach by 70 percent between 1990 and 1996 while its population increased by only 5 percent. During the same period, both Portland's built landscape and its population grew by 13 percent.

Beginning with the 1995 legislative session, conservative lawmakers made numerous attempts to overturn and weaken Senate Bill 100, the framework for Oregon's land-use laws. Although most of the bills never got out of committee, Governor John Kitzhaber used his veto to turn back those that he deemed unacceptable. Fearing the governor's veto power, the 1997 legislature was less aggressive in attempting to overturn S.B. 100. Toward the end of the decade, Oregonians in Action (OIA), a property-rights organization, began developing strategies and orchestrating a direct assault on the state's planning system. OIA successfully placed an initiative measure on the November 2000 ballot that would amend the state constitution to require state and local governments to compensate landowners in instances where land-use restrictions reduced property values. Although several former governors, the Oregon Business Association, the League of Women Voters, and several county commissioners spoke out against Ballot Measure 7, nearly 53 percent of the voters approved the amendment on a very crowded ballot.

Governor Kitzhaber immediately asked Oregon's attorney general for an opinion on the measure, and the state's land-planning agency met in special session. In a parallel development, Audrey McCall, Governor Tom McCall's widow, and Hector Macpherson, the author of Oregon's pioneer land-use legislation, filed a legal complaint, arguing that Measure 7 violated the "single question" requirement for constitutional amendments. In February 2001, Marion County Circuit Court Judge Paul Lipscomb ruled in behalf of *McCall et al.*, declaring that the ballot measure violated the Oregon constitution's requirement. The case eventually found its way to the Oregon Supreme Court, where the justices unanimously upheld Judge Lipscomb's ruling.

While property-rights groups charged Oregon's high court with judicial activism, the Eugene *Register-Guard*, speaking for many public officials across the state, called Measure 7 a "stealth effort to undermine Oregon's landmark land-use planning system." Voters, the newspaper argued, were deceived by the proposal's "deceptive populist appeal" and distracted by the more than two dozen measures on the ballot in 2000. But Oregonians in Action and other property-rights interests, most notably large timberland owners, pressed forward again, this time with an initiative petition placed on the 2004 ballot. Measure 37 would require local, city, and state governments to compensate owners when regulatory policies reduced the fair-market value of their property, or the governments could "modify, remove or not apply" the new law to allow the owner to develop the property for a use permitted at the time the property was acquired. Approved 60 to 40 percent, Measure 37 threatens to undermine Oregon's grand experiment to protect its livability through land-use planning. Because Oregon's roll-back in regulating land use has captured national attention, the state has already suffered damage to its reputation as an environmental pacesetter.

During the last half century, women and minorities have made modest gains in Oregon's elective politics. After Nan Wood Honeyman, the state did not have another congresswoman until the election of liberal Democrat Edith Green, who represented the Third District from 1955 to 1975. By the mid-1960s Green was a powerful force on the House education committee. Only two other Oregon women have been elected to the U.S. House of Representatives. Liberal Democrat Elizabeth Furse represented the first district between 1993 and 1999, surviving three very close election campaigns; and Democrat Darlene Hooley, elected to the Fourth District seat in 1996, has served three terms. Maurine Neuberger succeeded to her husband's U.S. Senate seat when she was elected in 1960. Neuberger decided against reelection in 1966, in part, when the *Oregonian* and other newspapers in the state accused her of neglecting the state's business. Her short-lived marriage to Boston psychiatrist Philip Solomon in 1964 added to the perception that she was out of touch with her home state.

Women candidates also have made modest strides in their attempts to seek statewide elective office. Norma Paulus, the first woman to be elected as Oregon's secretary of state, served two terms (1977-1985) and then ran for governor, losing to Neil Goldschmidt in the 1986 election. She later was elected to two terms as superintendent of public instruction (1991-1999), a period of considerable ferment in public education, when the state adopted new graduation requirements for Oregon high-school students. Barbara Roberts, secretary of state from 1985 to 1991, became Oregon's first woman governor in 1990; she served one term, deciding against another campaign when Senate President John Kitzhaber challenged her in the primary. Governor Roberts' stepdaughter, Mary Wendy Roberts, served a long period as commissioner of labor and industries from 1979 to 1995. A good case can be made that women have been most influential in the Oregon House of

Representatives, where Vera Katz (1985-1991), Bev Clarno (1995-1997), Lynn Snodgrass (1999-2001), and Karen Minnis (2003-2005) have all served as speaker of the lower house.

The ethnic makeup of Oregon's statewide and congressional officeholders has also become more diverse in the last several decades. Republican Victor Atiyeh, of Middle Eastern ancestry, served in the state senate before defeating Robert Straub for the governor's office in 1978. Voters reelected Atiyeh for a second term in 1982. Jim Hill, the first African American elected to statewide office in Oregon, served two terms as state treasurer between 1993 and 2001; and David Wu, a Chinese American, succeeded Elizabeth Furse in Oregon's first congressional seat in 1999. Wu, who has been successful in subsequent elections, lost the *Oregonian*'s endorsement in 2004.

Oregon's demographic profile has become increasingly more diverse since 1940, and especially so since 1960. The state was on the receiving end of the remarkable African American diaspora to West Coast defense-industry jobs during the Second World War, with most newly arriving Blacks taking jobs in Portland and Vancouver shipyards. Although Washington's numbers have always been higher, Oregon's African American population increased from 0.2 percent in 1940 to more than 1 percent in 1960 and to 1.6 percent in 1990. The 2000 census enumerated 1.6 percent of the state's population as "Black or African American," with another 2.1 percent listed as both African American and one other ethnic group. This cohort continues to concentrate in Portland and along the I-5 corridor.

American Indian and Alaska Native residents, who comprised 1.3 percent of the state's population in 2000, also identified with more than one group: 2.5 percent reported American Indian and Alaska Native and one other racial identity. People with Asian ancestry comprised 0.6 percent of the state's population in 1940, 0.5 percent in 1960, and then increased sharply to 2.4 percent in 1990. The 2000 census lists 3 percent of the population as Asian in a broad category that included Asian Indian, Filipino, Chinese, Japanese, Korean, Vietnamese, and "other Asian." Another 3.7 percent of Oregon's population identified themselves as Asian and one other category. Between 1990 and 2000, the number of minority people in the state doubled, increasing from 9 to 15 percent of the total population.

Among the state's ethnic groups, Oregon's Hispanic population has shown the most striking gains since the Second World War. Although Mexican muleskinners began running pack trains to Pacific Northwest gold mines in the 1850s, Mexican immigration to the Pacific Northwest was limited until immigrants began coming to the region early in the 20th century to work as agricultural fieldhands, especially in Idaho and eastern Washington. Those numbers have grown with each passing decade, but especially during the Second World War when the *bracero* labor program, a guest-worker plan, brought large numbers of Mexican agricultural laborers to work in the region's fields and food-processing plants. The *bracero* program partially alleviated Oregon's serious labor shortage during the war, with more than 15,000 Mexican workers entering the state between 1942 and 1947. With the end of the war, large numbers of Mexican families from the Southwest and northern Mexico remained in the region as low-paid agricultural workers. In the succeeding decades, hundreds of additional migrant workers from Mexico and the southwestern United States made the annual trek north to work fruit and vegetable harvests, to labor in the region's rapidly expanding Christmas tree plantations, and to take jobs in service industries. In contrast to other ethnic groups, Oregon's Mexican population has always been widely dispersed across the state, reflecting their employment in agricultural and service jobs.

Although Oregon's postwar Mexican American communities were isolated from one another—in Ontario, Nyssa, and Vale in the far eastern part of the state and in Willamette Valley communities such as Woodburn, Cornelius, and Hillsboro—with the passing years, service and cultural organizations have emerged to assist Mexican Americans and Mexican immigrants. The earliest of those groups, the Valley Migrant League, was established in Woodburn in 1964 to support and speak for immigrants and their families to local and state officials. During the 1970s, a decade of Hispanic activism in Oregon, a Roman Catholic priest, Arnold Beezen, and his congregation formed the Centro Cultural of Washington County to provide services to local agricultural workers, a failed small college in Mt. Angel opened for a time as Colegio Cesar Chavez, and Mexicans in the Cornelius area founded a local health clinic, the Virginia Garcia Memorial Health Center. A more formidable, militant, and influential worker organization emerged in 1985 with the founding in Woodburn of Pineros y Campesinos Unidos del Noroeste (Northwest Treeplanters and Farmworkers United), or PCUN. The union has been very active in organizing Oregon's Mexican workers.

Hispanics made up 1.9 percent of Oregon and Washington's population in 1970, a number that increased to 2.7 percent in 1980, making them the largest minority group in the two states. The 2000 cen-

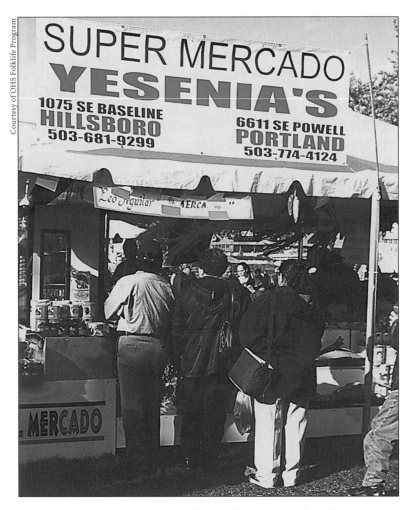

Yesenia's supermarket at Portland's Cinco de Mayo festival, 2002

sus shows Hispanics increasing to a surprising 8 percent of Oregon's population, a number that also suggests a growing political influence. Based on the 2000 census, Oregon's secretary of state created a newly redistricted state legislative seat covering the heavily populated Mexican American area between Salem and Woodburn. Although other Hispanic ethnic categories are included in the census figures, Mexican Americans are by far the largest of those groups. In Hood River County, Mexican Americans made up 20 percent of the population and 25 percent of children enrolled in the public schools in 2000. While

Oregon's population has historically been overwhelmingly Cauca-sian, the new immigrant groups moving to the state since 1940 have considerably broadened and enriched that state's cultural and ethnic makeup. Overall, the new immigrant groups have increased the state's minority population from 3.6 percent in 1960 to 13.4 percent in 2000.

Oregon's growing number of Hispanics has also influenced the state's cultural institutions. The Oregon Historical Society has been actively involved through its Folklife Program in documenting the stories of Mexican immigrants in an effort to preserve the traditions and cultures of people who have made Oregon their homeland. At the outset of the 21st century, the Society initiated a multiyear project, Las Artes Tradicionales en la Communidad, to assist recent Mexican im-migrants in preserving their arts and culture. The program celebrates crafts and craftsmanship, dance, celebrations, Mexican foods, and Mariachi music. As Oregon enters the new millennium, the Mexican presence is apparent everywhere across the Oregon landscape. When I walked into a Umatilla grocery store in June 2003 to purchase a bagel and cheese for lunch, there were no bagels and only a few loaves of white bread; but there were rows and shelves of tortillas and burritos and a lot of ingredients for making Mexican dishes. *Supermercados* (markets), *panaderías* (bakeries), and *tortillerías* (tortilla companies) can be found in places such as Umatilla, where there are large concen-trations of Mexican people. But while people of Mexican ancestry may easily find their preferred foods, like many other minorities they still face discriminatory practices and low wages.

Oregon's centuries-long struggle with issues of race has lingered through the high-tech boom of the 1990s and into the 21st century. Af-rican Americans, Hispanics, Southeast Asians, African immigrants, and other people of color have struggled with issues of equal access and service, racial profiling (especially while driving), and discrimi-nation in the workplace, charges that appear regularly in the news. In one extreme incident in 1988, a group of Portland skinheads brutally beat and killed Mulegeta Seraw, an Ethiopian immigrant. The per-petrators, who were members of the openly racist White Aryan Re-sistance (WAR), were convicted and sentenced to prison. In a widely publicized trial, the Southern Poverty Law Center, representing Se-raw's family, successfully sued and won a major judgment, bankrupt-ing WAR and its California leader, Tom Metzger.

Occasional police shootings of African Americans periodically stirred discontent in Portland, with the Black community charging

that law-enforcement personnel are too willing to use deadly force
when suspects are African American. In the aftermath of the shootings, grand jury findings have usually exonerated the police, further
exacerbating tensions among Blacks. Mexican immigrants living in
Corvallis revealed to a graduate student interviewer that they took
circuitous routes around the city to work or visit with friends; they
reported that local police regularly stopped them for some perceived
defect in their old and shopworn vehicles. Articles in the *Corvallis Ga-
zette-Times* have periodically addressed the issue of Hispanic profiling
in traffic stops.

No recent issue, however, fanned the flames of ethnic bigotry
across the United States and in Oregon more than the visual images
of airliners crashing into New York City's World Trade Towers and
the Pentagon on September, 11, 2001. The 9/11 terrorist attack and the
subsequent American troop commitments to Afghanistan and Iraq
provoked a series of individual and group assaults against people of
color. The incidents in Oregon were of a piece with assaults committed against minority people across the nation, as anxiety, racism, and
xenophobia combined to foster hatred against certain ethnic groups.
When Oregon followed the nation and descended into deep recession
in 2002, the pressures of a badly slumping economy worsened those la-
tent prejudices. Hate crimes increased in communities from Portland
to Medford, with a particularly vicious attack taking place in early
2003 against a Medford motel clerk from India. Owner Nick Patel, also
a native of India, charged that three National Guardsmen involved in
the unprovoked and brutal assault mistook his employee for an Arab.
Patel told a news reporter that his ethnicity seemed unimportant until
the terrorist attack on the World Trade Towers: "After September 11
people ask, 'Are you Pakistani?' And I say, 'No, I'm an Indian.' They
ask, 'Are you a Muslim?' And I say, 'No, I'm a Hindu.'"

Southern Oregon University historian Jay Mullen, from nearby
Ashland, told an *Oregonian* reporter that people become anxious and
strike out at those who are different during times of economic and
social difficulties. He added that U.S. Attorney General John Ashcroft
worsened matters when he told the American people to report any
individual who looked suspicious. Pedro Cabrera, who has lived in
the Rogue Valley since leaving East Los Angeles in 1973, has also noticed increased suspicions since 9/11 from people who wonder if he
is Arab. We are all "more sensitive to people of other colors now," he
told a reporter. While the events associated with September 11 have

stepped up the public's awareness of people who come from different countries, Darrell Milner, a long-time professor of Black Studies at Portland State University, argues that the problem is an old one. The propensity to see people as members of a group rather than individuals, he remarked, "comes straight from American history."

During the last two decades of the 20th century, Oregon's politics have become increasingly volatile, with environmental and natural-resource issues, field burning, gay rights, tax-limitation measures, doctor-assisted suicide, and vote-by-mail elections among the more contentious questions before the public. With sharply declining salmon runs in the Pacific Northwest and the federal government's decision to list several salmonid stocks as threatened or endangered, rural citizens have sometimes felt themselves under siege to decisions made in Salem and Portland. In an effort to restore salmon populations and to fend off further endangered-species listings, Governor John Kitzhaber initiated a salmon restoration plan through the formation of local "watershed councils." As volunteer and cooperative bodies designed to reach decisions through consensus agreements, the councils have met with mixed success in persuading landowners to restore salmon habitats. In those watersheds where there are large timberland ownerships, company representatives—who seldom miss the monthly meetings—control council agendas by default. In watersheds where there are more mixed ownership patterns, councils have sometimes adopted truly progressive measures to restore the ecological health of salmon-bearing streams.

Urban and rural Oregonians have also differed over the question of field-grass burning, a practice that seed-grass farmers use every autumn to cleanse their fields of debris. Urbanites in the Willamette Valley argue that the annual smoke spiraling into the autumn skies is ruinous to the public's health and tarnishes the state's reputation for livability. Although Governor Tom McCall declared a brief moratorium in August 1969 during an especially acute smoke inversion that obscured the sun and smothered the upper valley in an acrid odor, authorities have allowed burning to continue when wind conditions were more favorable and less likely to blow smoke over the heavily populated Eugene-Springfield area. Oregon State University and seed-grass growers experimented with mechanical burning machines, and farmers cooperated in restricting field burning when weather conditions were unfavorable. When heavy smoke billowed across Interstate

5 near Harrisburg on August 3, 1988, the dense smoke caused a huge pile-up involving 23 vehicles, killing seven people, and injuring 37 others. The accident resulted in further restrictions against burning near highways. Through the 1990s, seed-grass farmers have continued to refine burning techniques, removing stubble from fields to minimize fuel loads, and using propane burners to reduce smoke. Open field burning dropped sharply from 83,000 acres in 1995 to 52,000 acres in 2001. The seed-grass industry has changed in other ways; farmers have concluded that it is unnecessary to burn stubble every year, and growers now sell huge bales of straw to Asian buyers.

While Oregon's high-tech spectacular was capturing news headlines as the stock market boomed at century's end, there were indications that troubling times lay ahead. Reflecting the historically significant changes in the state's economy during the 1990s, Oregon newspapers increasingly drew attention to issues of class and rural-urban divisiveness. By the mid-1990s, high-tech manufacturing jobs had surpassed Oregon's long-time staple, lumber and forest products employment, and timber harvests on private and public lands had plummeted to a 70-year low of 3.53 billion board feet by 1998. The declining timber industry paralleled generally downward shifts in the region's other extractive economies. Since the 1970s, 500 forest-products mills have closed in the greater Northwest, 5,000 boats have been lost to the fishing fleet, and more than 10,000 farms and ranches have gone out of business.

Even in the face of the declining timber economy, however, the booming high-tech sector provided a powerful counterforce and pushed the state's unemployment to a 25-year low in the mid-1990s. But the economic boom disproportionately benefitted upper-middle and upper-income groups, especially in the greater Portland metro area where computer-related manufacturing prospered. Beyond the Willamette Valley's urban centers and Deschutes County's flourishing economy, high unemployment, growing income inequality, and social distress have persisted. And then national and global events combined to send Oregon's economy into a tailspin. A national recession beginning in the summer of 2001 severely disrupted Oregon's high-tech sector, placing the state at the head of the nation's unemployment rankings for several months. Those distressing circumstances further aggravated Oregon's already divisive politics and contributed to an exodus of people looking for work in other states. Roseburg,

Klamath Falls, Coos Bay, La Grande, The Dalles, and Ontario actually lost population by the close of 2001. Although Oregon led the nation in unemployment and the number of hungry people, an improving economy in 2004 reduced the jobless rate and set the state on the path to recovery.

In the midst of the booming economy of the 1990s, Oregon experienced its version of the culture wars as anti-gay initiatives began to appear on the ballot. The measures—which found greater support in rural areas than in Willamette Valley cities such as Eugene, Corvallis, Salem, and Portland—further deepened the state's rural-urban divide. The Oregon Christian Coalition and Lon Mabon's Oregon Citizens' Alliance (OCA) supported measures in 1992 (Measure 9) and 1994 (Measure 13) condemning homosexuality and targeting the state's gay and lesbian population. Voters said no to the restrictive Ballot Measure 9 by a margin of 56 percent to 44 percent but turned away Measure 13 by only 51.5 percent to 48.5 percent. Similar efforts by right-to-life groups to drastically restrict the right to abortions have also been turned back. Since the failure of the second anti-gay initiative, Lon Mabon and the OCA have been unable to mount a successful initiative campaign, and the organization's legal and financial difficulties have sharply diminished its role in Oregon politics. The emergence of gay and lesbian marriages in early 2004, however, put the question squarely before the public in the fall election, when voters approved initiative Measure 36—a constitutional amendment defining marriage as between one man and one woman—57 to 43 percent.

The most divisive issues before the Oregon public in the last decades of the twentieth century, however, centered on the state's tax policy. Anti-tax activists—led by Don McIntyre, a Portland-area athletic club proprietor, and Bill Sizemore of Oregon Taxpayers' United—sponsored two successful initiatives during the 1990s to reduce taxes. Although Oregon had turned back several property tax limitation measures during the 1980s, voters narrowly approved Ballot Measure 5 in 1990, a law that severely limited the fiscal ability of local governments to support schools and other services. In an ironic twist, the state's more liberal urban areas provided the majority of the support for Measure 5. Five years later voters restricted local property taxes even further with Measure 47, which shifted even greater responsibility for public school funding to the state legislature. Measures 5 and 47 have also redirected much of the remaining property-tax burden from businesses to individuals. In each legislative session since the passage of the two measures, Oregon legislators and the governor's office have grappled with the increasingly contentious funding issue, with the most combative arguments taking place during the recession-ridden and revenue-short years of 2002 and 2003.

Although statewide elected offices were once the exclusive province of moderate Republicans, the Democratic Party has been successful in most contests since the election of Governor Neil Goldschmidt in 1986. But in the state legislature, where Democrats had been in control, the party suffered a reversal of fortunes in the 1990s, some of it attributed to rural voters who have associated the Democratic Party with environmental issues harmful to natural resource industries. Since then, voters have elected socially conservative, anti-tax Republican legislators who have blamed the Endangered Species Act and Oregon's land-use laws for the state's troubled economy. In the wake of the foundering natural-resource sector during the early 1990s, timber and agricultural interests attacked Governor Barbara Roberts (1991-1995) and attempted three times to recall her from office. Voters targeted other scapegoats for the state's problems through the state's initiative system, approving term limitations for state legislators in 1992 and passing tougher crime laws in 1994.

New visual signs of money and power, a kind of contemporary gold-rush phenomenon—have been reshaping a few Oregon and Northwest communities since the 1980s. While the symbols of new capital have largely bypassed towns such as Coos Bay and Burns, new forms of technology and an influx of highly educated, affluent people have been remaking some of the region's old natural resource communities. Recreational, leisure, and information-age capital have transformed many old mining, lumbering, and fishing communities into gentrified settings for the educated and wealthy. New golf courses, gated communities, and upscale cafes and boutiques have socially divided rural Oregon between affluent newcomers and long-time residents whose occupations have been marginalized by the new economy. Oregon has experienced its own process of deindustrialization where good-paying and skilled blue-collar jobs have been eliminated, while new ways of doing business have forced former primary products workers into low-wage, service-sector employment. Long-time residents of these communities often suffer the social costs of such dramatic changes in rising real estate prices, property taxes, and rental prices.

The greater Bend area has been Oregon's pacesetter, flourishing as a symbol of the new economy. When Brooks-Scanlon closed its big sawmill on the Deschutes River in 1992, Bend was already in the midst of an expansive, fashionable, and thriving economy whose success centered on upscale winter and summer recreation and a new generation of upper-middle-class telecommuters. Black Butte, Sunriver, and Inn of the Seventh Mountain—destination resorts constructed on cutover company timberlands—were the first of several vacation retreats to appear in central Oregon. The influx of affluent newcomers to central Oregon also brought sharp increases in service-sector employment and growing disparities in wealth, characteristics of the new economies elsewhere in the West. In addition to the tourists who visit Bend in summer and winter, the community has attracted affluent retirees and a wave of professional people whose business life depends on telephones, faxes, computers, and access to air travel.

Many newcomers to places such as central Oregon were people who sold high-priced California homes or otherwise benefitted from the booming stock market of the 1990s. In their new homes on Oregon's high desert, they have contributed to widening the gap between rich and poor, placing Oregon among a group of states where lower-income people actually lost ground during the 1990s. Deschutes County's surging population and sharp increase in service-sector employment reflect those growing disparities in wealth. As a center for tourism, Bend is similar to other areas enjoying an economic boom. Once prospering through the pine lumber it shipped to the city, Bend now thrives by marketing charm, scenery, winter and summer recreation, and the amenities of upscale living.

Deschutes County led the state in population growth during the 1990s, with an increase of 42 percent. The transformation of its labor force from blue-collar workers and bosses to service-related and tourism-industry jobs signaled a changing civic order where newly arrived professionals have emerged as an influential force in political and cultural life. At the close of the 20th century, the Bend area was repeating patterns established in Aspen, Colorado; Ketchum, Idaho; and Jackson, Wyoming—places where newcomers and seasonal migrants have changed the social and cultural landscape. In Bend, Brooks-Scanlon's real estate spin-off, Brooks Resources Incorporated, led the local market in property sales, converting former timberland into residences for expensive homes and golf courses and building time-lease condominiums upriver from its old sawmill grounds.

By the 1990s it was obvious that Bend was losing its former work-ing-class character. Older residents feared that the community was becoming divided into two classes: the well-to-do and the people who drove the busses and shuttles, labored in restaurants, worked as carpenters, landscaped the heavily watered lawns and flower gardens, or clerked in local retail stores. Most worrisome to long-time residents was the concern that they would be priced out of the housing market. Bend was not alone in facing such fears. The southern Oregon com-munity of Ashland, home to the Oregon Shakespeare Festival, has ex-perienced similar changes, with one resident describing the commu-nity as "all charm and no substance; a town built for the visitor, but impossible for the resident; a stage set." Because working-class people found it increasingly expensive to live in Ashland, one city council member proposed a local real estate transfer tax to encourage low-cost housing and rentals. The city council refused to adopt the measure. Beyond the Willamette Valley's urban centers, however, Ashland and Bend are the most striking examples of the emergence of a very differ-ent and new Oregon.

EPILOGUE

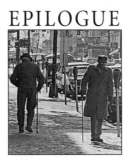

Still an Immigrant Society

Shortly after Oregon entered the new millennium, its commercial life began to slow, and then—with the national business downturn in the fall of 2001—the state's economy went into a tailspin. Oregon's unemployment reached a 17-year high in June 2003, with the jobless rate at 8.5 percent, much of it reflecting the sharp decline in technology manufacturing and related employment. For several months the state led the nation in the percentage of jobless and hungry people, giving Oregon the dubious distinction of making national news while policymakers at home were grappling with school funding, tax issues, and troublesome environmental questions. Because of the state's problematic tax structure (its dependence on income-tax revenue), its budget shortfalls contributed to a loss of 1,400 teaching positions by 2003 and another 6,800 jobs in state, county, and municipal employment.

The Oregon Health Plan (OHP), a controversial and revolutionary piece of legislation pushed through the state legislature in 1989 by then Senate President John Kitzhaber, suffered severe budget cutbacks during the recession. The nationally touted plan, a legislative measure that promised health services to all people below the poverty level, was under attack from the beginning. The Republican-controlled legislature repealed the employer mandate in 1997, a section of the OHP requiring employers to contribute to the health coverage of employees who worked more than 17.5 hours a week. When Oregon's economy

foundered in 2001-2002, additional legislative cuts reduced the OHP
to little more than the coverage provided by the federal-state Medic-
aid program for disabled, vision-impaired, and senior citizens. With
the legislature politically divided through the 2005 session, the health
plan remained on fiscal life support.

Although Oregon's economy was on the road to recovery in 2004,
with businesses setting statewide records in generating new jobs, the
number of people entering the workforce continued to outpace job
growth. A sizable in-migration to Oregon, largely from California
and other western states, has compounded the state's difficulties in
reducing unemployment. An Oregon Department of Employment
study in late 2004 revealed another alarming statistic: most of those
record job-growth advances took place in the low-wage service and retail sectors. To further complicate matters, when some manufacturing
and research companies began shifting their operations to Asia, those
corporate moves eliminated some of Oregon's better-paying jobs, especially in the high-tech sector. "No state is an economic island," Ted
Sickinger wrote for the *Oregonian* in November 2004. Sickinger urged
critics to look beyond the state's political leadership to national and
international economic forces that were shaping the future.

If global forces have been the major factor shaping Oregon's economy over the last several decades, the acrimony in the state legislature and the nasty charges hurled in noisome talk-radio shows suggest
otherwise. Oregon's experience bears testimony to the truth in the
late Speaker of the U.S. House of Representatives Tip O'Neil's famous
remark, "All politics is local." The state's ongoing quarrels over tax
policy, school funding, economic development, gay and lesbian rights,
assisted suicide, medical marijuana laws, property-rights controversies, and environmental and natural-resource issues seem never-end-
ing. In the revenue-short years of 2002 and 2003, a frustrated long-
time legislator and moderate Republican, Ashland's Lenn Hannon,
worried that the state had lost its sense of civic commitment: "We've
lost our can-do attitude in Oregon. And we've replaced it with a cannot do attitude." As he was leaving office in January 2003, a frustrated
Governor John Kitzhaber reflected that the state was becoming "un-
governable."

Oregon's increasingly fractious politics, especially since the mid-
1980s, has eroded civic discourse, polarized legislative proceedings,
and accelerated strident partisanship across the state. In the 2004
election, anti-tax zealots in the Republican Party purged moderate
members for cooperating with Democrats in the 2003 legislative ses-

sion, thereby further widening the ideological differences between the two political parties. David Fidanque of the Oregon chapter of the American Civil Liberties Union remarked in June 2005 that the state's political climate reflected trends across the nation: "There are fewer people in the middle, fewer people looking for ways to bridge the gap." Northwest Environment Watch, a non-profit Seattle-based think-tank promoting sustainable living, reported in 2002 that Oregon's divisive politics can be attributed to a widening income inequality that has weakened shared values, increased economic anxiety, and frayed social cohesion.

The sharp edges to Oregon's political discourse in the last two decades reflects a broader cultural/political shift in the nation towards an individualized, atomized society—including a more aggressive assertion of property rights. The increasingly combative advocacy of property rights in contemporary Oregon presents the strongest challenge to the progressive accomplishments of Governor Tom McCall's administration (1967-1975) and the state's proud tradition of livability and advocating for public space. Led by developers, real-estate interests, and free-enterprise think-tanks, unregulated property use threatens the state's open spaces, its air and water quality, its salmon restoration efforts, and its valuable agricultural and forest lands.

Although there has been some erosion in Oregon's commitment to the greater common good—shared beliefs that value equity, *public* ends, and civic responsibility—the state's politics continue to mirror progressive elements from the past. Since the early 1980s Oregon's minimum-wage law has been consistently above the national average. Voter approval of Ballot Measure 25 in November 2002 raised the minimum wage to $6.90 and provided for annual adjustments based on the Consumer Price Index. Effective January 1, 2005, Oregon's minimum wage was $7.25 per hour, the second highest in the United States to Washington's $7.35 per hour. The law survived the Oregon Restaurant Association's attempt in the 2005 legislative session to exempt restaurant workers from the minimum wage law because of the tip money they earn. In a parallel development, the U.S. Senate defeated a measure that would raise the federal minimum wage from $5.15 to $6.25 per hour but would override state laws on tip credits. Oregon's own Senator Gordon Smith voted with the minority.

Oregon's tradition of grassroots progressivism surfaced in two other successful initiative measures in the 1990s, a physician-assisted suicide law—known as the Death With Dignity Act—passed in 1994 and the Oregon Medical Marijuana Act, approved by voters in 1998. The Oregon Medical Association quickly adopted physician guidelines to implement the medical marijuana law and the Oregon Health Department assumed administrative responsibility for coordinating the measure. While the state legislature and the Oregon attorney general's office have made minor adjustments to the law, the medical marijuana initiative remained largely intact until the U.S. Supreme Court ruled in June 2005 that only Congress had the authority to regulate drugs nationwide. The ruling affected Oregon and nine other states permitting the use of marijuana for medical purposes. John Walters, the federal official in charge of drug-control policy, announced that the decision marked "the end of marijuana as a political issue." To avoid running afoul of federal law, Oregon officials stopped issuing medical marijuana cards following the court's decision.

The Death With Dignity Act has been even more controversial, with Oregon joining Belgium and The Netherlands as the only places in the world permitting physician-assisted suicides. Under the 1994 initiative, which passed 51 to 49 percent, physicians are allowed to write prescriptions for lethal medications for terminally ill patients who have less than six months to live. When opponents attempted to repeal the physician-assisted suicide measure in 1997, voters turned back the effort 60 to 40 percent. Qualified patients and physicians make choices under the law on an individual basis, with Oregon's Department of Human Services mandated to issue annual reports to assure compliance with the measure. The U.S. Justice Department under Attorney General John Ashcroft challenged the Oregon law in 2004, arguing that it violated federal law in allowing the use of controlled substances to terminate human life. The U.S. Supreme Court has agreed to hear the case during its fall session in 2005.

Oregon's grassroots politics also found expression at the local level when several cities passed resolutions opposing certain provisions of the controversial U.S. Patriot Act, enacted after the terrorist attack on the World Trade Center in 2001. The Multnomah County Library in Portland joined the fray early in 2002 (with libraries across the United States), objecting to turning over to prosecutors data about its patrons. The City of Eugene joined 14 other cities across the nation in November 2002 urging repeal of Patriot Act provisions that violated civil liberties. Corvallis became the second Oregon city to oppose the Patriot Act when the city council passed a resolution in April 2003 to "refrain from collecting or maintaining information about the political, religious, social views, associations or activities" of people unless demonstrated criminal conduct was involved. And Portland City Commissioner Dan Saltzman drafted a resolution on October 2003 (passed by the City Council) urging the federal government to revise the Patriot Act to better protect the civil liberties of its citizens.

Although Mayor Vera Katz and the Portland City Council voted in the spring of 2003 to permit the Portland Police Bureau to cooperate with the FBI in the local Joint Terrorism Task Force, that cooperation ended in April 2005 with the election of new Mayor Tom Potter. With the support of the City Council, Portland revoked its participation in the task force when the FBI refused to grant elected officials security clearance to oversee joint-task force operations. The Eugene *Register-Guard* also joined the growing unrest with the U.S. Patriot Act in April 2205 when it published an editorial urging Congress to drop the temporary and controversial "sunset" provisions of the 2001 law. The newspaper charged that some of the anti-terrorism provisions in the act authorized intrusive searches and violated citizens' civil liberties, such as allowing court-ordered wiretaps to follow calls from cell phones and to collect data from libraries and medical offices. The Bush administration, the newspaper predicted, could be expected to intensify its "drumbeat of fear" as Congress took up the issue of renewing the Patriot Act. Lawmakers should remember that the fight against terrorism could be achieved "without sacrificing fundamental American liberties."

To paraphrase historian William Cronon, all of us—Native American and immigrant alike—inhabit a storied landscape. We live in a place rich with complex social, economic, cultural, and ecological meaning. Unlike many states, Oregon's first peoples still exercise meaningful influences across the land because of their significant land holdings and treaty-guaranteed rights. The state's federally recognized Indian tribes are also becoming important players in the modern Oregon economy through their gambling casinos, cultural centers, and various development projects. There are still other approaches to understanding the way Oregon's historical antecedents have shaped its development. Although its once highly productive natural-resource industries have given way to high-tech manufacturing and outdoor recreation, issues related to those activities continue to resonate through the state's political culture, influencing special interest groups to push a variety of ballot measures, such as those to preserve state-owned forests (defeated in 2004), to ban the use of dogs to hunt bear and cougar (approved in 1994), and to protect streams from livestock grazing (defeated in 1996).

There is still more continuity to Oregon's story. Present-day tensions between rural and urban sections of the state also has 19th-century precedents in the long-standing jealousy of Portland's economic and political power. Portland's extensive banking influence in the late 19th century fostered hostility, bitterness, and political insurrection in rural areas of the state. While today's visitors to the state marvel at the attractive make-over of Portland's waterfront and its other amenities, many rural residents see the city's expanding MAX light-rail project and its attractive trolley lines as examples of urban extravagance and wasteful of taxpayers' money. Referred to as "little Beirut" by a recent American president, Portland has come under attack for its left-liberal politics, its social and environmental activism, and its support for gay and lesbian rights.

In several respects, therefore, contemporary Oregon is at one with its past. The state's 21st-century population is more diverse than it has been since the 1840s, a decade when the demographic profiles of immigrant Euroamericans and Native Americans were moving in inverse proportion to each other. Modern Oregon is still a place made up of people who were born elsewhere. I remember feeling at home when non-native-born Oregonians pushed beyond the 50 percent mark of the state's population sometime in the late 1970s. As many personal stories attest, the immigrant tide to Oregon accelerated during the Second World War and has remained above the national average for each succeeding decade. One war émigré was young red-headed James Brewer from Winfield, Louisiana, whose tour of army duty included a stay at Camp Adair, a mid-Willamette Valley training base. While attending a United Services Organization dance, he met Patricia Skaling, a student at nearby Oregon Normal School in Monmouth. Before Jim took ship for Europe in the summer of 1944, the two were married in a quiet ceremony in Salem. When Jim mustered out of the service, the couple lived for a brief time in Louisiana before returning to Salem where they decided to make their home. One of their seven children, red-haired Karla became my wife (after I, too, discovered Oregon at a later time via the U.S. Navy).

Although today's immigration pattern includes sizable numbers of people who have relocated to urban counties within the state, most newcomers are migrants from California and other western states. The 2000 census for Oregon lists 45.3 percent of the population native-born with another 45.4 percent from other states and more than 9 percent born in other countries. But the most striking feature of the state's 2000 enumeration is the sharp increase in the minority population to nearly 15 percent. While those newly arrived immigrants have inflamed tensions among some constituents, there is little question that the newcomers have enriched the state's ethnic make-up and helped diversify its cultural environment. Today's resentment directed toward undocumented immigrants reflects similar antagonisms once leveled against Chinese, Japanese, African Americans, and other ethnic groups across the American West.

For more than 150 years, therefore, Oregon has been a point of destination for people from elsewhere. Coming first by wagon road and ocean sea lanes and then railroads and eventually interstate highways, immigrants came to work in the fields, in the forests, in the canneries, and in recent decades, the growing number of microchip plants in the Portland metropolitan area. Although the agricultural potential of the western valleys provided the initial attraction, later immigrants flocked to mineral finds in the interior, to the Columbia River salmon industry, and finally to the logging camps and mill towns in the Douglas-fir and ponderosa districts. Beginning in the 1830s, with fanatical visionaries like Hall Jackson Kelley, promoters and developers offered up glowing descriptions of an Oregon Eden, a land abundant in natural resources ready for the taking. With only slightly less fervor, later enthusiasts touted Oregon as a Pacific wonderland—or, as the Oregon State Highway Commission advertised in 1939—"a land of giant forests, of rushing rivers, mirrored lakes and waterfalls, of mountains eternally white." The Depression-born Oregon Writers' Project publication, *Oregon: End of the Trail*, praised the state as "still the most unspoiled and most uncluttered spot in America." During and after Tom McCall's tour in the governor's office, national magazines continued to commend Oregon for its environmental achievements and its livability.

My earliest visions of Oregon—filled with images of emerald-green western valleys, lush forests, salmon-choked streams, and spectacular high-mountain lakes—have lost some of their romance and innocence during more than four decades of living in the state. Although I have yet to travel to some of Oregon's more remote corners, I still find its people, places, and stories endlessly fascinating. I wonder with Molly McFerran, one of my graduate students, who wrote in a 1991 essay that she would give up luxuries and creature comforts if she could "see the Columbia River before it was dammed to servitude." Oregon's contrary mix of progressive and reactionary politics continues to fascinate me and to beg for explanation. Although today's scholarly interpretations of Oregon and the Northwest are considerably less celebratory in assessing progress and achievement, this more somber mood suggests that we still have much to learn about the place we call home. When the late novelist Don Berry was visiting the Oregon coast in the mid-1980s, he wrote with great feeling about a special place as the sun was disappearing over the western horizon:

> With the moon rising over my shoulder and the sun setting before me, I stilled my mind and tried to feel only the truths of this place – the eternal ones of tide and wind and sun and moon, the forest behind me, the sea before.

Suggestions for Further Reading

Introduction: Of Forests, Water, and Sky

Cox, Thomas R. *The Park Builders: The History of State Parks in the Pacific Northwest.* Seattle: University of Washington Press, 1988.

Foner, Eric. *Who Owns History? Rethinking the Past in a Changing World.* New York: Hill and Wang, 2002.

Hobsbawm, Eric. *On History.* New York: New Press, 1997.

Oregon Trout. *Oregon Salmon: Essays on the State of the Fish at the Turn of the Millennium.* Afterword by Gov. John Kitzhaber. Portland: Irwin-Hodson, 2000.

Robbins, William G. *Landscapes of Promise: The Oregon Story, 1800-1940.* Seattle: University of Washington Press, 1997.

Walth, Brent. *Fire at Eden's Gate: Tom McCall and the Oregon Story.* Portland: Oregon Historical Society Press, 1994.

Williams, William Appleman. *History as a Way of Learning.* New York: New Viewpoints, 1973.

Chapter 1: Beginnings and Native Cultures

Aikens, C. Melvyn. *Archaeology of Oregon.* Portland: U.S. Department of Interior, 1984.

Ames, Kenneth M., and Herbert D.G. Maschner. *Peoples of the Northwest Coast: Their Archaeology and Prehistory.* London: Thames and Hudson, 1999.

Baldwin, Ewart M. *Geology of Oregon.* Eugene: University of Oregon Books, 1964.

Beckham, Stephen Dow. *The Indians of Western Oregon: This Land Was Theirs.* Coos Bay, Ore.: Arago Books, 1977.

Boyd, Robert. *The Coming of the Spirit of Pestilence: Introduced Infectious Diseases and Population Decline among Northwest Coast Indians, 1774-1874.* Vancouver: UBC Press; Seattle: University of Washington Press, 1999.

———. *People of The Dalles: The Indians of the Wascopam Mission.* Lincoln: University of Nebraska Press in cooperation with the American Indian Studies Research Institute, Indiana University, Bloomington, 1996.

Buan, Carolyn M., and Richard Lewis, eds. *The First Oregonians: An Illustrated Collection of Essays on Traditional Lifeways, Federal-Indian Relations, and the State's Native People Today.* Portland: Oregon Council for the Humanities, 1991.

Cressman, Luther S. *The Sandal and the Cave: The Indians of Oregon.* Corvallis: Oregon State University Press, 1981.

Fagan, Brian M. *Ancient North America: The Archaeology of a Continent.* New York: Thames and Hudson, 1999.

Hunn, Eugene S. *Nch'i-wána, "The Big River": Mid-Columbia Indians and Their Land.* Seattle: University of Washington Press, 1990.

Oregon State University. *Ecology and History: Landscapes of the Columbia Basin.* Corvallis, Ore.: Video Course, 2001.

Ramsey, Jarold, comp. and ed. *Coyote Was Going There: Indian Literature in the Oregon Country.* Seattle: University of Washington Press, 1977.

Ronda, James R. *Astoria and Empire.* Lincoln: University of Nebraska Press, 1990.

———. *Lewis and Clark among the Indians.* Lincoln: University of Nebraska Press, 1983.

Ross, Alexander. *Adventures of the First Settlers on the Oregon or Columbia River, 1810-1813.* 1849. Reprint, Corvallis: Oregon State University Press, 2000.

Swan, James. *The Northwest Coast, or Three Years' Residence in Washington Territory.* 1857. Reprint, Seattle: University of Washington Press, 1977.

Chapter 2: The Coming of Other People

Allen, John Logan. *Lewis and Clark and the Image of the American Northwest.* New York: Dover, 1975.

Ambrose, Stephen E. *Undaunted Courage: Meriwether Lewis, Thomas Jefferson, and the Opening of the American West.* New York: Simon and Schuster, 1996.

Barker, Burt Brown, ed. *Letters of John McLoughlin, Written at Fort Vancourver, 1829-1832.* Portland, Ore.: Binfords and Mort, 1948.

Clayton, Daniel W. *Islands of Truth: The Imperial Fashioning of Vancouver Island.* Vancouver: University of British Columbia Press, 2000.

Cox, Ross. *The Columbia River.* Edited by Edgar I. and Jane R. Stewart. Norman: University of Oklahoma Press, 1957.

DeVoto, Bernard. *The Course of Empire.* Boston: Houghton Mifflin, 1952.

Dillon, Richard. *Meriwether Lewis: A Biography.* New York: Capricorn Books, 1965.

Harris, Cole. *The Resettlement of British Columbia: Essays on Colonialism and Geographic Change.* Vancouver: University of British Columbia Press, 1997.

Johansen, Dorothy O. *Empire of the Columbia.* New York: Harper and Row, 1967.

Moulton, Gary, ed. *The Journals of the Lewis and Clark Expedition.* 13 vols. Lincoln: University of Nebraska Press, 1983-2001.

Ott, Jennifer. "'Ruining' the Rivers in the Snake Country: The Hudson's Bay Company's Fur Desert Policy." *Oregon Historical Quarterly* 104 (2003): 166-95.

Schwantes, Carlos A. *The Pacific Northwest: An Interpretive History.* Lincoln: University of Nebraska Press, 1996.

Thompson, David. *Columbia Journals.* Edited by Barbara Belyea. Seattle: University of Washington Press, 1998.

White, Richard. "Discovering Nature in North America." *Journal of American History* 79 (1992): 874-91.

Chapter 3: Creating an Immigrant Society

Boag, Peter G. *Environment and Experience: Settlement Culture in 19th-Century Oregon.* Berkeley: University of California Press, 1992.

Bowen, William A. *The Willamette Valley: Migration and Settlement on the Oregon Frontier.* Seattle: University of Washington Press, 1978.

Bunting, Robert. *The Pacific Raincoast: Environment and Culture in an American Eden, 1778-1900.* Lawrence: University Press of Kansas, 1997.

Clark, Malcolm. *Eden Seekers: The Settlement of Oregon.* Boston: Houghton Mifflin, 1981.

Douthit, Nathan. *Uncertain Encounters: Indians and Whites at Peace and War in Southern Oregon, 1820s-1860s.* Corvallis: Oregon State University Press, 2002.

Jeffrey, Julie Roy. *Converting the West: A Biography of Narcissa Whitman.* Norman: University of Oklahoma Press, 1991.

Johnson, David Allen. *Founding the Far West: California, Oregon, and Nevada, 1840-1890.* Berkeley: University of California Press, 1992.

Langston, Nancy. *Where Land and Water Meet: A Western Landscape Transformed.* Seattle: University of Washington Press, 2003.

McLoughlin, Virginia Duffy. "Cynthia Stafford and the Lost Mining Town of Auburn." *Oregon Historical Quarterly* 98 (1997): 6-54.

Palmer, Joel. *Journal of Travels: On the Oregon Trail in 1845.* 1847. Reprint, Portland: Oregon Historical Society Press, 1993.

Robbins, William G. *Hard Times in Paradise: Coos Bay, Oregon, 1850-1986.* Seattle: University of Washington Press, 1988.

———. "The Indian Question in Western Oregon: The Making of a Colonial People." In *Experiences in a Promised Land: Essays in Pacific Northwest History,* edited by G. Thomas Edwards and Carlos A. Schwantes. Seattle: University of Washington Press, 1986.

Schwartz, E.A. *The Rogue River Indian War and Its Aftermath, 1850-1980.* Norman: University of Oklahoma Press, 1997.

Simpson, Peter K. *The Community of Cattlemen: A Social History of the Cattle Industry in Southeastern Oregon, 1869-1912.* Moscow: University of Idaho Press, 1987.

Chapter 4: Emerging Social, Economic, and Political Relations

Allen, Barbara. *Homesteading the High Desert.* Logan: Utah State University Press, 1987.

Blair, Karen J., ed. *Women in Pacific Northwest History.* Seattle: University of Washington Press, 2001.

Collins, Cary C. "The Broken Crucible of Assimilation: Forest Grove Indian School and the Origins of Off-Reservation Boarding-School Education in the West." *Oregon Historical Quarterly* 101 (2000): 466-507.

Daniels, Roger. *Asian Americans: Chinese and Japanese in the United States since 1850.* Seattle: University of Washington Press, 1988.

Duniway, Abigail Scott. *Path Breaking: An Autobiographical History of the Equal Suffrage Movement in the Pacific Coast States.* Portland: James, Kerris, and Abbott, 1914.

Foster, Doug. "Refuges and Reclamantion: Conflicts in the Klamath Basin, 1904-1965." *Oregon Historical Quarterly* 103 (2002): 150-87.

Hummasti, Paul George. *Finnish Radicals in Astoria, Oregon, 1904-1940: A Study in Immigrant Socialism.* New York: Arno Press, 1979.

Kessler, Lauren. *Stubborn Twig: Three Generations in the Life of a Japanese American Family.* 1994. Reprint, Portland: Oregon Historical Society Press, 2005.

MacColl, E. Kimbark. *Merchants, Money, and Power: The Portland Establishment, 1843-1913.* Portland: Georgian Press, 1988.

Moynihan, Ruth Barnes. *Rebel for Rights, Abigail Scott Duniway.* New Haven: Yale University Press, 1983.

Reddick, SuAnn M. "The Evolution of Chemawa Indian School: From Red River to Salem, 1825-1885." *Oregon Historical Quarterly* 101 (2000): 444-65.

Schwantes, Carlos A. *Railroad Signatures across the Pacific Northwest.* Seattle: University of Washington Press, 1993.

Victor, Frances Fuller. *All Over Oregon and Washington: Observations on the Country.* San Francisco: J. H. Carmony, 1872.

Chapter 5: Into the New Century

Abbott, Carl. *The Great Extravaganza: Portland and the Lewis and Clark Exposition.* 3rd ed. Portland: Oregon Historical Society Press, 2004.

Dubofsky, Melvyn. *We Shall Be All: A History of the Industrial Workers of the World.* Chicago: Quadrangle Books, 1969.

Langston, Nancy. *Forest Dreams, Forest Nightmares: The Paradox of Old Growth in the Inland West.* Seattle: University of Washington Press, 1995.

Minto, John. "From Youth to Age as an American." *Oregon Historical Quarterly* 9 (1908): 127-73.

Pomeroy, Earl. *The Pacific Slope: A History of California, Oregon, Washington, Idaho, Utah, and Nevada.* New York: Alfred A. Knopf, 1965.

Robbins, William G. *Hard Times in Paradise: Coos Bay, Oregon, 1850-1986.* Seattle: University of Washington Press, 1988.

———. "The Lumber Industry in the West: A 20th-Century Perspective." In *Major Issues in 20th-Century Western History,* edited by Gerald D. Nash and Richard W. Etulain, 233-56. Albuquerque: University of New Mexico Press, 1989.

Taylor, Joseph E., III. *Making Salmon: An Environmental History of the Northwest Fisheries Crisis.* Seattle: University of Washington Press, 1999.

Chapter 6: Cultural Politics, Depression, and War

Abbott, Carl. *Portland: Politics, Planning, and Growth in a 20th-Century City.* Lincoln: University of Nebraska Press, 1983.

Barker, Neil. "Portland's Works Progress Administration." *Oregon Historical Quarterly* 101 (2000): 414-41.

Burton, Robert E. *Democrats of Oregon: The Pattern of Minority Politics, 1900-1956.* Eugene: University of Oregon Books, 1970.

Clark, Malcolm. "The Bigot Disclosed: 90 Years of Nativism." *Oregon Historical Quarterly* 75 (1974): 109-90.

Gamboa, Erasamo. *Mexican Labor and World War II: Braceros in the Pacific Northwest, 1942-1947.* Austin: University of Texas Press, 1990.

Haynal, Patrick. "Termination and Tribal Survival: The Klamath Tribes of Oregon." *Oregon Historical Quarterly* 101 (2000): 270-31.

Lowitt, Richard. *The New Deal and the West.* Bloomington: Indiana University Press, 1984.

Maben, Manly. *Vanport.* Portland: Oregon Historical Society Press, 1987.

Mullins, William H. *The Depression and the Urban West Coast, 1929-1933: Los Angeles, San Francisco, Seattle, and Portland.* Bloomington: Indiana University Press, 1991.

Neal, Steve. *McNary of Oregon: A Political Biography.* Portland: Oregon Historical Society Press, 1985.

Patterson, James T. *Grand Expectations: The United States, 1945-1974.* New York: Oxford University Press, 1996.

Pearson, Rudy. "A Menace to the Neighborhood: Housing and African Americans in Portland, 1941-1945." *Oregon Historical Quarterly* 102 (2001): 158-95.

Pierce, Walter M. *Oregon Cattleman, Governor, Congressman: Memoirs and Times of Walter M. Pierce.* Edited and expanded by Arthur H. Bone. Portland: Oregon Historical Society Press, 1981.

Schwantes, Carlos A., ed. *The Pacific Northwest in World War II.* Manhattan, Kans.: Sunflower University Press, 1986.

Skold, Karen Beck. "The Job He Left Behind: Women in the Shipyards during World War II." In *Women in Pacific Northwest History,* rdited by Karen J. Blair, 158-80. Seattle: University of Washington Press, 2001.

Tamura, Linda. *The Hood River Issei: An Oral History of Japanese Settlers in Oregon's Hood River Valley.* Chicago: University of Illinois Press, 1993.

Toy, Eckard V. "The Ku Klux Klan in Oregon." In *Experiences in a Promised Land: Essays in Pacific Northwest History,* edited by G. Thomas Edwards and Carlos A. Schwantes, 269-86. Seattle: University of Washington Press, 1986.

White, Richard. *"It's Your Misfortune and None of My Own": A New History of the American West.* Norman: University of Oklahoma Press, 1991.

Chapter 7: The Postwar Boom

Beckham, Stephen Dow. "Federal-Indian Relations." In *The First Oregonians,* edited by Carolyn M. Buan and Richard Lewis. Portland: Oregon Council for the Humanities, 1991.

"Crater Lake National Park at 100." Special issue, *Oregon Historical Quarterly* 103 (2002).

Drukman, Mason. *Wayne Morse: A Political Biography.* Portland: Oregon Historical Society Press, 1997.

Harmon, Rick. *Crater Lake National Park: A History.* Corvallis: Oregon State University Press, 2002.

Haynal, Patrick. "Termination and Tribal Survival: The Klamath Tribes of Oregon." *Oregon Historical Quarterly* 101 (2000): 271-301.

Lang, William L. "Failed Federalism: The Columbia Valley Authority and Regionalism." In *The Great Northwest: The Search for Regional Identity,* edited by William G. Robbins, 66-79. Corvallis: Oregon State University Press, 2001.

McKay, Floyd J. *An Editor for Oregon: Charles A. Sprague and the Politics of Change.* Corvallis: Oregon State University Press, 1998.

Munk, Michael, "Oregon Tests Academic Freedom in (Cold) Wartime: The Reed College Trustees Versus Stanley Moore." *Oregon Historical Quarterly* 97 (1996): 262-354.

Neal, Steve, ed. *They Never Go Back to Pocatello: The Selected Essays of Richard Neuberger.* Portland: Oregon Historical Society Press, 1988.

Robbins, William G. *Landscapes of Conflict: The Oregon Story, 1940-2000.* Seattle: University of Washington Press, 2004.

State of Oregon, Postwar Readjustment and Development Commission. *Progress Reports, 1943-1949.* Salem.

Walth, Brent. "No Deposit, No Return: Richard Chambers, Tom McCall, and the Oregon Bottle Bill." *Oregon Historical Quarterly* 95 (1994): 278-99.

Chapter 8: Education, the Arts, and Letters

Bingham, Edwin R. "Pacific Northwest Writing: Reaching for Regional Identity." In *Regionalism and the Pacific Northwest,* edited by William G. Robbins, Robert J. Frank, and Richard E. Ross. Corvallis: Oregon State University Press, 1983.

Bingham, Edwin R., and Glen A. Love, eds. *Northwest Perspectives: Essays on the Culture of the Pacific Northwest.* Seattle: University of Washington Press, 1979.

Chittick, V.L.O., ed. *Northwest Harvest: A Regional Stock-Taking.* New York: Macmillan, 1948.

Gunselman, Cheryl. "Pioneering Free Library Service for the City, 1864-1902: The Library Association of Portland and the Portland Public Library." *Oregon Historical Quarterly* 103 (2002): 320-37.

Herbert, Bob. "Oblivious to the State's Dire Straits." *New York Times.* Reprint, *Oregonian,* July 1, 2003.

Layman, William D. "Riverplaces as Sacred Geography: The Pictographs and Petroglyphs of the Mid-Columbia River." In *Great River of the West: Essays on the Columbia River,* edited by William L. Lang and Robert Carriker. Seattle: University of Washington Press, 1999.

Montague, Martha Frances. *Lewis and Clark College, 1867-1967.* Portland: Binfords and Mort, 1968.

Robbins, Tom. "Why I Live Where I Live (Tom Robbins discusses Burlington, Washington)." *Esquire* 94 (1980): 82-4.

Simonson, Harold P. "Pacific Northwest Literature: Its Coming of Age." *Pacific Northwest Quarterly* 71 (1980): 146-51.

Venn, George. "Soldier to Advocate: C.E.S. Wood's 1877 Diary of Alaska and the Nez Perce Conflict." *Oregon Historical Quarterly* 106 (2005): 34-75.

Warren, Sidney. *Farthest Frontier: The Pacific Northwest.* New York: Macmillan, 1949.

Chapter 9: From Natural Resources to a New Economy

Abbott, Carl, Deborah Howe, and Sy Adler, eds. *Planning the Oregon Way: A Twenty-Year Evaluation.* Corvallis: Oregon State University Press, 1994.

Abbott, Carl, Sy Adler, and Margery Post Abbott. *Planning a New West: The Columbia River Gorge National Scenic Area.* Corvallis: Oregon State University Press, 1997.

Dodds, Gordon B., and Craig E. Wollner. *The Silicon Forest: High Tech in the Portland Area, 1945-1986.* Portland: Oregon Historical Society Press, 1990.

Findlay, John M. *Magic Lands: Western Cityscapes and American Culture after 1940.* Berkeley: University of California Press, 1992.

Knapp, Gerrit, and Arthur C. Nelson. *The Regulated Landscape: Lessons on State Land Use Planning from Oregon.* Cambridge, Mass.: Lincoln Institute of Land Policy, 1992.

Lichatowich, Jim. *Salmon without Rivers: A History of the Pacific Salmon Crisis.* Washington, D.C.: Island Press, 1999.

McCormack, Win, ed. *Profiles of Oregon: An Anthology of Articles from Oregon Magazine, 1977 to 1987.* Portland: New Oregon Publishers, 1986.

Northwest Environment Watch. *This Place on Earth, 2002: Measuring What Matters.* Seattle: Northwest Environment Watch, 2002.

Robbins, William G., ed. *The Great Northwest: The Search for Regional Identity.* Corvallis: Oregon State University Press, 2001.

Index

About the Author

William G. Robbins is Emeritus Distinguished Professor of History at Oregon State University (OSU) in Corvallis. After serving four years in the U.S. Navy, he earned his B.S. from Western Connecticut State University and his M.A. and Ph.D. from the University of Oregon. After teaching for two years at Western Oregon State University, he joined the History Department at OSU in 1971. An expert in the history of the American West and environmental history, Robbins has written dozens of articles and is the author or editor of seven books, including *Colony and Empire: The Capitalist Transformation of the American West* and *Landscapes of Conflict: The Oregon Story, 1940-2000*. He served as editor of *Environmental History* from 1986 to 1988 and in 1997 received OSU's highest faculty award when he was named Distinguished University Professor. Robbins has also served on the council of the Pacific Coast Branch of the American History Association and the council of the Western History Association and on the editorial boards of the *Pacific Historical Review*, the *Pacific Northwest Quarterly*, the *Oregon Historical Quarterly*, and the Oregon State University Press.